How to Make Money

2ND EDITION

Philip Kadubec

ALLWORTH PRESS
NEW YORK

12   11   10   09   7   6   5   4   3

Published by Allworth Press
An imprint of Allworth Communications
10 East 23rd Street, New York, NY 10010

Cover design by Derek Bacchus
Page composition/typography by SR Desktop Services, Ridge, NY

Library of Congress Cataloging-in-Publication Data
    Kadubec, Phil.
    Crafts and craft shows: how to make money/Phil Kadubec.—2nd ed.
        p.   cm.
    Includes index.
    ISBN-10: 1-58115-470-4
    ISBN-13: 978-1-58115-470-2 (pbk.)
    1. Handicraft—Marketing.   2. Craft festivals—Planning.   I. Title.

    HD9999.H362K33   2007
    745.5068'8—dc22

                                        2006034578

Dedication

To my wife Judy, with all my love and deep appreciation. Without her, there would be no book, because there would have been no crafts business. It was her inspiration and creativity that first sent us on our crafting journey. Her dedication, perseverance, never-give-up attitude, and optimistic spirit were what kept me going, and her ability to relate to people was what made our business a success. I just built the baskets, wrote the book, and was part of the odyssey on which she took us.

My everlasting thanks also to our son Mark, who stained thousands of baskets, enjoyed the journey during his young years, and so stoically endured it all as he grew to maturity. You kept me on schedule, son, and kept me laughing. As we stood side by side through all your young years, it was a joy to watch you grow up.

"The manufacturer who waits in the woods for the world
to beat a path to his door is a great optimist.
But the manufacturer who shows his 'mousetraps'
to the world keeps the smoke coming out of his chimney."

—O. B. WINTERS

· · · · · ·

Contents

Acknowledgments

• • • • •

DURING THE SEVENTEEN YEARS that Judy and I participated in the craft world, numerous craftspeople assisted us in ways too varied to enumerate. Often we were ships in the night, passing by, never to meet again. To those people who may remember The Three Basketeers, and now read this book, our heartfelt thanks.

As I wrote this book, there were areas of the crafts business in which my knowledge was quite limited. It was therefore necessary to draw on the expertise of people who possessed that experience. I am deeply indebted to Wanda McAleese, group manager of Harvest Festival; Rhonda Blakely, promoter of Country Folk Art; Beth Weber, promoter for North Tahoe Fine Art Association; Rich Burleigh, promoter of Fire on the Mountain, and Rosie Lamar, for sacrificing their valuable time to answer my many questions, so that I might accurately represent the promotional and manufacturing side of the crafts business.

Throughout the years, some very special people provided advice and counsel, without which we would not have been successful. Our special thanks to Bill Campbell (Rocking Horse Bill), who was next to us in Arnold, California, on July 4, 1982, our first two-day craft show. What you taught us in two days, Bill, would have taken two years to learn.

To a most special couple, Jim (known in the business as Lord Jim), and Fran Seeley, we extend our deepest appreciation for the friendship, help, and advice you extended throughout our career. Thanks to you, we moved into the "Big Time" arenas where the real money is to be made. We regret that our friendship must now be conducted across the so many miles that separate us. We miss and will always cherish the jokes, the laughs, the fun, the debates, and the work we enjoyed together. May your much deserved retirement in Maine fulfill your dreams.

Editor's Note to the Second Edition

• • • • •

I AM LOOKING AT a letter, dated May 18, 1999, that I sent to Phil Kadubec, regarding his unsolicited submission of a short manuscript entitled *So You Want to Be a Crafter*. I wrote that, while the book had potential, it was too short and was missing a number of things that would make it, in my view, publishable. A short time later, Phil resubmitted, having taken many of my suggestions to heart, and we deemed the book worthy of the Allworth imprint. *So You Want to Be a Crafter* morphed into the very successful *Crafts and Craft Shows: How to Make Money*. (Although Phil wasn't too keen on the "How to Make Money" part of the title, he never denied that profit was one way to measure success.)

The aspect of *So You Want to be a Crafter* that captured our interest, and that was even stronger in the latter-titled rendition, was really what made the book, not my organizational suggestions. That aspect is Phil's voice. Rereading this book, I am once again struck by the amount of useful advice that it contains—about the crafts business and about the humanity—all filtered through a point of view that is alternately philosophical, bemused, curmudgeonly, generous, wise, and practical.

The world has changed since May of 1999. We wanted to update this book to reflect the way in which changes—to the Internet, the economy, foreign trade, fashion, national and international politics—have impacted craft shows. Sadly, Phil is no longer with us to revise his own work. So, with the intent of preserving everything that is classic and universal about the voices, stories, and advice in *Crafts and Craft Shows*, we asked crafter/designer Brauna Rosen to read and revise it.

All factual and contact information has been updated throughout the book. New sections about the Internet, mailing lists, pricing, street fairs, retailing, and wholesaling have been added. Profiles of crafters who are currently out there and other informational nuggets have been inserted as boxes. Much of the book is timeless; certainly the lessons about human nature and art and commerce are just as true now as they were then, and the inspiring, cautionary Tale of The Three Basketeers who traveled the craft fairs of the 1980s and 1990s is still vibrant. —NPT

Preface to the Second Edition

• • • • •

A DAY AFTER TURNING thirty, I quit my job as a manager of a fabric importing company in New York City to take up the nomadic life of a street vendor. Despite giving up a regular salary and cozy office for a hand-to-mouth subsistence, the decision did not give me a single sleepless night. It was the eighties, and the streets of Lower Manhattan where I plied my trade were a ferment of artistic activity. My friend and I set up a table in the East Village (at the time, a low-rent version of Greenwich Village) and began selling handmade jewelry.

Although I had been an ardent crafter since my mother first gave me a pair of scissors and a little pot of paste at the age of three, I had never sold anything I made before and I was a novice to the rules of the street. In the beginning, I was clueless as to how to claim my bit of street turf or how to defend myself against would-be interlopers. Fortunately, I was a quick to learn and my friend was quite a bit more street savvy than I.

Looking back at what now seems like a considerable leap of faith, I can truly say that I never regretted making my break for freedom. In those early days, I had little money, but I enjoyed the challenge of creating wearable art—literally out of trash. When I was short on cash, the garbage dumpsters in the garment district provided a treasure trove of material. There were always plenty of leather and fabric scraps of all descriptions to be rescued after factory hours for making "soft" jewelry. Rubber gaskets and chains from the hardware store could easily be transformed into collars for late-night club goers. By working through the night, I was always able to make enough merchandise to sell the next morning. The trick was rising early enough with the completed jewelry so I could stagger downtown to jockey for a position on the sidewalk.

As my skills improved, so did my sales. When my friend decided to follow her own dream and move to California, I moved my table to a well-known outdoor arts market, which meant that I only had to set up on weekends, freeing up time to create more jewelry. I approached boutiques and was able to place my jewelry in several on a full-time consignment basis. Later, I began showing my wares at the wholesale tradeshows and found that my retail experience on the street translated very successfully in the arena of selling to small specialty boutiques across the country. Eventually, following in the footsteps of other designers, I opened my own store.

The store, located in my now familiar territory in the East Village, seemed an elegant solution to my long-term dilemma of how to combine a schedule of craft shows and tradeshows and still sell directly to a steady flow of my personal clients. Unfortunately, September 11 abruptly put an end to this dream. I closed the store after a good run with a fond farewell to the many customers who had come to be a neighborhood of friends.

The last few years have been difficult for many craft-related businesses. Major trade shows are not as lucrative as they once were. Even the smaller, local craft shows, which were consistent and dependable for many years, don't seem to pack their customary punch. Veterans of the craft show circuit who once counted on one or two big shows to bring in the largest proportion of their income have been forced to rethink their strategy. Survivors in the market place interpret these changes correctly as a sign that if you wish to flourish, you must diversify and reinvent yourself.

The number of crafters and the number of craft shows in this country has surged since the original edition of this book was written. Phil Kadubec's insights into human nature, sales tactics, show selection, and product display continue to be as useful today as they were a decade ago. Today's craft professional, however, will need to branch out and not depend solely on one approach to sales in order to be effective. Professional crafters who know more about art than business must become skilled marketers, savvy both about cultural trends and technological innovations. The biggest obvious change in the scenery is the advent of the Internet as a tool for spreading the news about your business. In spite of their reputation as Luddites and technophobes, crafters are learning to use new media and new technology to get their work out there.

Let's face it. Crafters may have to do a little image enhancement if they want to thrive. In the United States, we have come to think of crafts as only the province of hippies and hobbyists, a remnant of the counterculture. Just as with any other product field, crafts needs to be seen as cool and inviting to stay on the consumer map. This may be a marketing challenge—or it could be an opportunity to invent a whole new craft or way of using craft techniques.

As we wend our way through the early part of the 21st century, the crafts profession needs to hold onto the traditions that have worked for it in the past, but it also needs an infusion of new blood—perhaps yours? I hope that, armed with advice of the veterans, the readers of this book will bring a fresh approach and new enthusiasm to our art and profession.

—BRAUNA ROSEN

Introduction to the First Edition

· · · · ·

DURING THE THRIVING ECONOMIC conditions of the past two decades, an increasing number of individuals have ventured into creative, entrepreneurial businesses. Nowhere is that more evident than in the world of crafts. Everywhere you look, there is evidence of modern renderings of yesterday's treasures. Makers of furniture, wall coverings, home design, clothing, bedding, even cooking utensils, seek to reflect and imitate in their products the timeless love and attention to detail that the craftsmen of long ago put into their work.

This book is the product of our experience in the craft world. During the seventeen years that we devoted to it, Judy and I traveled the length and breadth of California and Nevada selling our creations in as many as thirty-five craft shows a year.

As it so often happens in the crafts business, our eventual product line and successful business began as a hobby. It then developed into a means to supplement my retirement income and quickly developed into a thriving, full-time occupation. We were known as The Three Basketeers.

There are thousands of such craft names throughout America today. The names represent the many people who design a unique product and assert their desire to be independent of systems, bureaucracies, and corporations by venturing out on the road to sell it. Throughout the years, we met doctors, lawyers, carpenters, engineers, teachers, plumbers—members of almost every profession and vocation. All had walked away from their planned and established careers to express a newfound talent and independence.

As we are being moved daily, sometimes kicking and screaming, into this new, highly technological society—sometimes referred to as a disposable society—the public's resistance to it may explain the endurance of the craft show and its thousands of exhibitors. More profound explanations we leave to social scientists.

We can only say that at every craft show, as our customers searched nostalgically for prized examples of a simpler period in our lives and in our history, we sensed them seeking durability and craving yesteryear. The crafts business may well be one of the last true vestiges of our nation's Free

Enterprise System, alive and well every weekend across our land. Craftspeople probably influence the current trends in every marketplace far more than is recognized by the public or than craftsmen themselves may realize.

Maybe you are already one of these people. Or, perhaps you are just now considering entering the crafts business. If you are, whether you expect to do only a few shows a year, are already a veteran craftsman, or are newly entering the business on a full-time basis, we believe this book will assist you in your quest for financial success.

Of course, no book can help those who take a negative view of themselves or their product. We cannot help people who find excuses for their failure (and craftspeople have dozens) or those who waste time and energy complaining about how they are not appreciated. Nor is this a book for those who enjoy a nice hobby and then make a few gifts for family members and select friends at Christmastime. And this book definitely cannot help those who believe in creating "art for art's sake."

This book is directed to those individuals who, at craft shows week after week, put their talent on the line without sufficient financial reward. It is also dedicated to those who have yet to do their first show, but, believing in their product, are ready to test it in the marketplace and expect to earn a good living by doing so. Both must have faith in their creative abilities and must not be afraid of hard work—the two essential ingredients necessary to earn a substantial living. For, like every business endeavor, the crafts business is about making money, and there is plenty to be made. But, to make it, you must also be prepared to deal with reality.

Through the years, Judy and I met many people who possess a romantic, enchanted vision of the crafts business. Truthfully, that never-never land doesn't exist. To make a success of the business, that vision must be tempered with practicality and good judgement. There is nothing fascinating, enjoyable, or romantic about setting up your booth in some desolate parking lot or community park at five in the morning. Nor is there anything pleasurable about lugging your wares up and down the stairs of a vast convention center, or a weekend in the rain with few, if any, customers. The satisfaction comes from a full wallet at the end of a tiring, but productive weekend. Then the drive home is fun!

To achieve that feeling, another reality must also be faced. Craftspeople are uniquely independent and, while we may share our experiences and volunteer our assistance on a weekly basis within the closed circle of our industry, we also never forget that we are competing with each other every weekend, on a year-round basis.

During our early years in the business, my wife, Judy, and I learned most lessons the hard way. It is our hope that this book will save you a great deal of the time and money we lost. It can, if you are open to adopting the philosophy and attitude we recommend and applying the lessons we share. It is especially vital for all would-be craftspeople who are starting on their journey. Our hope is that the journey Judy and I took will encourage—not discourage—you from pursuing a similarly gratifying career. If by chapter 3 you have become discouraged, turn quickly to the epilogue. But, if you need such a boost, maybe you don't have what it takes to succeed.

You should also be aware that we acknowledge and honor the independent streak that we in the crafts business possess. We know it might sometimes inhibit the reader's openness to advice and cause her to take a "Who are you?" and "What are your credentials?" attitude. Hopefully, a little background about us, presented in the first chapter, will answer those questions to your satisfaction.

I will not pretend that we can provide all the answers to every problem you will encounter as you produce and sell your merchandise. Some questions or concerns you have may be exclusive to specific crafts, and you no doubt will experience circumstances and problems that even we, after seventeen years, never ran across. However, I do believe that in this book we treat—both generally and specifically—all the major and minor areas of the business in which you will engage. If you learn to deal with them, you will be well prepared to handle other circumstances that no one can anticipate. You will also be much further down the road to developing a successful business. Remember these words!

The right merchant is one who has the just average of faculties we call common sense; a man of a strong affinity for facts, who makes up his decision on what he has seen. He is thoroughly persuaded of the truths of arithmetic. There is always a reason, in the man, for his good or bad fortune . . . in making money. Men talk as if there were some magic about this. . . . He knows that all goes on the old road, pound for pound, cent for cent—for every effect a perfect cause—and that good luck is another name for tenacity of purpose.

—RALPH WALDO EMERSON

1

A Little about
The Three Basketeers

EIGHTEEN YEARS AGO, LIVING in the mountains with the snow piled high, Judy lined a few wicker baskets to give to friends as gifts. One couple was so impressed with Judy's talent that they invited us to share a booth in a one-day Oktoberfest in Murphys, California. Bob made nice cutting boards, as a hobby. We split a thirty-five-dollar booth fee, stood up two sawhorses, threw a piece of plywood across them, slapped on a tablecloth, and put out our merchandise. Judy and I displayed about twenty baskets, earned $235, patted ourselves on the back, and I said, "What an easy way to occasionally supplement my retirement income."

With that naïve idea in mind, the following summer, on July 4, 1982—my birthday—we tried our hand once again at a two-day show in Arnold, California. Unable to find sufficient wicker baskets, I designed a wooden, slatted picnic basket and a small breadbasket. We set up the same plywood table, covered with the same old tablecloth, and without even a canopy over our heads, were in business.

As luck would have it, it began raining just after we had set up, so I ran to a hardware store, bought a roll of black plastic and covered everything. I guess it made people just that much more curious. Like a feeding frenzy, customers scrambled under the plastic and bought almost every basket we had. I don't recommend depending on rain as a sales technique, but that day it worked. I think we displayed some thirty baskets that Judy had lined with scrap material my mother had found at Goodwill. We sold out on Sunday, grossing about $500. That was almost all profit. What a simple, easy way to make money, I thought, and stupidly made the statement, "If I can make $500 every weekend, I'll make baskets all day." I didn't know how prophetic that would be. For the next seventeen years, I was always working on my birthday!

During our first few years, we worked only small, local shows. We hit every nearby town, small club, and church event. The first time we grossed $1000, we were ecstatic, thinking we were making big money. Then we "graduated" to the Big Time. We added to our product line and improved our skills. Our inventory grew, as did our bills. Traveling more often and further, making more baskets, we needed and purchased bigger and better vehicles and equipment. We made more money and, of course, wanted and needed more. As the saying goes, we were "in for a penny, in for a pound."

Harvest festival shows, complete with costume; country folk art exhibitions; art and wine festivals all over the state; street fairs; we did them all—and sometimes lost money in the process. We took whatever advice we were offered, but scattered bits of information cannot generate immediate success. As beginners, we were not fully capitalized to sustain the cost. We learned that there is an inevitable trial and error process that is expensive. We would have made a lot more money, a lot earlier, if we knew then what we know now.

As we learned, we sometimes speculated on whether our organizational and creative abilities were a blessing or a trap. Probably they were both. Our youngest son grew up surrounded by the business. He made a lot of spending money, but it probably didn't compensate for the tedium and boredom of long hours on the road and thirty shows a year. We doubt if his future wife will ever be able to drag him to a craft show.

Over the span of our career, I guess we did approximately five hundred shows. At some of them, we weren't sure that we weren't taking part in a carnival or a circus. Through all those shows, I doubt if there were many setups or teardowns during which, at some point, Judy and I didn't have a disagreement or debate, often over the exact same thing we had discussed the week before. We listened to many a neighbor's arguments and noted that some marriages didn't survive. If you're single, you can swear at yourself. If you have a partner, you'll need to decide on each person's duties and responsibilities. I doubt if I ever satisfactorily placed a basket on a shelf where my wife wanted it. She invariably moved it to another spot.

The crafts business is a true test of any partnership. We were successful because we learned our appropriate roles and, more important, respected each other. Judy is a "people person," who possesses the enviable quality of smiling at adversity. I am more likely to get aggravated and my charm is singularly lacking during the early morning hours, during hectic selling periods, or under strict time constraints. Hell! I'm just not charming, so I made the coffee runs!

Judy and I survived it all and retired this year with enough in the bank to secure our remaining years. The crafts business exacts a physical and mental toll. It is not the casual, laissez-faire adventure it was when we began. Today, the little mom-and-pop booths doing a few shows a year and from whom you may purchase some specialty items are relatively rare. The business is now a highly competitive enterprise throughout the nation and much of the world. It is a billion-dollar industry. That is the arena in which you must be prepared to operate if you expect to make big money. So let's get on with learning how to compete successfully in that environment.

There is a market for any product that you as the craftsperson or artist manufacture well. As in fiction writing, where there really are no new plots—only variations on basic themes—so, too, in the crafts business. There are few crafts that someone else hasn't created or isn't already selling successfully. With thousands upon thousands of craftspeople throughout the country, that fact is inevitable and one to which you will just have to adjust. Later in the book, we will give you some examples of how we dealt with that reality when we were confronted with it.

The Three Basketeers was a successful business, not because there weren't other baskets on the market. There certainly were! Our business was profitable because we gave a new spin to an old standby. Our goal was to create baskets that people felt they wanted, needed, and couldn't live without. We created them to be beautiful and decorative, but also useful and functional and sturdy.

From the outset, The Three Basketeers emphasized uniqueness and attempted to personalize every item we sold. Nothing we produced was mass-produced or purchased ready-made, then simply embellished by us. You will see much of this at any show in which you compete, as you will also see many products produced overseas and therefore selling at a cheaper price than could possibly be asked if they were manufactured in the United States. Get used to it! That is the competitive nature of the business.

However, in conscientiously sticking to our own philosophy, we created an image that became "The Three Basketeers." If you take just that one bit of advice to heart—giving the customer something unique, and giving her as much value for her money as possible, year in and year out—you'll find there is a big, money-making market for you.

2
Marketing Yourself and Your Product

MARKETING AND SELF-PROMOTION can be tremendous obstacles for artisans and craftspeople. The very idea of having to put your work or your own person in even a low wattage limelight can be cause for discomfort and anxiety. Tooting your own horn does not come naturally to many of us. At the start of your craft career, it may have been possible to simply make what you love and sell it to supportive friends and family members. This positive initial response is probably what encouraged you to go into business the first place. As a result, crafters often are not obliged to confront the problem of self-promotion right away. After you do a few shows, however, you will want to expand your sales and you will be forced to take a more analytical look at your entire enterprise.

The subject of marketing, for those majoring in business, constitutes many individual courses. At the corporate level, experts with degrees in sales and advertising are hired to promote and merchandise a product, and they're fired when they do not produce revenue that satisfies directors and investors. On the other hand, marketing for the small home-based entrepreneur with a limited budget is, more than anything else, a matter of researching the current market, defining who you are, and identifying your best customers.

What You Are Not

You, as a craftsperson, are not a huge corporation. You are not Kellogg's or General Motors or Microsoft, competing twenty-four hours a day with like competitors for a share of the market. You are not selling millions of dollars worth of a product and usually cannot absorb the losses, as can a large business. Unlike a big business, you cannot afford to produce inventory that does not sell and then write it off as a loss. Most often, you do not have a financial consultant at hand to save you money.

A craftsperson must adjust to surviving independent of assistance. You do not have at your disposal an entire division staffed with college-educated professionals, trained in the latest techniques necessary to sell a product. You do not have a budget for advertising on billboards, magazines, newspapers, radio, and television. You do not have a supervisor to teach and coach you as you take your first business steps. You do not have twenty-four hours a day, seven days a week to sell your product. You do not have a huge distribution center to market your product throughout the countryside. You have only you, your product, and a few days a week to convince potential customers that they want what you have to sell. To sell successfully, therefore, you have to first learn what you do have at your disposal to sell—first your product and then yourself.

The Need to Develop Self-Reliance

What you are not is emphasized above to help you focus on one basic principle, relying on yourself. Most well-capitalized businesses can financially sustain some mistakes while developing and expanding. They have the experts in manufacturing, sales, and advertising to do so. Your success in the crafts business depends solely on your ability not only to produce an excellent product, but to sell it. Unless you have large monetary reserves, you must learn quickly. Nobody else is going to do it for you, and very few people are going to teach you. Your success will depend primarily on your belief in your product and in yourself.

When Judy and I began, neither of us had had the slightest training in any aspect of selling or marketing. Judy had an edge, as her personality lent itself to dealing cheerfully with people. It took me at least a year to understand that I also had to cultivate her natural talent. While I was a self-reliant person, I had little confidence that our new product could really sell and had even less confidence that I had any selling ability. I had to learn to develop this trait, realizing that it was essential to moving our product off the shelf and into the customer's home. We both learned a key lesson: At the same time that we were selling our baskets, we were also selling our individuality.

Judy and I quickly noted that selling ourselves was not a matter of turning on a phony smile at a moment's notice. It was about learning and practicing ongoing, pleasant, social interaction with the public. We imitated Jim and Fran Seeley, who did this from the moment the first person passed their booth until the last customer left the show site at the end of the day. From them, Judy and I learned that when we were not actively involved with the customer and the product at the same time, we were selling little or nothing. From a competitive standpoint, skills needed in the area of marketing must be developed quickly. Every promoter with whom I discussed the issue agreed that new people coming into the business are more experienced at marketing themselves and have more familiarity with the business skills necessary to do so. As Rhonda Blakely, a member of the family that owns and promotes Country Folk Art, expressed it, "Artisans who are changing their product, coming up with new and fresh ideas, are the people who are reporting increased business." That means that if you are a veteran and are still working on a hit-or-miss basis, the new competition is going to drive you out of business unless you develop new, improved products and better marketing techniques. If you are new to the craft world, you cannot afford to spend years learning these techniques the hard way, little by little, as Judy and I did.

What You Are

I must admit that self-promotion has been an area of my business that stymied me for many years. Recently I took a short seminar on marketing. I was amazed to realize that I had never really considered, in anything other than an intuitive fashion, who my customers were and why they bought my jewelry. Nine times out of ten, I could probably have told you within a few minutes after entering my booth whether a customer would buy from me but I had never put it into words, let alone in writing. In the workshop, I was asked to describe precisely what kind of jewelry I made and to whom I sold. In explaining the nature of my materials, where my inspiration came from, what type of woman purchased from me, I was able to define more clearly for myself who my target market is.

After coming to a deeper understanding of my product and my customer, I came to appreciate how important it was to design all of my marketing materials with these insights in mind. The connection between my business card, business logo, product tags and cards, brochures, and even my Web site design became a lot more significant to me. In this media savvy world, consciously creating your business image is essential. Simply going with the flow does not bring in those all important dollars.

Your first attempt at self-description may be a little disappointing. It is not always easy to pinpoint the crucial factors that set you and your work apart from the rest of the crowd. Remember that you are trying to make your product vivid to people who may not have encountered your work in the flesh. Think about your craft in the larger scheme of things. Customers are often looking for a new twist to an old theme to renew their interest in a product. What is the story behind what you make or a detail in your own artistic history that will arrest the attention of your potential buyer? Explain the nature of your materials and their quality, where they come from, and their historic usage. Do you work with your materials in a traditional fashion? If so, do you attempt to recreate a particular style or era? What is it about this time period that draws your attention? How is it different from contemporary attitudes toward this object?

If your work is contemporary, what makes it innovative? Have you reinvented a traditional form or converted a well-known object into something completely alien to its original purpose? (An example of a creative use of well-known objects would be a line of suitcases constructed out of old license plates or a line of bird houses or garden ornaments.) Has your product been inspired by an important current issue such as recycled paper and fabric or computer-influenced lifestyles? The more specific you allow yourself to be, the closer you will come to being able to convey the spirit of your work to the consumer in an effective fashion.

If you have been doing shows even for a short time, you will already have an idea of who your customer is. As you make a list of what your average customer wears, what they like to talk about, their lifestyle, even ethnicity and religion, you will begin to develop a word picture of who is most likely to buy from you. What do you think is the size of your market? How old are they? What is their income and gender? Where do they work, live, take their classes, and look for their indulgences? Why do they need this kind of product in general? Who else do they look at before buying from you and what factors are important in their decision to buy from you, in the end? Or if they choose someone else, why do you think they choose them over you?

Craft shows are primarily a venue for people buying gifts for themselves. Many people are afraid to buy an unusual gift for a friend or family member, but they will easily gravitate toward something they personally like. By understanding the basic character of your work and who your customer is, you will make it easier to introduce your work to your very own fan base. —BR

Naming Your Business

One of the least considered aspects of marketing your craft and yourself that we first encountered was naming our business. This can seem inconsequential and you may ask, "What does that have to do with me and my product?" Surprisingly, a great deal more than most people realize or stop to consider. Name recognition is paramount in creating a product and a business from which to sell it. Establishing a name that everyone knows is most, if not all, of the game in which advertising engages.

The name of your business defines who you are to the public, to the promoter, to other craftspeople, and even to yourself. The name you select can intrigue a promoter if he has never seen your work before. Your sign can attract potential customers as they walk by your booth. Your business name can define you and set the stage for sales, and it can provide a means of being remembered—or forgotten. It is a vital form of marketing.

At our first few shows, we never thought of giving ourselves a name and we immediately encountered our first major problem. To whom should the buyer make out a check? So we quickly came up with the name Sew Crafty. We used it for about a year, though we recognized that it was a little too cute. We also discovered that the name was being used by many others in the business. So, living in the mountains, we became Mountain Creations. Better, but not much!

As luck would have it, six months later, we learned that another business in our county was already registered under that name and threatened to sue us if we didn't change it. We did not know that there was a state agency with which a business name could be checked and should be registered. For the second time, we had to change all our checking accounts, business cards, signs, and everything else on which we used our business name.

Finding another name became a problem. Luckily, we had imaginative friends. Doing our first Harvest Festival show, produced by one of the bigger and better promoters of craft shows, we were required to wear costumes. This is another way to advertise yourself and to stand out. Just by happenstance, our young son Mark was reading *The Three Musketeers*. The book gave us the idea of using Musketeer costumes, causing a friend to suggest that we name the business "The Three Basketeers." The name stuck and identified us throughout all the years we sold our baskets. It had that catchy quality that appeals to customers. It was easy to remember, always sparked lively conversation, gave us a logo (a plume) for our banner and business cards, and thereby enhanced the sale of our baskets in many ways.

The image you present to the public contributes immeasurably to how well you will sell your product. You probably have attended many craft shows where most of the booths looked like they belonged at a flea market and their proprietors looked equally seedy. Booth design and your overall appearance will be covered extensively in later chapters. Here, we will treat the more subtle symbols that help you appear professional and contribute to marketing yourself and your product.

Your Personal Appearance

The first thing a customer sees as she enters your booth is you. Your appearance, even before any conversational exchange takes place, is extremely important. How you present yourself physically and verbally to the customer—the first impression you make—can make the difference between a sale and no sale.

Yes, we realize that today there is a tendency to try not to judge people by their looks and appearance, and, yes, I know this is the era of casual Fridays, even at IBM, but that doesn't change reality. One of the wealthiest women I ever knew, heiress to one of the largest fortunes in the United States, dressed like a slob. Fine! She could afford the eccentricity. You can't!

A craft show certainly doesn't require formal attire and your customers may look like they walked out of a rummage sale, but you shouldn't. Looking like a throwback to the sixties or a homeless person begging on a street corner is not going to inspire confidence in you or your product. Nor is it going to help you develop a rapport with your potential customers. Certainly dress casually, but cleanly and neatly. Customers definitely do notice. It also makes you feel better about yourself.

Your Tools Are Your Jewels

For the designer of accessories and clothing, one of the best ways to publicize your product is, of course, by wearing it yourself. Whether you are doing a show, or doing your daily rounds at the supermarket, you are a walking advertisement. The more flair you exhibit in your personal appearance, the more notice you will attract to your work. Those who have a natural flair for color, fashion, and drama will probably flaunt their peacock feathers as a matter of course. Those who are of a more retiring temperament will need to train themselves to the idea of using their own person as a perpetual display mannequin. You must learn to put your modesty aside and strut your stuff. More than one sale can be been made simply by sashaying by with a smile on your face and an extravagant hat perched on your head. Your customers are not only buying your work but a part of your personal style and panache. This is true for both men and women, so there is no gender discrimination here. Think of yourself as an art object. You are not trying to make a shocking display of yourself, obviously, but to draw attention to your booth and your work.

I myself tend to downplay my appearance. Some years back, I was taken aside by a kind-hearted jewelry veteran who whispered in a confidential tone, "Dear, you need a lesson on makeup and how to dress." She proceeded to teach me the rudimentary techniques of applying eye makeup and lipstick, of which I was blissfully ignorant.

She instructed me to construct an outfit that would allow me to wear an item in every category of jewelry I was featuring at the same time. I came to the next show decked out to the nines. For a short while, I became a show diva. Not surprisingly, my show totals soared and my confidence increased. In the end, I settled on a happy medium. I minimized the makeup as it made me self-conscious, but I made it a practice to buy a few fantastic new outfits for my shows and I always wear as many of my latest creations as I can. Shows are theatre. The same care you lavish on your designs and your booth appearance should go into your own personal appearance.

Weather Appropriate Attire

Sometimes, however, there are occasions when it is necessary to sacrifice beauty for practicality and comfort. If you are selling on the street or an outdoor market, weather is paramount. Always take into consideration and prepare for extreme heat or extreme cold. In the winter, layering is key. Cotton, silk, and wool protect against subzero temperatures far better than synthetics devised for outdoor sports activities, which are designed for body heat generated by a lot of movement. Protect your extremities. Your feet, hands, and head are the most vulnerable. I usually wear at least ten layers when I anticipate a full ten hours out in the ice and snow. People who have never seen me in my civilian clothes are often shocked to discover that I am actually a relatively small person and not the abominable snowman.

In summer, of course, the problems are quite the opposite. You must provide yourself with sufficient water to keep properly hydrated and remember to protect yourself against the sun. No matter your complexion, a full day in the direct sun is unhealthy. The good news is that summer offers many great opportunities to feature season-appropriate accessories.

—BR

Your Business Card

Seemingly a small item, business cards make an important contribution to sales and provide assistance in selling your product. Have them from the first day you open your booth to the public. First, business cards create the appearance of professionalism by sending the message that you are a serious businessperson. Many customers enter the booth, look around, and start to walk out. Don't try to detain them. Just thank them for dropping in and give them a card. Display the cards in a holder on your table. Some people will enter your booth, take a card, never look at your craft or say a word to you, and walk out. Children also like to collect them, but that's the price of doing business.

The main thing to remember is that business cards are a form of advertising. They are essentially a mini brochure. Many people leave the back of their cards blank. This is a missed opportunity. There is plenty of room to offer a list of your products or a photographic reminder of a featured piece. Having your card in their possession reminds customers of you and your product. They will often return to look again and maybe buy something. Many customers who regularly attend craft shows will keep your card as a reminder to look for your booth when they next attend a craft show.

The business card also enables customers to phone you and make a purchase after the show is over. Much of our business was generated this way. Sometimes people are not financially prepared to buy on a particular day. Sometimes the customer simply doesn't see anything that she wants right away. Then, when she gets home, she wishes she had purchased your product. Or, a few weeks later, she needs a gift for some special occasion and your card reminds her of you. So, if the customer does make a purchase, place your business card inside the bag in which you package the purchase. Spend the extra money to have a special card designed, one of good quality and with your logo on it. It definitely makes an impression!

The Most Trivial Things Can Be Important

There are two additional things that contribute to the aura of professionalism that you must try to create. They may seem trivial, but they are essential to the way in which your customers perceive you. The first is having something in which to package the customer's purchase. A brightly colored bag or an imprinted tag with your name and logo attached to the bag handle can add value to the purchase and remind the customer of your company. The second is a schedule of the craft shows in which you will be participating that year. In both cases you are marketing yourself and your business and establishing your professionalism.

To be sure, there are many crafts that are simply too large to be wrapped or packaged in any way. Some are also too bulky and heavy or awkward. If your craft puts you in that category, find some way to help the customer transport it to her car, if at all possible. This is particularly necessary on a rainy day. If assisting the customer in this way is not feasible, offer to store her purchase for her until she is ready to leave the show. That way, the customer doesn't have to lug it around all day.

Admittedly, this can be inconvenient when you are working in very cramped space, but assisting the customer in this way makes it worth your personal inconvenience. Often, too, when the customer returns later in the day to pick up her purchase, she may decide to buy something else. Rich Burleigh, whose promotion company is called Fire on the Mountain, told me that when he selects booths for his show, he also evaluates the craftsperson. He chooses people who subscribe to the idea of "doing it right." He calls it, "The merging of the spontaneous with the organized."

One word of caution here, though: Don't, under any circumstances, hold anything for anybody who hasn't paid for it. In the crafts business, customers who make this request are members of what are called the "Be Back Family." "I'll be back," "We'll be back," "She'll be back." They never are! They see something else they like, somewhere else, spend their money, and they are gone. Meanwhile, you have lost the ability to sell that particular piece of merchandise, perhaps for the entire day.

Your Craft Show Schedule

The show schedule I mentioned above can contribute immeasurably to your sales for the remainder of the year. Everyone who enters your booth should be given your schedule. This is especially important at street fairs, where customers have not paid to enter the show. They may be out for a Sunday walk and haven't brought enough money with them to buy. Or, before they even entered your booth, they may simply have spent all the money they had or intended to spend that day. The schedule tells them when and where you will be in the future. The schedule also provides them with your telephone number should they want to order by phone. You can develop, as we did, a very large customer base in this manner. A show schedule constitutes advertising, marketing, and good public relations all at the same time.

Along these same lines, many of the big, traveling shows—like Harvest Festival and Country Folk Art—will mail you, on your acceptance to the show, a stack of cards. These cards usually offer an entry fee discount and include the promoters' upcoming show schedule. You should place them in a conspicuous place on your counter at every show you do. Give them to everyone who enters your booth, whether they make a purchase or not. Drop them in the bag with every customer purchase. It is amazing how many people want that dollar off. They will thank you for the card and show up at that next show to buy at your booth. We had a rubber stamp with our business name and logo that we applied to every promoter's card. We would check the shows we were going to participate in. That card would act as an advertisement for both our business and for the particular promoter's upcoming shows.

The Importance of a Large Inventory to Your Sales

The next lesson that we learned was that it is essential that you have sufficient inventory. To an extent, this will also be discussed in more detail under the chapter on booth setup and display. It is, however, relevant here because customers want a large selection from which to choose. Sufficient selection of merchandise gives you greater sales potential, more with which to keep the customer in the booth.

As a novice, it is very difficult to judge just how much of your product you should bring to a show. Yet, many veteran craftspeople also neglect this area of their business. Of course, anyone may be limited by his own cash reserve and how much inventory he can afford to stock and have the physical capacity to produce. But, beyond that, there is a natural tendency to take too little simply because, to you, it looks like a lot.

Since you may not have ever produced in volume before, the amount of inventory to bring to a show is difficult to judge. Just how much is too much and how much is too little is a matter of trial and error but, because too little can drastically affect your sales ability, it is better to err on the side of too much.

This inventory predicament happened to Judy and me for the first two years we were in business. When we began, we displayed a total of perhaps thirty or forty baskets of three different designs and we usually sold out, but we weren't making much money. Then, as we expanded our variety, we set ten of each basket as our target for each show. What took time to realize, however, was that once we had sold five or six of each, we had sold the most desirable of our baskets and we had no selection left with which to entice the customer. The booth looked empty and that fact alone may discourage customers.

A virtually empty booth, no matter how fine your product, still looks a bit bare. Nobody wants what they consider leftovers. As a salesperson, no matter how good your sales ability, with nothing to sell, you might as well not be at the show. To experienced customers, an empty booth makes a poor impression.

Experienced customers know when the best merchandise has been taken and their perception of you as a craftsperson is that you have nothing much to offer. Furthermore, since our sale of baskets depended on color schemes and color coordination—something on which your product may well rely—if we had only a scant selection from which to choose, there was nothing to discuss with the customer. We couldn't sell ourselves and we couldn't sell our product. Or, as Rhonda Blakely of Country Folk Art aptly noted, "You can't sell from an empty wagon." She and her family have been promoting shows for eighteen years—fifty shows a year, from the Atlantic to the Pacific coast—so she knows. As a general rule, many craftspeople work on the principle that at good shows, you should sell half of what you bring to the show. Obviously, then, you can't start with an "empty wagon" if you are going to make money.

To sell correctly, we realized that if we wanted to make big money, we had to make it a full-time enterprise. Thereafter, we never stocked our booth with less than thirty and often forty or fifty of our bestselling baskets and half as many of the less popular, but still reliable sellers. Judy convinced me, and she was correct, that the more we took, the more we sold. We had lots to sell and a lot to talk about.

The Reality of the Craft Marketplace

From the beginning of our craft show venture, and regularly throughout, Judy and I reminded each other of one basic reality that can keep you humble, keep you productively creative, and keep your business life in perspective: Nobody needs what any craftsperson has to sell. That is a hard reality to face, but if you are too egocentrically involved in your craft and are unable to admit and acknowledge it, you won't be able to sell or market your craft successfully, and, inevitably, you will lose money.

To have a good grasp of this core reality, you must bury your artistic ego. The truth is that crafts, like most commodities, appeal primarily to a customer's wishes, desires, and fantasies. It is not far-fetched to say that the entire business and advertising world is based on understanding that fact. As a craftsperson, it is your goal, in attracting customers, to capitalize on your awareness of that fact and convince the customer that your product fulfills those dreams and fantasies.

Now you may never have considered this, but it is true: Most people who come to a craft show do not know what they want to buy. They usually walk around looking and waiting for that special something to "speak to them." Most often, they know that they would like to buy something, if they can find something that fits into their budget and appeals to them. Your product has to be that special something that tempts them to reach into their wallet and part with their hard-earned money.

It is important to remember that term: hard-earned. As you meet and observe your crafts competitors, you will be surprised at how many, during the course of the day, develop a resentful attitude when people are not spending their money. They seem to think that just because they have expended the effort to be at the show, the patron has some obligation to make a purchase. When a customer leaves the booth without buying, far too many crafts merchants act as if they had been personally insulted and become surly. They allow the customer's failure to make a purchase to affect their mood for the remainder of the day and thereby lose even more sales. So, if you find yourself taking that attitude, get rid of it. It will not help you to sell yourself or your craft.

A good way to evaluate yourself and your product, and to understand potential customers, is to ask yourself this question: Would I buy this? It is a simple, but sometimes very scary, question. Many, perhaps most, craftspeople never ask this question of themselves, because they wouldn't like the answer. As Judy and I learned to ask that question—and as we remembered to keep it in focus throughout our career, particularly when we designed a new basket—we began to engage in a ritual at every show that enabled us to evaluate the competition and our own product. This ritual provided insight into what we could anticipate over the next few days, which in turn helped us to maintain our composure and selling ability.

Before every show opened, one or both of us would amble up and down the rows of booths. Predictably, we would see what we came to refer to as Foo-Foo. There would be three or four vendors selling stuffed dolls, two or three selling dried flowers, another couple with a booth full of wooden stakes with cutesy-pie sayings and mottoes, a number with miniature ceramic figurines, junk jewelry, and the like. Then there would be five booths filled with birdhouses, six different potters, and numerous people selling reprints of their artwork, some with a conglomeration of a little of everything.

Cynical as it may sound, that was great for us. We knew that too many merchants were going to be competing with the same products, for the same customers. Since nobody sold a product like ours, because we created it, we knew we would get more than our share of the market. Of course, frequently there were other kinds of baskets, but none that were in competition with ours. Maybe nobody really needed our baskets, but if they desired one, we usually had a corner on the potential market.

On completing our walk, we immediately knew three things: If we treated every customer with courtesy and respect, our product was going to sell. We knew that, regardless of any adversity, we were going to make a good profit. And we knew we could count on hearing a lot of complaining about what a poor show it had been from those who didn't earn as much money as we did.

Later in the book, you will find a list of excuses and alibis that craftspeople regularly use to justify their lack of sales. However, if you are confident about your product and your ability to sell it, when you're having that inevitable bad day, you'll resist the temptation to use them. If you are producing a good product and selling your unique personality to the customer, the "bad days" will become less frequent. You won't need the excuses. Rationalizations may satisfy the ego temporarily, but they don't put money in your pocket. The mental energy expended in creating phony excuses engenders a negative attitude that hampers your salesmanship and can ruin what might have become a good day.

That term—a good day—leads to discussion of another problem that can affect your ability to sell: Except at very rare shows, for very specific reasons, most days start off slowly. People don't usually rush into a show and immediately start buying. Bill Campbell taught us this when I noticed that during the entire first day, he had not sold a single rocking horse. I suggested that maybe he was in the wrong area, to which he responded, "Wait until tomorrow." What Bill knew was that since he had a high-priced item, people needed to go home and think about the investment they were making. Women may buy expensive earrings on impulse, but not rocking horses. The next day Bill sold five at $750 a piece.

So don't start looking for excuses as to why your product isn't selling only a few hours after the show's opening. Give people time to look around, to think about what they truly want. We rarely sold much the first few hours, but we always went home with a good profit. If you have a good product, after they've looked at a great deal of garbage, they'll be back to your booth to buy. And you won't frustrate yourself unnecessarily.

Never Be Self-Satisfied

What I am now about to write may seem even more cynical, callous, or even greedy, but again, it is reality. As a craftsperson, as a merchant, as a vendor, or whatever you may call yourself, you must never be satisfied with the profit you are making. That attitude leads to stagnation and, eventually, profit loss.

As in any endeavor, but particularly in the creation of a product, you should always believe that you can make a better product and make even more money. Possessing that attitude is a reflection of your self-confidence. That self-confidence will then naturally and almost automatically be reflected in the quality and output of your product, your continued creativity, and your attitude when selling it.

Try to Produce Something Different

Would I buy this? Whether you are an "in the cradle beginner" or "a rocking chair veteran," if your product is unique, if you believe in it, and if you are positively involved in the selling process, you should be able to truthfully answer "yes" to that question. If you can't, ask yourself whether anyone else would. If the answer is "yes," then you're on your way.

This doesn't mean that you can't produce Foo-Foo. It does mean, however, that if you want to earn more than an average living, your Foo-Foo must be better produced than anyone else's and must capture the imagination of the customer in a way that another merchant's work does not. Even so, as good as your work may be you will still have to hope that a potential customer hasn't already spent her money at another booth like yours somewhere down the aisle before ever seeing your workmanship. This, then, may be a good time to discuss and define the term unique.

In the craft world, unique doesn't necessarily mean one-of-a-kind. Every promoter with whom I discussed this issue agreed that the one-of-a-kind craft is fast disappearing, noting that the pressure to do more shows has created a need to have more products that are easier to produce in order to meet greater demand. Oh, each new craft season you may occasionally see something that you have never seen before and it may be truly one-of-a-kind, but the reality is that by next year, or maybe sooner, someone will have copied it and created his own variation. It is not uncommon, as has happened with many inventions, that more than one artisan will develop the same concept at the same time. So, unique really refers to the way you personalize your product and the way you display it.

The greatest danger to the individual crafter in this day and age is actually large import companies who have the capacity to steal your idea and send it to a third-world country where it can be "handmade" at a fraction of the cost in materials and labor. Unfortunately, there is no way to protect yourself against this predator in the marketplace. Your best protection will always be your own creativity. If you are primed to generate as many new products as possible, you will keep your customers intrigued and leave your giant competitors in the dust.   —BR

Do you grow, dry, and dye your own flowers? If you're a potter, a unique approach may refer to the way you shape, color, or glaze a pot. Are your earrings distinctly different or can they be purchased at any dime store? Is your stained glass artistically individual or are your patterns and designs like everybody else's? Do you create your own clothing designs or truly different wooden shelves or merely take patterns out of a book? Many do this and make a living, but not much more than that.

Actually, one-of-a-kind is relatively rare anyway. It is found primarily in the fine arts but, even there, a painting is a painting; earrings are earrings. It is the uniqueness that the artist brings to the painting or the creation of the earring that makes it different. Most often, the one-of-a-kind piece is a gimmick item that usually doesn't survive more than a few years. What makes and sells your product as unique is what you give to the product that is genuinely you, and that includes how you sell "you" to the customer as you sell your product. Promoters all agree that customers like the interaction with the artist and like to talk with and get to know the person who created what they have purchased. The personal connection is very important, especially if your product is unique.

At our first shows, Judy and I observed that, though there were other kinds of baskets in the show, ours were unlike any others made. If you can say that, you can then capitalize on that fact. Then, if you can smile at the customers, show them that you enjoy their company, you sell yourself, your product, and your entire business. Your entire operation sells itself as unique.

Choosing the Right Product for You

While I agree with Phil that there is certainly a great deal of "Foo-Foo" out there in the marketplace, I feel that the buying public is always ready to embrace a truly novel product or concept. In fact, the search for something unique and exciting is more pressing than ever before. The "new" quickly becomes "old" as media exposure and mass consumerism increasingly promote to jaded taste buds. Before you launch yourself into the craft shows world, it is always a good idea to do the rounds and inspect what is already out there. You want to make sure that you are offering not only your own unique product but that it is a product that others will want to buy. As you stroll through the various craft shows, you will notice that there are actually very few categories being exhibited. Recently, I walked the Lincoln Center Craft Show, a high-end biannual craft show in New York City. I observed that, as usual, certain crafts dominated the show. Jewelry held pride of place, leading the pack by at least four to one. Here's a breakdown of what comprised the show:

> Jewelry
> Glass: vases, paperweights
> Jewish home blessings
> Mezuzahs
> Wooden vessels
> Wooden furniture
> Wooden toys
> Wooden games
> Chenille garments
> Pottery plates, kitchenware, teapots, mugs
> Handbags
> Photos

> Switch plates
> Masks
> Cards
> Raincoats
> Puppets (sock puppets)
> Kids clothing
> Mobiles
> Magnets
> Hand painted T-shirts
> Mirrors
> Boxes
> Fountains
> Wind chimes

- > Hats
- > Dolls
- > Scarves
- > Lamps
- > Frameable wall art

- > Notebooks
- > Shadowboxes
- > Dog products
- > Animal portraiture

Although jewelry is always a major category, and it is the one that I have specialized in myself, it is not always a surefire seller. As with anything else, there are ups and down. When I first started in the late eighties, accessories were very hot. The larger and more individualistic the piece, the quicker it sold. One year hair bows were flying off the table. I would fashion a hundred completely individual bows out of every conceivable material—feathers, leather, fabric, and metal. My bedroom floor was completely covered with hair accessories in various stages of completion. At the end of each week, I would be sold out. This particular trend lasted the length of an entire year and as quickly as the trend appeared, it died. I couldn't sell my remaining stock at half price.

An era of minimalist jewelry set in, which seemed to last an eternity. I would flip through all the major fashion magazines from end to end and wouldn't find a single necklace, bracelet, or earring in the entire issue. Most of the jewelry designers I knew turned to making home accessories to draw customer interest. Most businesses have their booms and bust. The same is true in the craft world. One year, glass is getting all the press, the next stationery is drawing the crowds' eye. No craft item that I can think of is perpetually hot and it is good to remember even when the customers are flooding into your booth that you need to constantly foster your creativity and revitalize your work.

While the birth of a new idea or product often feels spontaneous, in fact it is necessary to constantly nourish your artistic brain. Keep in the habit of searching for and experimenting with new materials and techniques. Talk with friends, visit craft shows, study consumer and trade magazines, take walks in nature, watch children or animals— even study what people are bringing to the supermarket checkout counter. Consider what you yourself use in your daily life and above all listen to your customers as you develop a following; they will tell you what they want. Keep a notebook and sketchbook with all or your ideas and even half notions, clippings, and photos. All of these activities will help you regenerate your line when direct inspiration fails.

Once you have done your market research, it will become obvious that it is far more difficult to make your mark in a craft category that is already flooded. It is even hard sometimes to get accepted into a well-established show if you are working in a very popular medium. A unique approach is vital to your success. Sometimes presentation and packaging can make the difference. Sometimes finding a way to merge two popular trends can do the trick.

In the eighties, I began to sell collage pins made out of dismantled watches. My watch pins sold moderately well but I knew instinctively that I had an "item," a product that could be a big seller. I just couldn't figure out what they were missing. A friend, who worked extensively with Austrian crystal and did a brisk business all the time, gave my pins one glance and said, "Jump up the glam. You would triple your sales if you just added crystals to your work." I was horrified. I saw my pins as wearable art. However, I desperately needed to meet my rent that month, so I bought a gross of AB crystals and glued them on to the center of the watch faces.

At my next show, the women were literally fighting three deep to get at my table. The combination of collage jewelry with just the right amount of glitter sealed the deal. It was the right look at the right time. One without the other would not have sold nearly as well. —BR

Try to Stand Out from the Competition

When you attend a craft show, particularly one that is outdoors, you will see row after row of canopies, all ten by ten feet, all virtually alike. One promoter told me laughingly that he thought that the invention of the portable, retractable canopy began the downgrading of outdoor craft presentation. Craftspeople ceased to be individual in the creation of their booth. And his point is well taken. It is not until the customer looks inside your booth that your product is defined. Once the customer steps inside, it is up to you and your product to keep her there.

So, for example, we always placed our largest and most colorful baskets at the front of the booth. We also kept a scrapbook with photos of us in every phase of production. It helped sell baskets because, in crowded conditions, it kept the customer interested and it verified that we made the product and that the baskets were truly original. The scrapbook was also a great conversation piece with which to break the ice.

For a few years, I wrote humorous poems that applied to every basket and gave the customer a copy with her purchase. Still another year, we designed a basket I called a Flambajobble. The name was a literary invention, but the fantasy story I told about the basket kept customers intrigued. The Flambajobble was an intentionally weird basket and we didn't sell many. But, we sold a lot of our other baskets. While we were entertaining them, our customers were also looking around.

As noted above, it is good to remember that you yourself are an original. If your sales seem to be diminishing, look to yourself as well as your product.

You must never be so wed to an idea, a product, or your image of yourself, that you are not open to modifying or changing it for the sake of product improvement and selling success.

Flexibility on your part is vital to success in the crafts game. That is why each year Judy and I created new baskets and discarded nonsellers from the previous year. One year we designed five new baskets and dropped four of them by July. We loved some of those baskets, but they didn't sell. The inability of so many craftspeople to part with their creations, and continue to sell the exact same product year after year, explains why so many of them either go out of business or just eke out a living.

Are there exceptions? Definitely! A good friend has been making large women's purses for twenty years. She has varied the basic style, pattern, or color very little. However, they are practical, durable, and washable. Nobody makes a purse the way she does and nobody has tried. Since all women have numerous purses for various occasions, Jessie's purses will always be desired and useful. Little girls, who once attended shows with their mothers, grew up and bought Jessie's purse. She has always had a market and always will.

Variety Is the Spice of Life

Success depends on what you are selling and how good your products are. Our customers would never need more than one sewing or picnic basket. Over the years they might buy one for friends and relatives, but we couldn't make a living just selling those two baskets. We had to develop many kinds of baskets. All were functional and utilitarian.

This constant process of invention and reinvention is an agonizing, personal process. We thought that many—maybe all—of our baskets were beautiful and useful. But, a craft booth is not a museum to which you are charging admission. I can't remember all the baskets we created and discarded. Since they didn't sell, they were worthless. We ate our losses and created something new. This approach generated the repeat business that made for our success. Henry Ford could not sell his Model T—today!

However, we tried to make the loss worthwhile. When a basket wasn't selling, we made it a practice to ask customers what they didn't like about it. We solicited their ideas and redesigned accordingly. The idea for a number of our baskets came from someone with a particular need. We had designed a jewelry tray that we thought was very pretty. It didn't sell. Then one day a customer picked it up and pointed out that slightly enlarged and with two dividers it would make a beautiful utensil tray for outdoor picnics and barbecues. We made the change and over the years we must have sold a few thousand.

Whenever that happened, if the basket turned out to be a financial success, we sent the customer who had suggested it a free basket as a thank you.

The customers appreciated that and kept coming back year after year—and made more useful suggestions.

Creating something unique and being able to market it successfully by applying the above approach has another advantage: There is nothing you can produce that someone else can't imitate. But the act of creating your product and doing variations on your own basic theme gives you a selling advantage. Let me give you an example.

The Copycat

One year a vendor next to us watched us have a big payday. Of the twenty different baskets we displayed, this day we were selling dozens of one particular style. His booth was an accumulation of other people's ideas and he was having a particularly bad year. Under financial pressure, he decided to copy and produce this one basket, hoping to make a lot of money selling our creation the remainder of the year. Forgetting his lack of ethics, he also forgot that we participated in many of the same shows.

Now, there is a phenomenon that takes place at craft shows that none of us in the business has ever been able to fully explain. On any given day, at any given location, for reasons completely unfathomable, every customer is attracted to the same item in your booth. Maybe it is simply that one customer sees another customer attracted to an item and so, having confirmation of her taste, she buys it. This can be contagious. Over the years, this basket had been a consistent seller, but never like this day. Copycat didn't know that.

About six months later, at another show, Copycat approached me and apologized. He had produced twenty of these baskets and hadn't sold one. He didn't sell them because he didn't have our experience, reputation, or variety in his booth. He had them displayed next to some cowboy-boot birdhouses. That basket sold for us because it was utilitarian. As a matter of fact, it was designed as a basket to hold French bread. A customer, having gone home and measured it, found that it happened to fit exactly on the tank of the standard toilet bowl. From that day on, the French breadbasket also became a basket to hold toilet paper and a tissue box. The result was that we also had some funny stories to tell our customers about it. Copycat knew none of this. I accepted his apology, but I wasn't about to buy up his stock. I also didn't tell him why he couldn't sell them.

There are many people in the business—veterans and novices—who have no real talent or creativity. That they make a living is all that can be said for them. Frankly, they are an asset to those who have talent. They fill up spaces at a craft show and, if you're good, you look even better by comparison. If that sounds a little too cynical, it is intentional.

The crafts business is as competitive as any other business, maybe more so. You have to decide if you want to just fill up the promoter's space or make money.

Know Yourself, Your Assets, and Your Limitations

Now, reading this, you may be saying to yourself, "I'm not sure that I am as talented as necessary, as imaginative, or as competitive." Well, definitely a certain amount of self-questioning and self-examination is natural—actually good. That should be part of the process when you enter the business and throughout your career. Judy is an optimist; I'm a pessimist, so I was particularly dubious about many things. Judy and I had no idea how successful we could be when we started. We are, however, both "stick-to-it" type people.

My knowledge of woodworking did not extend beyond the use of a hammer, saw, screwdriver, and jigsaw. Thousands of men and women are better woodworkers than I am. Judy owned a small sewing machine that she hadn't used regularly for years. She had little more than basic knowledge or experience about sewing as a craft. Little by little, we added equipment as we learned to use it and as we enlarged our product line.

The point is, you're probably more creative and capable of manufacturing and selling than you think. Creativity is rarely a spontaneous inspiration or a miraculous revelation. More often, creativity and salesmanship develop as a tiny seed, a germ of an idea that grows with nourishment. That nourishment is the practical use of your eyes, your ears, and your brain. Then you have to put into action what you have been taught.

To create something unique, you do not have to be an artistic genius. You are a craftsperson, maybe even an artist at your craft, but you are also a vendor, a peddler, a traveling salesperson. Some people don't like those terms and even resent them, but to one degree or another, they still apply to people in the business.

Many artists are introverts, accustomed to expressing themselves through their work. Not uncommonly, they are shy or uncomfortable with strangers. Questioning one's own talent and worth can lead to a reluctance to sell your work. It may feel as if you are putting your inner self out on the table for sale. Customers are not always kind. In fact, often, there seems to be a disconnect between their recognition of the work and the fact that you made it. Comments can be cruel or simply a bit oblivious.

In the early days when I was street vending, I found that customer response could run the gamut from cries of delight and approbation to comments such as "My ten-year-old daughter could have done better." My carefully chosen prices shaved to the lowest possible nickel might be met with derision: "I'll give you half the price." As if they were doing me a favor. Or the table might be swamped with enthusiastic buyers greedily grabbing up their favorites and exclaiming, "What a find! And your prices are so reasonable!" Luckily for my tender sensibilities, my early exposure was positive and I came home with a lined pocket. In time I came to understand that there would always be insensitive boors who couldn't keep their unkind comments to themselves. In addition, I recognized that customers speak through their wallets. I concentrated on figuring out what would lure customers to buy and tuned out negativity. In other words, I toughened up.

In the beginning, I expected all my ideas to be fully realized from their conception. It took me a while to understand that sometimes a perfectly good design might be slightly off. Perhaps the first pieces were too rough or unfinished looking. Experience taught me that a good design could carry itself while I matured the idea. Minor flaws would be forgiven if the novelty or "it" factor outshone the kinks that had yet to be worked out. At one point I created a series of wild leather necklaces that had a rather crude edge to them. I sold quite a few to clubbers and performers of edgy cabaret acts in New York City's East Village. As I moved on to the more refined atmosphere of trade shows, the store buyers demanded a slightly more polished version to complement clothing lines. Eventually, I figured out how to achieve a similar effect using metal castings and waxed linen. The tamer version was the result of a greater familiarity with fashion jewelry techniques I had acquired during an apprenticeship a more experienced designer. The additional perspective new technical skills can offer has often proved advantageous in the final stages of designing, allowing you to add that necessary polish to a slightly raw product.   —BR

Your goal in the business is making money. Your product must be durable: It should not fall apart before the customer leaves the building or parking lot, and we've seen that happen. But, you are also not creating and selling to museums. As Beth Weber, a promoter for North Tahoe Fine Art Association, pointed out to me, "Over the years the craftspeople who remained in the business were those who 'got better and better' with experience." Beth also thought that this fact helped to rid the crafts business of its "flea market image." She was concerned that newcomers to the crafts industry seemed to be "less concerned" with quality and perhaps placed too much emphasis on making money. And she was right! Money is the goal, certainly, but you must put care and attention into the means of acquiring it.

Another promoter pointed out the reality of decreased attendance at craft shows over the years. Craftspeople are now not just competing with others in the crafts business. They are competing with other craft shows on the same weekend. The malls and warehouse stores carry variations on products once almost exclusively found at craft shows. Many have created venues within their stores to resemble the craft show atmosphere and ambiance. Mail order and Web catalogs have cut into the craftsperson's retail business. The result is that in order to compete successfully, your goal—to earn a substantial living—must be first to produce a substantial product and then fully market yourself and that product. Do that and the money will come.

Reevaluate the Crafts Business

Go to any craft show. You've probably already been to dozens or you wouldn't be thinking of going into the business. If you're already in the business, go to your next show with a new eye, a different perspective. Look at every booth in the show and see how many are producing basically the same product, with a few different wrinkles.

For example, suppose you make pretty, dried-flower arrangements for wall display. Your friends have told you how beautiful they are. Well, there are probably at least a few hundred craft merchants selling such arrangements in California alone, and some of them will be at any show in which you participate. So, you immediately face competition with far more experience than you do, if you are a beginner.

Now, face financial reality. Even at well-attended shows, there is just so much money in people's pockets. Every person is not your potential customer. You want your share of those who are looking for something to cover a space on their wall. The key to that is in your product. If you can develop a dried-flower arrangement that the buying public doesn't see everywhere, you will stand out from the competition. If you're planning to produce or are already selling a well-established craft, no better or different than anybody else's, reevaluate yourself and your product. If it's being done, it's probably already being done better than you can do it. However, if you're convinced you're dried-flower arrangement is truly different, go for it, but be prepared for the competition.

Some customers walk an entire show, making a list of booths that interest them, before they ever make a purchase. Still others, on impulse, will buy the first thing that they see and like. You can't do anything about that. If they see another potter, on another aisle, before they get to you, you may miss that potential customer. Your location at a show may also reduce your chances for sales. Except under special circumstances, to be explained later, you can't do much about that either. It's the luck of the draw. So observe and then change the things you can do something about—your craft and yourself.

Set Your Standard High

Whether you are a veteran crafter or a beginner, starting at your next show, make it your primary goal to establish a reputation for quality and excellence in your product. Ask yourself these questions: Did I make my product of the highest quality materials available? Will the customer be happy to put it in her home? Would I put it in my home? Did the customer leave the booth with a lasting, positive impression, whether she made a purchase or not? Are customers likely to recommend me to their friends? Will the customer return?

Initially, Judy and I didn't recognize that the answers to the above questions involved marketing and selling. We thought it sufficient to aim for a quality product, thinking the baskets would sell themselves. Not so! You will lose money allowing a product to sell itself. What we discovered was that most customers at a craft show are not impulse buyers. They are very discerning and, according to promoters, becoming more so, particularly when they are paying an admission price to enter the show in the first place. They don't come just to look, another promoter pointed out. They may buy cheap knickknacks on impulse, but most spend their money carefully and examine a product with a cautious eye. Those were the customers who came back looking for us year after year and those are the customers you want to cultivate through the standards you set for yourself, the quality of the product you produce, and, as a result, the reputation you achieve.

Keep Up with the Trends, Fads, and Even Eccentricities of Your Public

As you develop your product and create a demand for it, you should also be researching the latest trends as they may apply to your craft. That doesn't mean you should fall into line with every fad. But, you want to keep up, for instance, with what color schemes are currently popular, still making sure you have enough variety to appeal to every taste.

Trends are playing an increasingly important role in the crafts business. They are changing more rapidly now. As the crafts business expands nationally, as there are more and more arts and crafts shows, and as more people enter the field, the demand to produce more products is leading to mass production. Mass production can quickly bore the buying public because it uses up new ideas at a faster rate, which, in turn, leads to a need to be more and more creative and generates a new demand. In essence, you can't sell what people don't want.

We had a customer we called the Lavender Lady. She dressed from hat to shoes in lavender. Even her cat was clothed in lavender. Eccentric yes, but with a very big lavender purse. Every year we made sure to have one of every new basket in lavender. We set them aside for her. Then we'd pray she would show up or we were stuck with those lavender baskets for the year. Almost nobody likes lavender—or canary yellow for that matter.

We took a gamble, but it was well worth it. The Lavender Lady never failed us. One year she picked up our fifty-dollar picnic basket, put the cat in it, and paid happily. I was even happier! We sure couldn't sell the basket to anyone else after the cat had been in it! However, the loss would still have been slight, because the Lavender Lady had lots of friends she brought along with her. They turned out to be the regular customers with whom we did a continuing, repeat business for many years. Keeping up with one customer's desires gained us many more, each with her own particular taste.

That is the essence of selling yourself and your product. Selling your craft is not just how much inventory you move or how much money you make today. Marketing is about building a reputation for quality and friendliness that repeatedly brings your customers back to you. The latest fad—the craft item that suddenly appears—is something over which you have no control. For a time, it may seem to be taking money out of your pocket. The guy who sells a baseball hat with a propeller on top may be very annoying when you watch him raking in the cash while you have a rotten day. The person who sells out of some trash item, while you, with a unique, high-quality product to which you have devoted endless artistic effort, sell very little, can engender feelings of envy. But mostly, the sellers of tawdry, whimsical items will not be in business long and do not hurt you in the long run. You must, however, be conscious of trends, particularly if they relate to colors, fashions, and furniture—anything that will have a fairly long-lasting effect on your business. You may still see a few people around selling tie-dyed T-shirts, but not many and not making much money. Your T-shirts had better have some different saying on them and be fashionably up-to-date. At first, our baskets were ultra-country, but as trends and tastes changed, we gave them an updated look in color and design.

As a jewelry and accessory designer and kitchen table manufacturer (meaning my manufacturing process takes place on the table, not that I have diversified into woodworking), I have had plenty of ups and downs. Only sheer compulsiveness and the stubborn desire to work for myself have kept me from throwing in the towel during the inevitable tough times. In the past, I considered myself a generalist, a bronco rider in the rodeo of crafts. I have tended to discover a trend and ride it to its natural conclusion, switching to the next trend once the old one has collapsed on the ground in exhaustion. These days, I have come to see myself a little differently. My customer has an eye for the unusual and is looking for an accent piece to set off her existing wardrobe. Whether I am working in "soft media" such as Fimo, leather, fabric, or papier-mâché or I am working in fine metal, my customers seem to like my slightly offbeat sensibility. I am not every one's cup of tea and I have found that this can work to my advantage. Rather than trying to appeal to the many, I now try to understand my own corner of the craft market and sell exclusively to it.   —BR

Continue Evaluating Yourself

Assuming you are convinced that you have a great, marketable product that can produce a good living, the next thing you have to do is evaluate yourself, once again. This may be more difficult than evaluating your craft. It is perhaps the most difficult thing we all have to do in life.

The crafts business is just a microcosm of the larger world. We have discussed many marketing and sales techniques needed to succeed financially. But, have you considered and assessed the pros and cons of your own personality in relation to the crafts business? Can you face them honestly and then change those things about yourself in order to substantially improve your income potential? To help yourself figure this out, ask yourself these questions: How committed am I? How hard am I willing to work? Will I or do I enjoy a gypsy lifestyle? If I don't, can I adjust to it, and for how long? Do I enjoy people? Can my physical and mental health sustain long hours, physically demanding effort, and a frantic pace? Am I capable of maintaining the necessary positive frame of mind? How long, based on my previous experience, can I sustain my ambition? Am I likely to quit when the business gets tough or am I a fighter? How long do I generate enthusiasm? Am I quickly bored? Knowing the honest answers to these questions is vital to marketing yourself as well as your product.

As acknowledged in the introduction, Judy and I just stumbled into the business and never considered these questions in relation to selling. Most craftspeople we met never did until they were deeply involved in the business. Sometimes, by then it is too late. We were simply lucky, as we were older, had experienced other professions, and knew our capabilities. We had never dodged hard work and had proven to ourselves that we had the tenacity to stick to it and make the necessary adjustments. Do you? Because once you make the financial commitment, you have no choice but to be dedicated. And, once you've made the financial commitment, you may find that you still are not able to generate the necessary energy. Try to avoid such a forced choice. Know your strengths and your limitations.

Travel, for example, is wearing and time consuming. Maybe you hate motels. If that's the case, reevaluate your show schedule. You may be in a rut, doing the same shows year after year out of habit, but not necessarily because they generate the most net income. Such circumstances can impact negatively on your selling ability.

Pay attention to the pressures under which you are selling yourself and your product. How is it affecting you? Among serious professionals in the business, unless you do at least twenty shows a year, you're considered a dilettante. That doesn't mean you should start by doing that many shows. To the contrary, our recommendation if you are new to the business is to schedule no more than ten shows the first year, possibly fewer. Selection of craft shows is addressed in chapter 5, but I mention it here because it is important as you evaluate yourself.

The first year, you need the time to analyze your product, yourself, and the shows you're participating in. Once you are doing twenty or more shows (many of us do more than thirty), you are stressed in ways you cannot foresee. That many shows require twelve-to-fifteen-hour days, seven days a week, almost fifty-two weeks a year. We rarely had more than a week's vacation a year. You will eat, sleep, and literally dream the crafts business.

That is not fun! There is nothing glamorous about the crafts business. The craft world is about making money and what you have to know and do to make it. We do not wish to discourage you with that bit of realism; we just want you to recognize the pressures that exist and the commitment you have to make to sell your product successfully.

Time constraints and pressure are especially acute during the latter part of the year. Your ability to sell yourself and your product will be affected by these factors. Most of the year, you will earn enough to pay for your business expenses, cover your personal budget, and, hopefully, take in some additional profit. But, the big money is always earned during the holiday season. You must be gearing yourself and your business toward this time of year, even while preparing for next week's show. For those shows, you must produce inventory in advance, adding to the pressure under which you must produce and sell all year. The last thing you ever want to do is sell out. That means you didn't have enough inventory to sell and you lost potential income.

Friends of ours sold their entire stock of candy on the first day of a Harvest Festival show—$2500 worth of sweets. They could not take down their booth and go home because of the promoter's tear-down rules. They sat there for two days earning and producing nothing. To say they were angry and frustrated is to put it mildly. Such frustration can easily contribute to physical and mental deterioration that, in turn, can affect the quality of your product and your ability to sell it. Helen and Tom worked twice as hard the following week and were behind schedule for the remainder of the year.

We suggest that newcomers to the business do no more than ten shows their first year. And if you are a veteran who is experiencing the Law of Diminishing Returns, reduce the number of shows that you schedule. In both cases, this will allow you time to evaluate your competition, your product, and yourself. Do your bookkeeping carefully. Learn how much money you must earn to be content, creative, and productive. Test your price line. Develop your public relations skills. Practice your new selling techniques and approaches. Be consciously aware of what you are saying and doing. Start off slow, but start off right.

When the season ends, decide the degree to which you desire to continue or expand your schedule. You must determine whether you can sell and market competitively at an increased rate, which means getting your share of the market. You can't produce and market your best product, or greet your customers with your best foot forward, if you're burned out creatively, frustrated, despondent, or lack enthusiasm.

During lunch hour, when business gets slow and the day is very hot, it is easy to nod off. One such day, I fell asleep in the booth while Judy was off having lunch. I was in my Musketeer costume, which made me look even more like a statue. I awoke to hear a little girl ask her mother, "Mommy, is he real or is he a dummy?" Judy returned at that moment and readily provided the answer. Luckily, the woman was interested in our product, in spite of my inattention, so we did not lose a sale, but we should have, and would have if it hadn't been for Judy. Staring into space, your mind in a netherworld, doesn't entice a customer into your booth. If you're not prepared to greet the customer with a smile, you're not prepared to sell yourself or your product.

3 Pricing Your Product

HAVING ESTABLISHED WHAT YOU need to do to sell successfully, and assuming that you have a good product, a good variety, and that you're working hard to build your inventory and that you've followed our every direction and subscribed to our best advice, you're probably poised to make a lot of money. Well, maybe, and maybe not.

The Difficulty of Pricing Your Craft

If there is a stumbling block in the crafts business, one that drives the most experienced craftsperson crazy, it is the pricing of your product. This may well be the most difficult, and could arguably be considered the most important aspect of your business. It is also a question for which there are no pat answers. There is no mathematical formula that you can apply to this problem.

If you hired Judy and me to come to your booth to assist you in pricing your product, after we knew your cost of production, compared it to similar products on the market and at craft shows, considered your craftsmanship and the quality and durability of your product, we could then give you a rough estimate of the price that you might charge. However, we could never give you a guarantee that it would be the best price for which the merchandise should be sold. The price we set may still be too low or too high and therefore affect your profit margin either way. Regardless of how good your product and how charming your sales personality and technique, price your product incorrectly and you will make fewer sales and less money.

Since the subject of marketing includes anything that involves the placing of your product in front of the buying public, pricing is considered part of marketing and, as such, could have been included in the previous chapter. The price you place on your craft is vital in determining whether you attract or discourage customers. Some people will enter your booth and the only thing they will really look at is the price of your merchandise. It will be their sole determinant as to whether to buy from you or not.

When Judy and I began our business, we not only had no idea what to charge for our baskets, but we hardly even discussed it. We knew, as should you, what it cost to produce a basket and how much time it took to complete each unit. But, how much to charge for each basket, how much profit we could fairly request—these were questions that, in our former professions, we had never had to consider. How much profit would the traffic bear? For us, it was an unknown quantity.

A Variety of Factors Affect Your Price

The fact is that there is no exact and precise answer to the quandary of pricing. Assuming that you have a wonderful product, price is still affected by the economics of the area in which you are selling. The season of the year strongly impacts and determines your income potential on any given weekend. The fall season prior to the holidays presents your biggest potential for income. After the holidays, the beginning of the year will be your slowest time, as people have spent all their money and don't want to run up their credit cards any further. However, you can't adjust and readjust according to these continual variables.

The type of customer the show is attracting will affect your weekly income. If you are in a depressed economic area, people will naturally have less money. Should a normally solid financial area have been hit by industry closings, layoffs—or, in a farm area, drought or flood—you will find that your income potential will fall off from the previous year.

Even very large, overall cultural changes will affect your pricing over a period of years. Smaller promoters cannot and needn't bother to survey this kind of information, but a large organization like Harvest Festival regularly conducts surveys in an attempt to understand and explain how changing cultural patterns may affect the way craft show customers are spending their money. Harvest Festival promoters have found, for example, that there has been a definite change in the spending behavior of what is referred to as the DINK (double income, no kids) generation. In the past, married couples would spend $500 to $2000 a year at Harvest Festival shows and could be counted on to return each year. Now that group of people is not spending as much and may actually be disappearing as a distinct entity. It is believed that downsizing of major corporations has had an impact on these couples, since both family members may not be consistently working now. Then, too, they may simply have had children, which, obviously, drastically changes where a married couple spend their money and how much money they have left to indulge their every desire. Country Folk Art has found that while their attendance at shows has not diminished, because of oversaturation of the marketplace (too many shows in the same area), the individual customer may not be buying as much at any given show. There is always another show next week. Therefore, your pricing may be a paramount element to your success.

Even the nature of your craft will impact your pricing scheme. Toys may be in more demand than stuffed teddy bears. In the spring, floral arrangements are going to be better sellers than Christmas ornaments, and vice versa in the fall and early winter.

To the greatest extent possible, try to evaluate these factors before applying to a show in certain areas at certain times. Just because you did well last year, or even over the last five years, is not an absolute indicator that you will make money this year. Whether it's the beginning or the end of the month and people have or have not received their pay or retirement checks may also have an impact on your sales. Income tax time may make a big difference in your sales as well.

You have to learn to try to anticipate such factors whenever possible. The way you present your product to the public is still another variable in the prices you can command, and it's something to which you must pay close attention. There will be more detail on this in chapter 7 on Booth Setup and Booth Display; however, the following is especially relevant to this subject.

The Loss Leader

There is in the retail business a concept known as a loss leader. This refers to an item or items on which you are prepared to accept a minimal loss. They are used to attract customers into the store or, in this case, into your booth. They should be quick and easy to produce and particularly eye-catching. Sometimes a loss leader may be a gimmick item or a small sample of the craft you produce, or something that is very inexpensive and appeals to children, drawing their parents into the booth. And, as a matter of fact, if you select and manufacture the right product, it may not even have to be a loser. But, winner or loser, the advantage of the loss leader to your pricing is that it can give you a price measure to compare to the other items you are selling. If you are only selling your loss leader, something is usually wrong with how you are pricing the rest of your merchandise.

Very early in our career, Judy came up with the idea of selling plant stakes. We traced hearts, rabbits, bears, and other figures on our scrap wood, cut them out, decorated them, put them on a stick, and never had less than a hundred sitting in large vases at the front of the booth. We never charged more than $2 apiece for them, sometimes only a dollar if we thought that money was in short supply. Most often, we sold enough of them to pay for our booth fee. However, if all the first customers who entered the booth purchased only plant stakes, we were usually in for a bad day, which meant either that we were in a depressed economic area or our prices were off base.

A few years later, Judy suggested a very small, wooden, slatted basket with painted wooden tulips in it. Plant stakes were out and Judy thought this might be a better loss leader. I thought it was the dumbest idea she had ever had. "Who would want to buy wooden tulips?" I foolishly asked. Nevertheless, I made them. We put the basket on a shelf at the front of our booth and charged $10 for them. We sold ten the first weekend and thereafter rarely sold fewer than twenty a show, sometimes thirty or forty.

These baskets were easy to produce, requiring very little time, and were made mostly of scrap material. They were almost pure profit. Those tulip baskets became one of the mainstays of our inventory for about six years and, according to the Law of Supply and Demand, we found that we could raise the price to $20 and still sell just as many. You can be sure that Judy never failed to remind me of what I had said and you can be equally sure that I never again questioned her judgement as to what women prefer. Truthfully, I never did like the tulip baskets, but they made money, so I set aside my personal distaste for the baskets and made them.

You Can't Make Constant Price Adjustments

Unfortunately, as noted above, the one thing you cannot do is adjust your prices according to many of the variables mentioned. Too many customers travel each weekend from show to show. Today's customers will remember not only what they paid last week, but also what they were charged the year before. Nor can you test what the traffic will bear on Saturday and reduce or raise your price on Sunday. Many customers come to a show both days and you'll catch hell from somebody who paid more yesterday than you are charging today. We did that once and had to make a refund. Occasionally, perhaps yearly, "cost of doing business" increases are tolerable and will be understood by your repeat customers. But, you cannot make drastic price changes from day to day or even week to week.

As with everything else in the crafts business, there is an exception. An artist friend of ours, who worked in oils, taught me this. In front of his booth he always had a very large painting that he priced at $5000. That may seem like an unusual price for a loss leader, but in this case the goal was different. He knew, just as well as I, that virtually no one goes to a craft show to buy a five thousand dollar painting. If they are going to spend that much money, they'll go to a reputable, established art gallery. He never did sell that painting at a craft show, as far as I know, but he sure sold a lot of small paintings and prints. Customers looked at and admired the five thousand dollar painting; somehow the price established his credentials as an artist. Then they thought they were getting a bargain on anything that they did purchase.

I thought I'd try that sales technique and built a giant basket for which I charged $200. The idea didn't work for us. Two hundred dollars is a long way from $5,000. Someone bought the basket the first day of the show. That was not what I wanted. There was far too much work, time, and money involved in producing it to make it really profitable, nor did we have enough room in our truck to transport a number of such baskets. So, I never made another.

The Hourly Wage Issue

A special word of advice: Never, never, never determine your price on the basis of how much you think your work is worth on an hourly basis. There is a strong temptation to do this and you must resist it. Over the years, we cannot count the number of craftspeople with whom we discussed this issue and who tried to apply that pricing strategy and lost a lot of money or quit the business.

Sometimes, these craftspeople had worked in previous jobs that paid on an hourly wage basis. Millions of workers do. So, when you are new to the business, this approach may seem logical. The veteran who insists on it simply hasn't done her homework or is allowing her ego to get in the way of her better judgment. This approach simply does not apply to the crafts business. All successful, veteran craftspeople know that if they priced their craft using hourly wage as a criterion, they would be charging Macy's prices. People don't come to a craft show to pay such prices. Attempt to apply that formula and you will price yourself right out of business.

Quite naturally, you may ask, "Why can't I charge what I think I'm worth on an hourly basis?" Well, the answer is simple, if you can handle it. Essentially, in the craft world, the customer, far more than you, determines what your product is worth. We all have an inflated idea of the value of our work and time. It's human nature, particularly in the craft and art world.

When you work for an employer, he sets the hourly wage and if you don't believe it's sufficient recompense for your labor, you simply don't take the job, you quit, or maybe you go on strike. Now, of course, you can quit the crafts business, or not go into it in the first place, but the strike option is not available to you.

More to the point, you are now in the crafts business and have made a big investment. You're not likely to throw that out the window. Besides, you like the business. Unlike most jobs or professions, you are your own boss, you make your own hours, you go where you please, you set your own standards, you create what you want to create, and you move in a world in which you want to move. You probably don't want to give up all this freedom for a few extra dollars an hour.

Customer Reaction Can Help Determine Your Price

Since you cannot and should not attempt to explain to a customer why an item costs what it does or how many hours of labor you put in, the product must speak for you. Place too high a price tag on your craft, and the product's message to the customer is "too much." Conversely, price out of fear that you won't sell anything and the message to the customer is "too low." The customer becomes wary of the quality of your product and may not buy at all or will recognize a great bargain and buy you out. That can put you out of business, too. I'll give you an example.

In 1982, when we designed our first picnic basket, we priced it at $28. We sold out at every show. We were as happy as the proverbial clams. We'd gross between $500 and $800 every show and thought we were doing great. The trouble was, I couldn't make baskets fast enough. It took the first year and advice from a veteran craftsperson to learn that those customers realized they were getting a tremendous bargain.

Eventually, we realized we were giving this basket away and, with much trepidation, raised the price to $40. Sales decreased! But, since our profit margin was higher, we made more money with less work. Then we got greedy and tried $50. Sales evaporated! We went back to $40, realizing that was the proper price at the time. Some sixteen years later, that basket still sold best at $48. Every time we raised it to $50, sales dropped. That fact involves another intriguing, mystifying, and often annoying pricing phenomenon with which you must learn to deal.

The Numbers Game of Pricing

There are in every business certain whole numbers that act like a wall or barrier beyond which the customer will not, for a given item, dip into her wallet or purse. Marketing and advertising people realized that years ago. You run into it every time you go to buy anything. Just remember how many products cost $4.95, $9.95, $19.95, $99.95, or $19,995.

I'm not suggesting that you use this technique. It is too much trouble in the crafts business. You don't have the time on a busy day to always be dealing with nickels and dimes. However, the idea points to the psychological phenomenon I mentioned.

Sometimes, just a dollar less will increase your sales, while a dollar more will reduce them. To give you a specific example: That first year in business, I had designed an odd-shaped fruit basket with a rope handle. It was very unusual, but it didn't sell. We carried fifteen of them with us to every show and every show we came home with fifteen. We priced them at $16 apiece. Exasperated, as I was tired of packing them in and out of the truck and having them take up valuable space on our shelf, I put a sale sign on them. We explained that we were no longer making that design and reduced the price to $15. We sold every basket that show. I, of course, then continued to produce that basket and $15 became the successful and appropriate price. Why $15 was right and $16 was too much, I'll never know. That is an intangible, even psychological phenomenon, involving every product in every marketplace.

Test Pricing

It was then that we learned that you must test price every piece of merchandise that you sell. This price testing is a never ending process and you must be ready to make adjustments for the reasons already noted. Sometimes, in a really bad year, you may have to adjust downward in the middle of a season, sacrificing some profit as opposed to realizing no profit. But the longer you can keep your price structure steady, the better off you are.

Granting that testing your prices engages you in a nebulous, intangible, and often frustrating aspect of your operation, there are several ways to go about it. If you are producing a product that can generally be found at craft boutiques and other stores, one approach is to check the prices in those venues. You can count on the fact that the stores will have doubled the price on any item. It is necessary to their profit margin, since their operating expenses are much higher than yours. Therefore, you can probably assume that you can sell at half their price and be making a reasonable profit.

A second method of testing your prices is to evaluate the price your competition is asking. Since we already know, based on what we said earlier, that many craftspeople will be charging too much, if you think your version is as good or better than theirs, undersell them. This was something that we never had to do, as no one made a basket like ours. But, be warned: This may not make you popular with your competition, particularly if they follow the hourly wage approach, and they usually do.

During the hundreds of shows we did, we had many neighbors, at many shows, griping to us that they weren't selling because somebody else in the show was selling the same item "too low." Usually they would complain that the other guy "just had to be selling at a loss." The truth was, that was never the case. "The other guy" had simply found a way to produce the product for less and more efficiently, or perhaps his lifestyle required less profit, or perhaps he was simply not as greedy.

Whatever the reason, the craftsperson had no ethical right to complain. The crafts business is highly competitive, and such tactics are just a realistic part of the business. You are not in business to win popularity contests with your competitors. And you certainly are not going to go around discussing your prices with the competition so you can agree on setting the same price. Do that and your competitor could be reaping real financial benefits while you lose money. You are in business to make the money you need to survive and profit. If you can satisfy your needs by underselling the competition, do it. You won't see the other guy that often anyway.

Once Again, Variety

A third factor in pricing—and perhaps one of the most important—is to offer a wide variety of sizes and designs in all price ranges, but to make sure you can still produce a profit. This allows you to display a range of choices that can suit almost everyone's budget. Rhonda Blakely of Country Folk Art strongly urges craft artists to have a range of prices.

You will find this advice very helpful, especially when you are doing a show in an economically sluggish area or where economic forces have changed financial conditions. Our baskets ranged in price from $10 to $48. Therefore, we were able to retain our share of the market no matter where we were and no matter what the economic situation. We didn't always make as much as we might have wanted, but who is always satisfied in life? Very often it was the smaller items that sold and kept us from losing money at a show.

Adjust Your Inventory

Think not only about how much inventory you should bring to a show, but also about what price range inventory you should carry with you. You may recall that I discouraged the idea of changing prices on a week-to-week basis and indicated that there were other ways to handle this problem. Here is one way:

Suppose you are scheduled for a show and you belatedly learn that there has been a downturn in the local economy. It is pointless to stock your booth with merchandise in your highest price range. As a matter of fact, no matter where we went, we never put more than one example of our highest-priced basket out front. People walk by, bend over, check the price tag, and walk on.

This is especially true in areas with a depressed economy. Don't even bring those high-priced items with you. Seeing the price will just discourage and often sadden potential customers. It reminds them of what they cannot afford. Better to have a fully stocked booth of items that are affordable to the people in the area, so everyone can feel they are getting a bargain. In the long run, you'll make more money and more friends.

The Special Order

Now a word about special ordering. It is inevitable and very probable that no matter how much inventory you have in your booth and how varied the selection open to the customer, a customer will be looking for something that you don't have. She may want a different color, a different size, a different something. That is a sale that is escaping you, unless you are prepared to take the order and ship it to the customer.

In some cases, if what the customer desires is not something that you have on the shelf, you may have the item at home. But, much more often than not, to provide the customer with what she is specifically ordering is going to cause you some inconvenience. You may have to go out and buy a special fabric or paint or wood or whatever. The customer may want a special design or size or any other number of possible changes. You can refuse and lose a customer or agree and establish a lasting relationship. We chose the latter, but remember that you will probably be forced to consider some change of price.

When taking a special order, it is perfectly legitimate to inform the customer that you will have to charge more. Tell the customer the increased price and don't forget to inform her that the price includes not only the cost of shipping, but also of packaging for shipment. You should have these special order prices ready and easily available for reference. If your merchandise is of varying size and weight, it will cost more or less to ship and will require more or less expensive packaging. Therefore, you should know the weight and size of every product you could be asked to ship, so that you can simply refer to a document on which you have the total cost already calculated and can quickly inform the customer of how much extra this service will cost. If she agrees, and she almost always will, though it means a little extra work, it also means another sale now and often many sales in the future.

Early in our career, when Judy had to pack something for shipping, we ran around trying to find boxes at the supermarket, or wherever, trying to save money. We saved money, but lost time. We never had the right size box at the right time. We soon found that there are dozens of catalogs available that provide you with every conceivable means of shipping your merchandise in every size. You can purchase boxes, bags, cellophane wrappings, labels, shipping tape, scales—just about anything you can think of relating to shipping a package.

We just received a catalog of this type in the mail from Uline, a firm that operates out of Waukegan, Illinois. Uline has telephone, fax, and Internet capability to take your order. Another packaging materials company specializing in bagging material and protective wrappings is Northeast Poly Bag, located in Sterling, Massachusetts. There are many more such manufacturers all over the country. However, if you cannot sustain this cost at the beginning, go to any flea market and you'll find someone selling plastic bags to use for packaging, or just hunt around the shopping mall, early in the morning, as we did, for empty cartons in which to ship your product. You can meet a lot of nice people at the rear of big stores, especially at Christmastime.

Another Reason to Review Your Pricing Structure

One last suggestion we would make regarding pricing has to do with record-keeping, a task that can be very helpful in making price adjustments. Maintain a record of the price you place on every type of product you manufacture and review it on a quarterly basis. The purpose of this is twofold. It will provide you with a record of the number you have sold of each item in your inventory. More importantly, it will establish your leading sellers and what merchandise is selling poorly. If, based on your discussions with your customers, you are convinced that your pricing is affecting your sales, you can make the necessary price adjustments accordingly. Usually such adjustments are small, but they are very important to sales.

Cash Flow

Having read all these pricing techniques, perhaps you think we forgot that problem of hourly wages. We haven't, but we wanted to show you as many ways as possible to improve your sales and take your mind off that concept. However, if you insist on thinking in hourly terms, be reminded that the crafts business is about cash flow. It is a business that, when you are successful, will regularly put large amounts of money in your pocket. Your theoretical hourly wage is irrelevant. The hours you work will always be far more than you would at any nine-to-five job. But so is the money you can make. We often made $5,000 to $6,000 at many shows and many crafts merchants make a great deal more. If we worked an average of twelve hours a day, seven days a week, we were averaging almost sixty dollars an hour. Not many jobs pay that.

Realistically, if you are new to the business, you will probably not be making that kind of money until you perfect your manufacturing, selling, marketing, and pricing techniques, to mention only what has been discussed thus far. So, if you are dissatisfied with your profit margin and expect to increase your profit (not your hourly wage), reevaluate your manufacturing techniques and cost of materials.

Ask yourself if you have done the necessary research to find new suppliers where you can purchase your materials for less money but of equal quality. Can you find short cuts in the manufacturing process without sacrificing quality? Years into the business, we never ceased being surprised when we suddenly found an easier, less time-consuming way to do something and would wonder, "Why didn't we think of that before?"

Concentrate on your successes and weed out the failures. Often enjoying what you're doing and the lifestyle you can now lead is the best reward.

An Update on Pricing

The approach to pricing that the Kadubecs used in the eighties and nineties is sound. Their practical, unemotional attitude toward pricing cannot be faulted. Nonetheless, I do differ on a few points and will weigh in for what it is worth. In the late eighties, the influx of sophisticated foreign handicrafts had only just begun to infiltrate the American market. While there were plenty of cheap goods available, importers had not yet taken the measure of the American markets taste for well-designed, affordable home furnishings with a crafted look. Canny companies such as Target; Bed, Bath & Beyond; Crate & Barrel; and Design Barn had not yet gotten the hang of it. Somehow, with the advent of craft cult divas such as Martha Stewart, elegance was suddenly affordable. The quality of available imported crafts shot up, but the price remained amazingly within reach of the common pocketbook.

Unfortunately, these prices, which the consumer likes to call "reasonable," were in fact so incredibly low that anyone who understands what goes into making something by hand stands mouth agape in shock when staring at the ticket price.

As a result of this shift in the market, many American designers began to go abroad to produce their lines. They started to realize that they could use their American design sensiblity to their advantage and still reap the benefit of low overseas production costs. This proved a successful gambit for almost all wholesale manufacturing. Very little is made here in the United States these days, as we all know. The consequence has been a plethora of alluring goods at prices that are impossible to beat.

The good news in recent years, however, has been that while many of these goods are manufactured cheaply, they are not in all cases sold cheaply. In fact, I have noticed that many high-end American designers will advertise their line as handcrafted without mentioning that the handcraft work is taking place overseas and the hands are not their own. They will refer to staffs of highly skilled craftspeople and ancient techiniques and every word of their advertising copy will be the honest truth, except for that one significant omission.

That Hourly Wage Question, Again

There is a market out there for American-made craft and design. And the customer is willing to pay the higher prices if the customer is convinced of the value of the product. In general, both retailers and crafters agree, the price a craft item can command is based primarily on perceived value. If you have an incredible product and can introduce your product into a venue where it will be appreciated for the quality item it is, you will be able to achieve much greater recompense for your work.

This does not mean that you should price your work too high, of course, but it does mean that you should not make the mistake of pricing your work too low.

When I put the question to Heather Skelly, editor of *The Crafts Report*, she said, "There are a lot of factors that go into pricing your work and one is most certainly paying yourself an hourly wage. Your time and creativity must be considered as factors in pricing along with supply costs and what the market can bear at the time. Keeping your prices fair to both your business and the market is essential. . . . If you keep your prices too low under the assumption that you'll be more successful, it's likely that you won't be in business very long."

While freedom of the craft lifestyle is in some way a compensation for a lower income, there is no question in my mind that a crafter must maintain an overall awareness of the hourly wage that is necessary to earn a reasonable livelihood. In my experience, many new crafters fail to consider the full amount of time involved both in creating and in selling their work. They tend to discount their overhead and the time spent in finding and preparing the raw materials. There are many invisible expenses that never make it into the final price of their work. As a result, when looking at their bank account at the end of the day, crafters often find themselves squeezed between that perennial rock and a hard place.

There is no one formula that will work for every crafter. However, I am in favor of factoring in an hourly wage and studio and health overhead. Design time should be charged at a higher hourly wage than your production time. This will help you differentiate between what you should charge if you are making a one-of-a-kind piece and a piece of which you are making multiples. For many years I did not include the cost of health insurance in my calculations, which meant that I went without insurance altogether for a long time. After arriving at a subtotal of all my costs (including insurance), I then add in my profit margin. I have been in the habit of doubling the cost of my materials. (Other crafters have recommended marking up the subtotal of all of your costs by 20 to 50 percent.) This becomes my wholesale price. Retail prices are generally considered to be double your wholesale price. Many stores will keystone your work, which means that they will mark up the wholesale price by 2.5 percent.

For a number of years, I made a particular style of pin I called an "image pin," which I was able to sell at both the wholesale and retail level. This is how I arrived at my wholesale price:

Pricing Out an Image Pin

Cost of raw materials per pin	2.00
Overhead (divide cost of studio rental by number of items you are able to make in a month)	2.00
Labor/production time ($10.00/hour) three pins created per hour	3.30
Design time ($20/hour) six minutes per pin for individual tweaking	2.00
Health overhead	4.00
Total	13.30
Profit margin	2.00
Wholesale price	15.30
	x2
Retail price	30.60

Making the argument for selling your work at elevated prices can be a stretch. You may be frightened to take the plunge. Obviously, the image pin was an inexpensive item in the first place and not a great challenge to the expectation of my customers. To my great surprise and delight, I have discovered that my customers are comfortable with prices higher than I had anticipated.

As I said earlier, the price of arts and crafts is primarily a matter of perceived value. The first part of your job as a crafter is to create these works and the second half is to inspire your customer to accept your prices. If you believe in the value of your work, so will the customer.
—BR

4 Strictly Business

"Being good in business is the most fascinating kind of art. . . .
Making money is art and working is art and good business is the best art."
—ANDY WARHOL

NO DOUBT, ANDY WARHOL was correct. Judy is an artist at manipulating, keeping track of, and multiplying money. I've just wished that I could avoid writing this chapter, for if money management had been left to me, we never would have retired. While for some, managing money may be an "art," for most of us it is the most tedious and even threatening aspect of business. Too much creativity can lead not just to a lot of trouble with the IRS, but, more importantly, to financial instability and even bankruptcy. Therefore, managing money may be the predominant reason why so many craftspeople fail to be successful. Creative and artistic people rarely think along the mechanical, logical, and practical lines necessary in a good accountant.

Finances boggle most of our brains. It takes a special kind of personality to be an accountant or tax consultant and to pore over figures day in and day out. Neither Judy nor I had the necessary credentials. One of us had to learn, however. Since, thank goodness, Judy was by far my superior in this area, she took on the tedious duty of record keeping. If you have a partner, and you cannot afford expert help, you should then make a decision in the early stages of developing your business about who will be the money manager. If you are a solo act, I'm afraid that you are probably stuck with the job. We will try to give you some general tips. This chapter, however, will not be devoted to a technical dissertation on bookkeeping, tax law, or other mathematical formulae. Neither Judy nor I are qualified to provide that kind of expertise.

Get Professional Help

If you hope to be successful in the craft world, no matter how talented you are or how beautiful your product, if you do not come to grips with the practical aspects of the crafts business, you will not be in business long. Our suggestion? If you can't or won't do your own accounting and bookkeeping, and if you can afford it, consult a professional as soon as you enter the crafts marketplace. If you are already in business and don't have a financial advisor, we strongly suggest that you find one. He will know what records your tax consultant will need. Most often, a financial consultant and tax consultant is the same person. Sit down with him and learn what you have to account for and what records you have to keep.

Once again, Judy and I learned the hard way. For the first few years, we were not aware of all the ramifications that could have saved us money. However, regardless of how good your tax consultant, there are certain general things you must do or you won't have any records to bring to him at the end of the year.

Open a Business Banking Account

Before you've invested, made, or spent a dime on your business, and after you've chosen a name for that business, go to your bank and open a separate business checking account in your business name. Thereafter, write checks relating to the business only out of this account. In your checkbook or on your computer specify what kind of bill you are paying, such as: shop supplies, show fees, postage, advertising, office supplies, legal fees, and the like. This is essential to keeping an accurate account of your financial transactions and cannot be emphasized enough. Any large purchases, such as your computer, production machinery, or business vehicles, may be depreciated or used as deductions. Your accountant is the best one to advise you regarding this aspect of your accounting.

Keeping an accurate business account is absolutely essential when you sit down with your tax consultant to explain your expenses. He will always want those expenses broken down for IRS purposes. By breaking your expenses into categories (such as telephone, electronic, travel, cost of goods sold, etc.), you also create a helpful tool to evaluate how your business spends money. This should enable you to budget and, in many cases, cut back on expenses.

These expenses are enumerated on Schedule C of your tax form. It is best to consult a professional in advance to verify all expenses that you may legally take. Then, when you write checks to pay your business bills, identify to which of these categories they were applied. Keeping records not only saves time when tax deadlines roll around, but it enables you to better judge just what your product is costing and hence assists you in setting the most appropriate and fair price. That is, fair to both you and your customers.

An excellent discussion of income taxes can be found in *Legal Guide for the Visual Artist* by Tad Crawford, an attorney who represented many artists and artists' groups before becoming the publisher of Allworth Press (and this book).

Avoid Commingling Funds

Maintained both for legal and tax reasons, meticulous records are a must. You should always avoid commingling your business funds with money used to manage home expenses, food, rent/mortgage, entertainment, and the like. Commingling funds will make it impossible for you to know—and positively establish on your tax return—what money went into and out of the business and what did not. Never use your business account for any purpose other than your business or you will find your business and private financial dealings hopelessly confused. You will never know how much profit you are making or how much loss you are suffering.

Many one-person businesses choose to start off without a business account in order to circumvent the monthly fees that come with being unable to maintain the high monthly minimum balance required of a small commercial account (usually around $5000). However, it is good to know that many banks will waive the minimum for the first year. Due to the great increase in the number of small businesses opening up in the last few years, many banks are much more interested in helping the budding entrepreneur get off to a good beginning. Cultivate a relationship with your personal banker. There is quite a bit of competition between banks these days for your business; you may find you are able to get your banker to negotiate a better deal in order to prevent your leaving the fold.

Small Business Regulations, Resale Permits, and Licenses

Research your state's regulations on small businesses. You will probably need a resale permit or business license, as you will have to pay state sales tax on a yearly, biannual, or quarterly basis. In California, we had to pay sales tax quarterly; here this is determined by the State Board of Equalization. So as not to be caught financially unprepared, we recommend that you set aside the amount of money that you owe the government after each show; those monies might even be placed in a separate checking account earmarked for taxes and used only to make such payments. That way you will not be scrounging for money or depending on the next show to make a payment from the last show. That applies not only to money that you will eventually have to pay the federal and state governments in the form of income taxes, but also money you owe in the form of sales tax.

In some cases, as in California, where we primarily did business, you may start out paying sales tax annually and then, as we were, be set up by the state to make quarterly payments. Remember that sales tax is different from county to county and state to state. In some places you will pay city sales tax as well as state tax. So, depending on where you are doing business, you must know the tax laws and tax rates in that community.

As an example, in Nevada, the sales tax is paid only to the state of Nevada. But since the Nevada tax collectors do not want to wait until the end of the year for nonresidents to pay that tax or have to keep records of everyone who owes Nevada money, sales tax is collected at the end of each show by the promoter. When we did shows in Nevada, each craftsperson signed a slip indicating his gross income at the show and then enclosed in an envelope the amount of money or percentage of that gross that the state required for sales tax. The promoter then was responsible for submitting the total amount to the state.

Such tax is also subject to change from year to year, usually on the upward side, so you must remember to obtain a chart from the promoter of the show each time you are in a new city, county, parish, or state. The chart will give you the exact percentage you need to pay, wherever you are. In California, the State Board of Equalization, from whom we received our resale permit and to whom we paid our sales tax, also provided us with such a chart. We carried it to every show, sometimes providing the information to other craftspeople and even the promoter. You will have to check these regulations in your state to assess and add to the price of every item you sell.

Assessing Sales Tax to the Customer

Basically, there are two ways to impose sales tax: You can roughly include the sales tax in the total price you are charging for your product or you can apply the necessary tax to the price you put on your product at the time you ring up the purchase. We highly recommend the second option, and some states require it.

If you choose the first option and include the tax in the total price, you will be changing your price tags at every show that takes place in a county, city, or state that requires a different percentage than the last place in which you did a show. Very few locales impose the same sales tax, and because there are different regulations all over the United States, there is no way to provide you with general guidelines. Besides, the information usually changes from year to year.

As well, including the tax in the total price requires that you hang a sign informing the customers that your price includes sales tax. Psychologically, when people are comparison shopping, that addition to the total price may make a significant difference to many would-be customers—to your detriment. You are presenting your product as more expensive than, perhaps *too* expensive in comparison to, the products of your competition. Eight percent added to a $50 purchase is $4 more. Human nature being what it is, those few extra dollars on the sales tag may hinder your sales, even though people are paying the same total amount when they complete the transaction at your cash register.

The reason for the different reaction at the register is that once a customer is at the counter and ready to pay for something she has chosen, she rarely rebels against the tax or decides not to buy because of it. She is accustomed to paying tax for everything she purchases anywhere, so she doesn't notice the difference between your asking price on the price tag and the purchase price at the counter. Besides, once she has the product in hand, having decided that she wants it, she is psychologically committed to the purchase and less likely to change her mind about buying it.

The Resale Permit

Having often referred to the resale permit, I should mention that it may or may not be required in your state. When such a permit is required, as in California, it is very important. Carry it with you whenever you are purchasing materials for your business. Most suppliers will defer sales tax if you have such a permit. The resale permit works in the following way:

If you have a resale permit, you should not have to pay sales tax when you purchase materials that you are going to use in making your product. The merchant selling you your materials will need to see the permit and will fill out a form with your permit number on it. You will sign this form and the merchant will then sell you the material without charging you the sales tax. This is because the item or material is going to be "resold" at a later date, at which time sales tax is added by you to the purchase price of your merchandise. You as the seller are then merely forwarding the required amount to the necessary agency, city, county, state. Remember that it is then actually the customer who is paying the tax. You are only collecting it for the agency. Whether such resale permits are required or optional in your state or are referred to by a different name is something that you need to research. It's worth your time to do so.

In our case, such materials as lumber, fabric, paint, stain, glue, and the like—all the materials that became part of our product—were subject to this sales tax exemption. Later, as baskets, the finished product was "resold," and the sales tax was collected at that time. As a manufacturer, this exemption may allow you to lower the price you put on your merchandise.

Since you deferred the sales tax until the time of sale, your product cost less to produce, thus benefiting both the consumer and you. The total cost of all that sales tax on material, if purchased and paid for by you without a resale license, would add a great deal more to the price of your product, and you would necessarily have to charge the customer more. Since you can sell it now for less, that makes your product that much more attractive, especially if competitors are not using this method and are therefore setting higher prices. Judy and I cannot stress enough that attention to these kinds of financial details is essential if you are to be competitive and successful in the craft world.

Your Suppliers and Your Accounts

Line up your suppliers and establish accounts with them under your business name. With most suppliers, you can work out a standard discount based on how much you expect to spend in their store. This is a discount separate from the sales tax benefit mentioned above. Inform your suppliers that part or most of your purchases will be with a resale permit. You can set up the account so that your purchases are divided into "costs of goods sold" and other general shop or production supplies.

If you are just starting out in the business, you may not be able to immediately establish the arrangements specified above. If your credit rating is good and you can establish a dependable financial track record with your suppliers, receiving a discount should be easy. They need only see that you are spending a great deal of money in their business establishment and regularly paying your monthly bill. When the lumber company near us realized that we would be spending $500 to $1,000 a month in their lumberyard, they quickly gave us a 10 percent discount rather than see us go up the road and buy our lumber elsewhere. Depending on your age, you might also find that the store grants a senior citizen discount that can further reduce your costs.

While you are establishing these accounts, check every resource for your supplies. This applies to veterans in the business as well as newcomers. Maybe even more so to veterans, for once accounts are established for a few years, your busy schedule and the convenience of the accounts you already have tend to cause you to forget or get lazy about looking for new suppliers.

New competition is always out there and may give you a better deal. Most often, there are many companies making the same product at different prices, or there are discount dealers who supply on a broad national or even international level in such volume that the cost can be as much as 50 percent less than your neighborhood store.

The Internet has become an invaluable tool for seeking suppliers who price competitively. If one supplier won't accommodate you, another will.

Catalog Suppliers

With our busy schedule, whenever possible, we found it much easier to order our supplies by phone and have them shipped directly to our doorstep. Nowadays, in many cases, you can go to the Web, look at the virtual catalog, and use the provided shopping cart to complete your purchases. Saving such time and energy assists in manufacturing and also saves money, thereby increasing profits.

Many companies sell fabrics, wood—every conceivable material you may need—and most provide catalogs describing their product line. One company mailed us swatches of fabric on a regular basis as samples from which we could select and order. We ordered bolts of fabric, and when we ordered by phone, if the material was in stock, the bolts of fabric were usually on our doorstep within a week.

Of course, when you start out, you may not want to order in such large quantities, but as you become increasingly successful and develop confidence in your product, the larger the quantity of material you buy, the less expensive it is. Hence, ordering in bulk is cost effective and time efficient. It will help you to keep your prices down and still maintain quality and profit.

Once your accounts are established, be sure to pay all your bills out of your business account. If you run out of money, transfer funds from your personal to your business account, but make sure you keep a record of the transfer. Later, when you start making money, pay back the personal account. Always deposit money made from your crafts business into your business account. If, due to some circumstance, you need to withdraw money from your business account for some personal use, remember to always make a note of the transfer and the reason for it. And pay it back! You may in fact want to pay yourself a salary and write yourself a check, just as you may do for anyone working for you. That will depend on your cash flow in the beginning.

Keeping Your Records

It is essential that you keep comprehensive and accurate records of all transactions relating to your business. Getting yourself organized in every aspect of your business is vital to your success, but nowhere more essential than in this area. Therefore, we suggest that you establish a filing system separate from any other personal account records you may keep. If you don't have a computer, you may simply buy a standard and traditional accounting records book at any stationery store. If you have never used such a book, you might want to take a basic course in accounting at a local community college or buy one of the many textbooks on the market.

If you already have a computer and you are comfortable using it, you should set up any one of a number of programs designed for business accounting. The nice part of such programs is that they will do all of the figuring for you. You just have to plug in the numbers. If you keep records after every show, as you should, you will have a running record of exactly where you stand financially in relation to your business at any given moment you need the information. Into the computer go all your expenses for postage, legal and consultant fees, gasoline and oil, vehicle repairs, advertising, food and lodging costs, equipment purchases—everything relating to the business.

When you are selling at a craft show, make sure to give every customer a receipt for her purchase and keep a copy for your records. That way, you will have a running account of every transaction in which you have engaged and know exactly what profit (hopefully) you are making or how much money you are losing. Make sure you keep the actual receipts and other paperwork, long after you have filed your tax returns. Should you ever be audited (a hideous experience), the IRS agent will want to see them.

While on the subject of what records to keep, we suggest that you keep your inventory records of production broken down by month. In other words, keep a record of just how many of each item you made each month. We discovered the advantage of this by happenstance early in our career. Keeping track of this information enabled us to review those records the following year, compare them with our sales record for the same months the previous year—when doing essentially the same shows—and have a pretty good approximation of just how much material we had to buy and how much of the finished product we had to manufacture for a given show and even for the entire new season.

As we got older and our bodies were wearing out, I must admit that we hated reviewing and maintaining this list, as we dreaded knowing that we had to look forward to manufacturing some 4,000–5,000 baskets. But we did it, because it was useful and necessary. I told you it isn't all fun—it's about money.

As part of your record-keeping, know how much of a product you have made to date, week to week. As the year progresses, you will know how many of that item you have sold, and when, and where you sold it. This will also tell you immediately which items are selling well and which are selling poorly or not at all, as compared to the previous year. You don't want to waste money on materials or waste effort producing losing items.

If you wish to deduct the business use of your home for tax purposes, talk to your tax consultant to make sure that your business qualifies for the deduction and to find out how you should go about keeping the records necessary to take the deduction. With all this information plugged into your computer, you simply have to print it out at the end of the year and take it to your tax consultant. We should add that, if you are personally knowledgeable and proficient in doing your own taxes, certainly do so, since it saves you money. Judy chose to do it for us because, early on, she had learned the essentials and, later, with all the records at hand in the computer, she only had to fill out the forms. We also have a son-in-law who is a CPA. If you do your own taxes electronically, using forms from the IRS or forms supplied by one of the commercial software tax preparers, you will find that often the financial information that you've input into your bookkeeping program can be "poured" automatically into the electronic tax document, saving you number entry and number-crunching time. On the other hand, it still is time consuming—time you could be devoting to your product and being creative, or getting a much needed rest. Your choice!

Business-Related Use of Your Vehicle

In order to deduct use of your vehicle on Schedule C of your income tax return, you have to keep good mileage records on every business-related trip; that is, to and from shows, buying trips for supplies, even going to the post office to ship an order. Another approach is to use a standard mileage deduction specified by the IRS, but it won't add up to nearly as much as if you keep your own records.

Judy and I developed the practice of keeping a book in the glove compartment of our vehicle specifically to keep those records, using the odometer to give us exact mileage readings. We also kept a folder in the truck in which we placed all documents relating to repair, maintenance, gas, and oil expenditures, and the receipts for money spent in this way. If you follow our example, you will have accurate records, and at the end of the year you can simply note the total miles the vehicle was driven and subtract the total number of miles that were business related. If that figure is at least 50 percent of the total miles driven, you can take the business deduction for your vehicle. We would then just plug those figures into the proper place in our computer business program.

All of this advice relating to your vehicle is really very simple and made even simpler if you always use the same vehicle. Record-keeping is less likely to become confused. We virtually never used the truck for anything else—a good idea anyway, as it saves wear and tear on the vehicle that is essential to your business.

Oh! You should also remember and record your vehicle's registration fee and your insurance costs. Please keep in mind, though, that tax codes change yearly, so even the most minor advice we suggest here is subject to change. Tax requirements that were applicable a few years ago may no longer be applicable. Be sure to talk to your accountant for specific, up-to-date details.

Buy a Cash Register

Before you do your first show, go to any business supply store and purchase a cash register. Buy a register that supplies duplicate receipts and that is powered by battery or will plug into a standard wall outlet. Such registers come equipped with rechargeable batteries and are essential at outdoor shows, where there is never an available source of electricity. Sometimes, when we're indoors, the power may go out; then our register automatically switches over to battery power.

Using a cash register is the most professional way to do business, and that's the image you want to create. It is also the most secure. Working out of a tin box looks amateurish and gives the customer the impression that you are non-professional. The tin box also makes for unreliable record-keeping, often prompting you to commingle funds. At lunchtime, you are hungry, so you grab money from the box and run off to eat. Later in the afternoon, you leave your partner in the booth, remove some money from the box (you don't even count it to see how much), and run off to buy some supplies or make a purchase at another craft booth. By the end of the weekend you have no idea how much money you have spent in this careless way.

The cash register gives you a continuing record of your sales transactions. You will know exactly how many sales you made and for how much money. When you cash out your register at the end of the day, if your cash is less than your receipts, you know how much of your profit you already spent.

Not only will most good registers give you a total of the amount you earned that day when you cash out, but they can also be programmed to break down your sales receipts so you know your net sales, sales tax, and gross totals. This gives you the exact amount you should set aside to pay your sales tax.

Most importantly, your money is safer in a locked cash register drawer. There are times when you will just have to leave the booth unattended and, unless it is going to be for an extended period of time, you don't want to have to take all of your cash from the tin box or walk around everywhere with a tin box in your hand. A register that can be secured to your countertop is the most preferable. Let's face it, all kinds of people come to a craft show—particularly street fairs and festivals in the park where the beer and wine flows freely. I don't know how many craftspeople we met over the years who left their booth and returned to find that their cash box was gone.

This brings us to a final few words about the cash register. Remember to bring cash and change to put in the register at the start of the working day. More than once we forgot and one of us had to leave the show and go to the bank to withdraw operating money, especially change. Having to do this is very inconvenient and in some cases, impossible, if there is no bank or ATM in the near vicinity. Once we actually were forced to borrow operating capital, which is amateurish and embarrassing. Furthermore, bring a few hundred dollars. People seem to bring big bills to craft shows and it is not unusual for your first customer of the day to purchase a $10 item and hand you a $100 bill. By the end of a good selling day, your register will most often be jammed with big bills, while you will usually be hard-pressed for singles and change.

Design Patents, Copyrights, and Trademarks

If you have created a new product and are concerned that someone may copy and sell your idea, it is possible to obtain what is known as a design patent on your product. This is, however, a complicated legal procedure. There are attorneys out there who specialize in patent law and nothing else. We will make no attempt here to discuss it in any detail. It is possible to research it yourself at any library. You might wish to buy or refer to a copy of *The Patent Guide*, by Carl Battle (Allworth Press), an attorney specializing in the subject of patents. But we would recommend that you take no action in this regard without legal advice.

We had one occasion when we found it necessary to seek the legal advice of a patent attorney. It involved a craftsperson based in another state but selling at shows in our state. She claimed that we stole her design for a paper-plate holder, stating that her design was patented. The truth is we had never seen her work, but we went to an attorney for advice. Some $500 later, he had looked up her design and there was absolutely no resemblance between her product and ours, other than that they were both paper-plate holders. He wrote a letter with a picture of our paper-plate holder to her attorney, pointing out the many differences in design and material, and that was the end of the matter.

Obviously, it is a very expensive process and, frankly, for most products, rarely worthwhile. It is too easy for artisans to make enough variations in a product design they have stolen to make it legal. Lawyers will gain a lot more than you will. They make at least $100 an hour, and usually much more.

One technique that some craftspeople use to protect the design of their product is to mail themselves a certified letter marked "return receipt requested," describing the product and enclosing a picture of it. The letter may also include a description of how the product is produced and what materials are used. However, this "poor man's copyright" approach has no legal status and we strongly advise against relying on it. If your product is worth protecting, consult a lawyer so you can do it properly.

The question of whether or not your particular craft qualifies to be copyrighted is another complicated legal question that we cannot and should not go into here. Generally speaking, pictorial, graphic, and sculptural works are copyrightable. A definition given by Tad Crawford in *The Legal Guide for the Visual Artist,* which thoroughly covers copyright, is that "work must be original and creative." Clearly, this is a pretty broad definition and is actually far more specifically defined in the book. We can only refer you to the above-titled book, which also lists where you may seek the advice of specialists in this field of law. You should consult experts, for only they can tell you whether your craft can be copyrighted and what benefit that would be to you.

In the second chapter of this book we addressed the importance of the business name as a sales and promotional tool. Trademarks are names or logos that identify a particular business as the source of goods marked with that name or logo. A great book on this protection is *The Trademark Guide* by Lee Wilson (Allworth Press). If the public is going to know that goods with a certain name or logo come from your company, consider getting a lawyer's help in filing your trademark (but keep in mind that you may have protection even if you didn't file).

A Crucial Related Problem

The subject that is discussed next could be included in chapter 7, Booth Setup and Booth Display, because it will be when your booth is fully set up, your crafts on display, and you are engaged in selling your craft that you will be confronted with this problem. However, the subject is included in this chapter in that it specifically relates to design patents and protecting your product.

Sometimes you will notice a typical tourist type who is just taking a picture of his or her wife or husband standing in front of your booth. Or tourists will take a picture inside the booth as a record of their having been there and attended the show. This happened to us a lot at Lake Tahoe, where there are thousands of tourists from all over the world and the lake is a beautiful, scenic background. They would even take photos holding baskets in their hands that they had purchased from us and ask us to pose in the pictures. This is fine, no problem, and you should always accommodate your customers, if possible, when they compliment you by making such a request after a purchase.

The serious and difficult problem with which you will occasionally have to deal involves the person who walks into your booth with a sketch pad and starts drawing your designs or the person with a camera who stands outside, or even inside the booth, and starts to photograph every item. Because you are busy or the booth and aisles are crowded, you may not even realize that it is happening until it is too late. When that happens, there is nothing you can do about it except to talk to the person and ask him to stop taking pictures or sketching your product. This person is not a tourist; this person is a thief.

In some cases, people merely want to copy your design in order to go home and make the product themselves for their own use. There really is no harm in this; after all, they could buy your product, take it home, and do the same thing. There is really nothing you can do about that.

The serious problem and threat to your business is the people who intend to produce the product themselves and sell it (who knows where). They will certainly be in competition with you and will be using your creation. Such a person may be an agent for a manufacturing concern, most often overseas or across the border. The intent is to reproduce your product, taking advantage of the much cheaper cost of labor out of this country, and then ship it back to the United States and sell it here, undercutting your price.

If such people are inside your booth, you have every right to ask them to stop drawing or photographing. If these people refused, either Judy or I would then position ourselves in front of them, blocking their line of sight to whatever they were copying on paper or attempting to photograph. Most of the time, this prompted them to leave the booth, particularly if we told them (whether it was true or not) that we had design patents on our work and that if they reproduced anything we created, we would sue them.

In this regard, you may, unfortunately, have a few obstinate types who refuse to stop either drawing or taking pictures. They will usually assert that "This is a free country and I can take pictures anywhere I want." This is true, only to a certain extent. You do not have control of the aisles, especially at shows to which people paid admission. If they stand in the aisle or street, all you can do is be equally obnoxious and continue to block their view. We only had to resort to this technique twice. It takes a lot of self-control to deal with this problem, so be ready to adopt the necessary attitude.

As a merchant, however, you do have control of your booth space, as you have leased it for the time of the show. So, in both instances, in a polite manner and attempting to avoid an obnoxious incident, explain your rights, ask the person to leave, and if he doesn't, then do what you first politely threaten—call the promoter. The promoter or security personnel will take charge of the matter at any good show, sometimes escorting the interlopers off the premises. Many of the bigger indoor promotions don't allow cameras into the building in order to protect the craftspeople from this kind of intrusion. For this reason, I had to obtain permission from the promoter to take the indoor photographs you see in this book. I also obtained signed permission forms from every craftsperson whose booth display Judy photographed. Even for this book, some artisans refused, quite naturally afraid that their design or idea could be stolen by someone reading the book.

Small Business Insurance

As you travel from show to show, you are going to be faced with certain risk factors at those that serve beer or wine. Under these conditions, you may encounter annoying and disreputable members of the public or, sometimes, perfectly well-behaved people, either of whom may have some sort of accident in your booth. They may be drunk and disorderly and in this condition do damage to your booth, merchandise, or both. They might simply trip on the carpeting or some object in your booth space. Perhaps, in crowded, cramped conditions they are jostled, stumble, and fall. No matter how it happens, the individual could decide to sue you and your business for damages, should she sustain any injury.

During the years we were in business, we never covered ourselves with any form of liability insurance. Were we beginning our career in this far more litigious age, we might well do so and we recommend that you investigate the cost of this coverage. A number of insurance companies will give you ratings. The cost will depend on whether you want only liability insurance covering injury to people who are in your booth or you wish to also cover damage to you and your merchandise. Had we chosen to take out such insurance, it would have been liability only, as it would not have been financially worthwhile to cover our merchandise. The likelihood of the entire booth burning down or being swept away in a flood was pretty remote. Nor was it worthwhile to try to cover ourselves for the theft of a few baskets or some minor damage. Therefore, no attempt is made here to estimate costs to you for such insurance. How much your policy will cost, if you can find the appropriate insurance company that underwrites such liability, involves too many variables and is particularly dependent on the estimated value of the merchandise you take to a show and how high a coverage you decide to select. Remember, insurance is to protect against big losses that you can't pay out of your own pocket. If you do get coverage, consider lowering your premium by having a high deductible (the amount you have to pay before the insurance kicks in)—as long as you can afford to pay the deductible amount.

Merchant Charge Accounts

Customer reliance on plastic instead of paper (money) has only increased since the first edition of this book appeared. A credit card machine is now a must for any craft business. Establishing a merchant account with a local bank will allow you to consolidate all incoming payments from credit card, debit card, electronic check, and other payment services. These accounts are specifically designed to accept virtually all forms of payments from both retail and Internet sources.

Some crafters choose to take a manual swiper to the shows and reenter all of their sales for authorization when they get home in order to save on costs. It is also possible to subscribe to a phone-in method of transaction. I recommend, however, going to the additional expense of a wireless credit card machine. Wireless terminal processing allows vendors to process transactions through a wireless phone–based terminal in situations where power and phone lines are not available. This guarantees that you are able to complete all of your credit card transactions at any craft show and outdoor event as they occur. With this method, you are assured of an immediate authorization and spare yourself additional work at the end of a show.

Purchase of these machines and the accompanying cellular phone can vary a great deal in price. Top-of-the-line systems can run as much as $1,095. It is also possible to find a perfectly good swipe system with printer for about $585. As this book is being revised, the Way Systems MTT 1500 seems to be the system of preference, mainly because they have better "coverage" (wireless reception in rural areas).

The Way Systems MTT 1500 comes with an infrared printer, Siemans C56 mobile phone, and SAM card. There is a monthly cell phone fee of about $18.95. Leasing to own for a one-year lease tends to run around $73 per month. The system comes with a five-year sales warranty.

Beware of deals that sound too good to be true because often they are too good to be true. Free terminals may come with large monthly minimums or surcharges. In some cases, the vendors may break the system into two separate pieces, giving you the swiper for free and charging you for the printer.

Merchant service providers will charge a monthly basic service charge and a per transaction fee. In the case of some cards (such as the "reward" cards) there will be additional fees and surcharges. You will find in many cases that lower quotes conceal unmentioned fees. It is important to contrast and compare before making a decision as there are often considerable differences and you can save yourself a bundle by careful shopping. There is a great deal of information online on merchant service providers. Be sure, however, to check the reliability of any company before buying.

While it is hard sometimes to stomach the additional expense of a credit card machine, the cost of doing business with a wireless card swipe machine is more than worth the initial outlay and the 2 to 5 percent of each transaction taken by the credit card company. Like it or not, our nation's economy runs on credit and, as a business person, you'll need to take advantage of this economic reality. If you don't, you will be losing a great opportunity for expanding your business.

Increasingly, customers expect to be able to use their cards to purchase at a show and will not have enough cash in hand to buy expensive items. Depending on the area where you are selling, you may even find during the Christmas season that you do as much as 75 percent of your business on charge. Charge capability offers your crafts business numerous other advantages. Each credit card with which you contract will provide you with signs that are used to display what credit cards you accept. You should hang your signs at the front of and inside your booth, so that every customer is aware in advance that you accept charge cards. You will find that many craftspeople accept only cash and checks and some will not even take a check. They are sadly limiting their money-making ability: The fact that you do adds to yours.

Another advantage to you when you accept credit cards is that, unlike a check, you will know immediately if the customer's account is solvent. A printout in the window of the machine gives you that information. Naturally, this is very embarrassing to most customers as they fumble for an explanation, but rarely do you lose a sale. Usually, the customer just pulls out another credit card from her purse or wallet or she pays cash.

Relative to record-keeping, it is extremely important that you retain and file all your records of transactions made over the machine and that you do so faithfully, not only for tax purposes but also for your personal accounting system. On some occasions, you may receive a notice in the mail of a charge back. All too frequently, you have to respond immediately or lose the amount of money the sale represented. Developing a quick, easy filing system in this regard is a must. The reasons for a charge back are many, but most often it comes as a result of a customer simply forgetting that she made the purchase. Most crafts businesses have unusual names that give the customer no hint as to what the purchase might have been. She has made purchases in a number of craft booths, at a number of shows, and has simply forgotten the purchase she made in your booth. The card may have been used by the husband to buy a surprise present and so the wife, unaware of the purchase, challenges the charge on her statement.

In this case, you will receive notice from the bank that a customer has challenged a charge on her statement. You then have to quickly call the bank to show proof of sale. Your proof is your copy of the signed receipt the machine produced. You must keep all these receipts in order and readily accessible so you can expeditiously respond to the problem. Be very conscientious in this regard: If you can't prove that the customer made the purchase, you will be required to refund that amount to the bank, which will, in essence, have made a gift of your merchandise to some customer.

Accepting Checks

Many, many craftspeople are afraid to and often refuse to accept a customer's personal check, and so lose the customer. There is no greater bonehead approach to business. In seventeen years, some five hundred shows, and who knows how many thousands of checks, we had no more than fifteen checks bounce and only four that went uncollected.

Customers at a craft show are honest people. They don't come to a craft show to rip off the merchants. We found that when a check did bounce, it was most often because some husband forgot to deposit his paycheck or it was due to a simple, mathematical mistake, the kind we have all made at one time or another. Refuse to accept them and you will be giving away far more profit than you could possibly lose if a check does bounce. You will just be sending your business to a competitor, losing not just that sale, but any repeat business that customer might have given you.

Your Business Work Routine

Because it isn't fun and it's hardly creative, it is very easy to procrastinate about developing a business-related schedule, similar to your craft-producing schedule. Judy and I strongly recommend that it is best to quickly learn to make it part of your regular work routine.

Judy always did her accounting and bookkeeping on Monday morning, the day after a show. First, she did all the accounting work while all the information was fresh in her memory. Then she immediately went to the bank and deposited all the money. Usually, she completed all the business-related activity by noon and she could return to the creative work and concentrate on making baskets.

Granted, this part of the business is tedious and, for most people, not particularly enjoyable, but it is actually the most important aspect of your craft work because it represents your bottom line—money. You will lose a lot of it and never know where it went if you don't apply yourself conscientiously to this vital area of the business. As you become a regular participant in the crafts business, and each week you meet and observe many fellow artisans, you will instinctively know, just by looking at their operations, which ones treat this aspect of the business seriously and professionally and which do not. Imitate those who do, engage them in friendly conversation, and learn the tricks of the trade. We are sure that you will find that, invariably, those craftspeople who appear the most professional are the most successful, because they operate according to the same basic principles that we advise.

Staying Organized

Failure to keep accurate records and attend to them regularly and efficiently may mean not only wasted time later in the year when you try to catch up, but also the loss of considerable income. At year's end, when tax time rolls around, you don't want to be hunting for receipts you didn't save, trying to remember how many times you drove to town for supplies, or rummaging through a carton full of slips of paper just to answer your tax consultant's questions. Under the existing pressures we are describing, you will not be able to remember all the details of the preceding year, and you will have lost much of the corroborating evidence of the claims you wish to make on your tax form.

In every small business, the owner wears a number of hats. The difference between small business and big business is that big business hires people to wear each separate hat. As a craftsperson and a small businessperson, you must wear virtually every hat most of the time—and more than one at the same time—until you are well established and making a very good income. The reality is that you just can't afford to do it any other way, especially in the early years that you are in business.

As time goes by and you can afford it, decide what parts of the manufacturing process you enjoy and take the least of your time. Then decide what operation is most time consuming and laborious. No matter how creative a person you may be, when you are manufacturing a product repetitiously, it will become boring. Certain aspects of the process will always remain a challenge, while others you will dread. That is the time to hire someone to do the bookkeeping or bulk sewing or whatever part of the entire manufacturing process is the most tedious for you.

Because the crafts business is labor intensive and cannot, as we said before, be evaluated on an hourly basis, your cash flow provides the necessary financial leverage. If you've run your business correctly, you'll have the money to pay for extra help. You will then find that hiring someone to handle a specific aspect of your business enables you to generate greater profit, in spite of the cost. Your time and energy then can be better spent on creating a better product. You will also relieve some of the tensions and pressure that can be so frustrating and debilitating; as a result, you'll have more fun.

5

Selecting Your Shows

NOW YOU ARE READY to go into business and sell your product. You've worked hard and produced what you believe to be a sufficient amount of inventory. Your product is as beautiful as you know how to make it, the quality as good as money can buy. You haven't skimped on any of the materials in your product and you believe you are asking a fair price and can expect to make a fair profit. Now for the $64,000 question: Where do you sell it? How do you find the places where your product will be most marketable, where it will be most in demand? Where do you find that buying public anxious to make you rich? Note that all contact/locale information has been thoroughly updated for this revised edition. One of the biggest differences between crafting in the nineties and crafting now is that even more information is available via the Web; however, many of the criteria for choosing shows are timeless, and they remain unchanged here.

How Not to Pick Your Shows

Before we tell you what positive steps to take to find your market, we think it's crucial to explain to you first what not to do. Ordinarily, when instructing anyone on any subject, using the positive side of the teaching coin is preferable. But in the matter of selecting craft shows, we must show the negative examples first, to help you proceed with the necessary caution.

Caveat Venditor!

This has been a particularly fraught time in the craft world. As Greg Lawler, editor and publisher of the *Art Fair SourceBook* framed the issue to me in a brief e-mail:

"The reality of the ever-growing crafts business is that there are just too many shows out there every weekend—too many potentially costly mistakes—should you select the wrong shows. The trends over the past 5 years or so have NOT been very positive for most exhibitors reporting to me. The booth fees keep climbing (over 50% in the past 5 years), but sales at shows are actually declining. I guess if you wanted to put a positive spin on that, you could say that a lot of the old-timers are dropping out and making room for the new, younger exhibitors."   —BR

A novice is definitely navigating a mine field of potentially discouraging, non-profitable shows in the beginning. In order to learn the ropes, it is much easier to work by a process of elimination, scratching all the undesirable shows. Otherwise, you will find yourself at some, maybe too many, of those very shows. So, while no one can predict exactly where your market isn't, using this approach, with some important tips, we can help you find where your best markets are.

As in every other aspect of the crafts business, Judy and I had little guidance our first year in business. We had never heard of or seen a *Crafts Fair Guide* and so we chose our first shows essentially through word of mouth or because we saw a show being advertised on a poster. We were such rank beginners that, until we (quickly) learned better, sometimes we would just drive up to a show with our truck full of inventory, expecting that all we had to do was to show up, unload, set up, and sell.

A few times that approach was actually successful, because the promoter received a number of cancellations and no-shows. It was, as a matter of fact, one of those small promoters who explained to us that normally we had to apply in advance and gave us applications for his future shows. As a result, for most of our first year in business, we were doing nothing but little, small-town street fairs, twenty-five booths in a show, the town so out of the way that the only customers were the residents—all 250 of them.

What would happen at these shows was that Harriet, in the booth next to us, would tell us about a particular show for which she was booked two weeks later and she would expound the virtues of the show, claiming that last year it was a "great show." Two weeks later we would end up in another nearby, small-town community and there would be Harriet, waving and smiling brightly, but nary a customer when the show opened.

Another time it was Joe, happily selling his little wooden toys, who told us that a show he was doing the following week had always been a "great show"—for the last six years. Then Edna informed us that a certain show was a surefire winner and we shouldn't miss it. "The people will love your stuff," she would rave. And so on and so forth.

We took everybody's tips and recommendations, believed their every word, and innocently applied to enter, and when we were accepted, packed ourselves off to these shows—only to come home, if we were lucky, with $300 to $400 in our pocket. One time, our total take was $35. The only saving grace was that most of these shows were close enough that we could drive home each night and save ourselves motel and food expenses. That was all that was keeping us from plunging deeply into the red. But we continued to try these kinds of shows that first year, until we realized that they were always going to be a big bust.

During that year, each weekday, while anxiously anticipating and preparing more inventory for the next show, Judy and I discussed whether our craft was marketable and what it was that we were doing wrong. We reviewed and relived everything we were doing and agonized over whether our craft was good enough and whether there was a better way.

What we finally came to understand, after about fifteen of these kinds of shows, was that taking the advice of all those nice people whom we had never met before and knew nothing about was the only thing we were doing wrong. They were so helpful and sincere that we couldn't resist following their recommendations, particularly when we had no idea where else to go.

Fact! We were doing everything right, except applying to the right shows. The shows we were entering had cheap entry fees and no jury process involved, so we thought we were saving money. We weren't taking into account the financial realities of the real-life crafts business world.

Harriet sold ticky-tacky, knickknack items. Her highest-priced item was $10. She was applying to shows in a depressed economic area and that price range was right in the customers' ballpark. Harriet grossed $300 a show and, for her, that was a "great show." All that Harriet really wanted was a nice, pleasant, social day out in the park, where she earned a few extra dollars.

Joe sold wooden toys for small children, all also in a low price range. In the really small towns where we were trying to sell, we didn't realize that a craft show was a big event. It was a family day out in the local park or community center, where the show was traditionally staged. There would be a few hundred children running around and through the booths most of the day, pestering their parents (particularly Daddy, as daddies give in more easily) to buy them a toy wooden gun or train or truck or whatever. Eventually Daddy would succumb to the kid's pressure. At the end of two days, Joe maybe grossed $500 and, given his cost of production and expenses, Joe has also had a "great show."

Edna sold junk jewelry, basically in the same price range, and she did fine. We came to the show with our baskets ranging from $15 to $45. Kids weren't screaming for Mommy to buy them a basket. Mommy could only afford to treat herself to a cheap bracelet. So we grossed $350 and went home with long faces. Oh, everyone loved our stuff and "wished" that they could buy it, but they simply could not afford it, and we simply shouldn't have been doing a show in that town—or any town like it.

Our tip from this scenario is to remember to investigate the general economic conditions of the area in which you intend to do a show. Keep in mind that the bigger your business becomes, the higher your expenses—and your expectations. If you persist long enough in doing shows of the kind I have described, very soon you won't have any business at all—unless you are Edna or Joe or Harriet and that is all you desire financially.

On the other hand, it can be just as embarrassing to be in a show where the other sellers have higher expectations than you do. We did a show in Palm Springs, while visiting Judy's parents. We expected a good show to be a bonus. We set up with our line of baskets and found ourselves in a fine arts show, surrounded by $5,000 original paintings and $10,000 statuary. Palm Springs is hardly the place to bring wooden baskets, no matter how beautiful. We didn't belong in Palm Springs and we should not have been accepted into the show.

Unfortunately, you'll have to live with the fact that there are a few unscrupulous promoters who will accept anybody, if it enables them to fill another space in their show and collect another booth fee. This fact is becoming a real threat to the craft industry. This kind of promoter was rare when we started in the business, but three veteran promoters told me that monetary greed on the part of new promoters is a serious concern. If you are accepted to a show on the basis of your application alone, it usually means that the promoter is accepting you sight unseen, and generally it is not a show worth doing. But more about that in a later chapter.

Judy and I did learn something important, however, from this early experience besides what shows to avoid. We used the opportunity to discuss our craft with the customers who walked in and out of our booth. Their positive reactions to and comments about our product convinced us that we had a product that would sell, and that helped us maintain our confidence level. We learned that we just had to do a better job of selecting the shows we chose to attend.

A Great Show Is a Relative Matter

Perhaps, before I take you any further into this subject, we need to examine that phrase I keep using: "It's a great show." Remember Harriet and Edna and Joe? Well, they weren't lying to us when they said, "It's a great show." They were absolutely serious. The fact that we did not realize, or take into consideration, was that what may be a poor, good, or great show is purely subjective. Please remember that, and only under special circumstances put much stock in a strange vendor's advice. One person's "great show" is another person's "flop."

It is vitally important that you keep in mind that you know nothing about another craftsperson's operating expenses, much less his lifestyle, living expenses, or general expectations and philosophy concerning the crafts business. You will see many, many craftspeople who travel from show to show the entire crafts season, working in and living out of the small van in which they travel. Some began back in the sixties and have an entirely different philosophy of life than you may have. Many are quite content to make just enough money to pay their expenses week to week. They live hand-to-mouth. If that is all that you desire, you probably don't need to read the rest of this book.

The largest majority of craftspeople depend on the crafts business as their only source of income. Some are single and have only themselves to support. Others support large families; in fact, their business is a huge, family enterprise, involving brothers and sisters and cousins. Every relative works in the business. At shows like Country Folk Art, which is a nation-wide organization based in Michigan, or Harvest Festival, a huge, top-of-the-line enterprise based in Petaluma, California, you will see craftspeople who roll up in fancy motor homes followed by two or three eighteen-wheelers. They travel with a staff who will actually put their wares together and keep their booth filled as their merchandise sells. A $25,000 gross for three days may be a "poor" weekend for them and you'll hear them griping.

Still other craftspeople don't even travel with their booth or merchandise. When they are booked for the entire season with the Harvest Festival, for example—which primarily sponsors shows in the Midwest and the western United States—their booth display and merchandise is loaded on trucks by the show's staff and shipped on to the next show site. These crafts professionals either return home between shows to manufacture more merchandise or, more likely, have a staff at home manufacturing the product and shipping it to wherever the next show is scheduled. Most of these people started out small, just as some of you are doing, then expanded under circumstances that will be discussed in a later chapter.

Obviously, for crafts businesses that operate on this large a scale, the perception of a "great show" is going to be vastly different from yours. I don't want to make a cynic of you, because most people in the business are sincere in the advice they are trying to give you. You just have to keep in mind that their recommendations simply may not apply to you.

Then There Is the Liar

As in any other part of life and in every business, there are a few less-than-ethical types who have an axe to grind and will give out misleading and erroneous advice. Such a craftsperson regards every dollar spent in your booth as a dollar less spent in his. In economics, this philosophy is referred to as the zero sum concept, the idea that there is a finite amount of money to be divided up among everybody—the more I get, the less the competition gets. Some people in the business view all competition from that standpoint and so will steer you away from any good show, particularly if you have a product in the same category as theirs. You will be told that a show is rotten, simply to reduce the competition. So be wary. Get more than one opinion.

As you do in every area of your life, learn to evaluate whom you can trust and whom you can't. When the person touting a show is someone you respect and who himself produces a fine product, then the recommendation is usually worth taking. A good craftsman wants good competition, because such competition makes for a higher quality show. This, in turn, draws greater attendance and a more discriminating customer; plus, it stimulates spending.

If you produce a good product, you needn't be afraid of good competition. Good competition brings in more customers to the show. That is why a promotion like Harvest Festival or Country Folk Art, or similar top promotions in your part of the country, encourage and represent a level of craftsmanship and competition that you should strive to attain—even if you don't choose to apply to these particular shows. You may not wish to, and you don't necessarily need to, sell at the larger shows to make a good living. Many, many successful craftspeople never do shows at that level. However, those kinds of shows still represent the theoretical top, the ideal. Their criteria for who they will accept into their shows is quite strict, but if you make it, you know you're among the best in the business.

We cite the taking-recommendations-from-just-about-everybody method outlined above to demonstrate that this approach is, arguably, the worst way to decide where to sell your merchandise. Listening to everyone and anyone—just because they make a craft and set up a booth—will get you someplace and no place at the same time. Word of mouth is a hit-or-miss proposition. It is highly unreliable financially, and it gives you no ability to assess a projected income upon which you can depend and continue to invest in your business. If you proceed only on the basis of a craftsperson's recommendations, we can predict with assurance that you will just eke out a living, making very little profit, and will most likely become discouraged and quit. You cannot plan a show schedule a year in advance by acting on recommendations.

More Conventional Means of Selecting Your Shows

Another means of learning about which shows are being presented is one to which all craftspeople are subjected. It is the direct invitation that you will receive in the mail and, like every other option in this aspect of the crafts business, it has its advantages and disadvantages. A typical, unsolicited invitation can be found on the following pages. Particularly note that while there are numerous rules and regulations by which you must abide, the promoter is not even asking to see your product. To get into the show, you just have to fill out the application and send in your money.

These mailed invitations promoting a show will usually start arriving after you have been in the business a short while and out there displaying your product at some shows. Either some promoter has walked the show and has seen your work or he has purchased a mailing list containing your name from one of your suppliers. These mailed invitations must be considered very carefully and, once you are established for a few years, most often rejected for reasons to be explained subsequently.

Another very frequent occurrence that presents you with an opportunity to select a few new shows is the promoter who walks into your booth with an application in his hand. This is the personal approach. At many of the bigger shows, you rarely see and may never meet the promoter, much less receive a direct, personal invitation. In this case, the promoter is virtually guaranteeing you a place in his show. Most often, you will and should forget about doing this show, for reasons also to be explained.

Negatives about the Unsolicited or Personal Invitation

You can bet on this: When some promoter either mails you an invitation to take part in his craft show or personally walks into your booth and places an invitation in your hands, he is probably a brand new promoter just finding his way into the business.

When you are new yourself, hunting around for shows, rejected by others to whom you have applied, and you're becoming anxious because your future income is becoming very problematical, or you have a free weekend, or last week's show was a loser, it is very tempting to accept these kinds of invitations. Under these conditions, almost every craftsperson is susceptible to the flattery that this invitation represents.

The in-the-mail invitation you receive is tempting because you don't have to do any work finding this show. Flashing before your eyes is all that profit you are going to make and it is sitting in your mailbox, just waiting for you. All you have to do is fill out the application, mail it in with your fee (usually less than the big shows), show up, and sell your product. You know nothing about the area in which you are going to sell or the kind of people to whom you are going to sell. You especially don't know anything about the promoter, his or her motivations, ability, or the show's reputation. But you go because the whole process is so easy. We know, because we succumbed to this temptation—and got financially stung almost every time we did so.

The promoter who walks into your booth and presents an offer can make himself even more attractive. This promoter, in presenting you with his application, always makes it sound as if he has eyeballed every booth in the show and has selected just a chosen few of quality to invite to his show. How nice that he has appreciated your work and chosen you.

The actual fact is that this promoter has approached everyone, in every booth in the show, or, if the proprietor wasn't there, left his application on the counter. This promoter had to approach you this way because he is definitely aware that most experienced artisans have already scheduled their shows for the entire year.

If this individual's show had any previous reputation, it would be in some craft show guide or on some craft show schedule published in your part of the country. The promoter wouldn't have to be out soliciting your attendance. You would be sending for his application. So, this promoter's real appeal has to be to newcomers who are just learning about the crafts business, as is he. In this scenario, you will find that the show date is coming up soon and the spaces aren't filled. This alone is a bad sign. It suggests that many veteran craftspeople are either not anxious to do this show or don't even know about it. Therefore, never make an immediate commitment. You should just politely take the application, explaining that you have to review your show schedule. Then ask around about the promoter. If veteran craftspeople haven't heard of him, then the person is not a promoter of any note. Very frequently, you will find that the application presented to you at a show will be for a show scheduled in the very near future or even the following weekend. Again, the reason the promoter is soliciting you is that he hasn't filled all the booth spaces in his show. For any number of practical reasons, if you sign up for the show, you'll waste a weekend doing it, conclude it was a flop, and drive home disgusted.

In the process of going through this, you'll learn that the promoter was on a small budget, hadn't advertised well, was running the show in some godforsaken spot that was all he could rent, and the show had no history behind it to attract repeat customers. If you hadn't applied to it, you probably wouldn't have missed a thing. In fact, your time would have been better spent staying home and producing more inventory.

After you have been in business for a few years and you have established your reputation with recognized promoters, you will be on their mailing list every year and you will receive an application and schedule of every show they are promoting the coming year. You will receive the schedules well in advance of the approaching craft season and have plenty of time to make your decisions and apply for the shows. In this case, the promoter has in the past already seen your work and, to some extent, knows you and wants what your craft represents in his show. Two examples of these applications that we still receive are found on the following pages. Many craftspeople base their entire season on selecting all the shows done by just one or two major promoters. They are also usually rewarded for this by being given better booth locations at that promoter's shows.

Some craftspeople are even willing to do some promoters' poorer shows (that is, those in a poorer location) just to ensure that they are accepted into the good ones. Some in the crafts business might even recommend this approach, but we wouldn't. There are too many good shows around to waste time at any poor ones.

The Exception to the Rule

Here is the other side of the coin with regard to those unsolicited show invitations. The new promoter may be good at what she does but has no track record as yet and is advertising a "first annual." The "first annual" can present you with a very troubling dilemma.

As happened to us, the "first annual" that we chose not to attend turned out to be a huge success. All the craftspeople who took the risk not only made money but also virtually guaranteed themselves a spot in the next year's show because the promoter repaid them for taking the gamble. Having ignored the invitation, our chances of getting into next year's show were seriously reduced.

I hate to think of the money that some of our mistakes cost us. Judy and I turned down the First Annual Asparagus Festival in Stockton, California, years ago. I stupidly talked my wife out of doing it because I didn't think the people of Stockton would turn out. I missed the fact that the promoter was an experienced veteran, not a newcomer to the business. The show drew 100,000 people the first year and thousands more than that as the show grew in popularity and became a local, established tradition. Thereafter, craftspeople from all over the state of California and beyond were applying. Everyone wants to be part of a big success. That mistake on my part resulted in our never being accepted into the show after that first year, and after a number of years, we finally stopped applying. I never heard the end of it.

There is no right or absolute answer to how to make some of these decisions. It depends on how many shows you are doing, how many more you want to do, your financial status, the amount of inventory you have in stock, how much more you can manufacture, and how hard you want to and are physically capable of working. Then you just have to weigh the odds, make your decision, and live with it.

In fact, you may decide to participate in a "first annual" being put on by a new, inexperienced promoter, and it may turn out to be a great show. Every show is always a gamble to some extent. That is just the nature of the business. We can only give you lessons from our experience and remind you to try to keep the odds in your favor—and hope.

The Best Method of Selecting Your Shows

If you're a novice or a veteran to this business, far and away the best method of selecting the shows you will try to do is by subscribing to whatever crafting guide exists in your locale, state, or area of the country. Every craftsperson I have ever met subscribes to at least one, even when they have a long, established schedule that they do every year and are on the regular mailing list of dozens of promoters. People who sell their crafts at shows are always looking for new shows, always seeking to test new territory. These guides give you a better measure of the shows to which you want to apply than the gambling methods noted above and they provide you the means by which you can plan your schedule much further in advance than the above examples.

There are good, practical reasons to always be on the lookout for new shows: First and foremost, no matter how good your product, you can saturate a given area by appearing there too often. Suburban areas extending outside the big cities, sometimes called the "suburban sprawl," are good examples.

Most of suburbia is a series of once-small towns that, years ago, were miles apart, but with continuing expansion in every direction, now run into each other. The result is that, except for the population sign entering each township or mini-city, you can't tell one from the other. And yet, each area or town has a name and a history and each develops its own traditions.

One of those traditions is becoming the yearly craft show. It is often sponsored by the local Chamber of Commerce, and every community organization, such as the Rotary, the Lions Club, the Elks, the Masons, and the Knights of Columbus—all supporting charitable causes—dedicate their time and effort to staging a successful show. It is a community enterprise and, in recent years, these annual craft shows have developed into friendly, intercommunity competitions, very often in support of some community project for which the town is attempting to raise funds. Communities coordinate their efforts, so they usually do not hold their craft fair on the same weekend as a neighboring community, but there are just so many good weekends, so occasionally they will overlap.

In California, with so much of the state dedicated to agriculture, the last fifteen years have seen the development of every conceivable fair and festival celebrating some fruit or vegetable or nut. There's the Pear Fair, the Artichoke Festival, Cherry Blossom Time, the Apple Hill Fair, the Asparagus

Festival, the Garlic Festival, the Walnut Festival, and on and on. Offhand, I can think of only a few major fruits or vegetables or "nuts" that California doesn't raise—coconuts and pineapples. You fill in the fruit or vegetable or nut and we have a show in its honor. Amazingly, and thankfully, we don't yet have a Marijuana Festival! Every one of these festivals includes a craft show. The problem with all these shows is that while they give you a multiplicity of potential shows from which to select, because they are so close together in time and geographical location, many of the same potential customers show up at every one. People who love craft shows are like people who stop at every garage sale. They provide a crowd and can be counted on to patronize every food and beverage booth, but they only have so much money to spend on crafts. Whether you're in a highly paid yuppie community or out in the farm belt with hundreds of migrant workers, craft show patrons still operate on a budget. They can't afford to buy from you every week. The customers stop by to say hello because they come to recognize you, and you them. It's all very social, but it may not make you a lot of money.

Another reason to be looking for new shows is that you will inevitably experience the poor or losing show on which you gambled and lost. There are the rained-out shows and the occasional cancelled shows due to some regional catastrophe in the area like a fire or flood or such devastating heat that nobody comes out to the show. These occurrences reduce your potential gross income for the year unless you can find a good substitute for them on an open weekend. This is when you become susceptible to signing up for those dicey shows that we discussed above.

Another problem you'll face is the potentially good show that the promoter just didn't advertise sufficiently. You, of course, have no control over this. You can complain to the promoter when you find out about it, but that won't help you that weekend. Next year, don't sign up for that promoter's shows. You will have to learn from experience which promoters fudge on their budget in this way and which do not. Other promoters do eventually draw only the most desperate craftspeople to their shows, and you want to avoid that scenario.

Yet, it is a scenario that may become too common. Beth Weber of North Tahoe Fine Arts Association, one of the most concerned and experienced promoters we know, told me, "The reality is that fewer promoters are coming into the business and the veterans are becoming more complacent and less discriminating." Hopefully, while that may be happening in California, it is not necessarily the case everywhere.

The Guide Book

Whatever the scenario that sends you searching for shows, either at the beginning of the year or throughout the year for the various and sundry reasons mentioned above, a craft guide is still the best way to find the shows at which you will have a better than average chance of making a profit. If you are wondering where you find these guides, ask your neighbors at any show, and they will tell you what magazine they use and how to subscribe. Usually, they'll have a copy with them. There is a great deal of information to be uncovered on the Internet as well. If you search by locale, you will be able to find listings for shows taking place in any part of the United States and Canada.

Certainly, you can find out what shows are taking place in your area from your local newspaper, local events calendars, and Sunday supplements. Magazines, like the one published by the California Automobile Association, or the many travel and camper magazines, also list events for the year throughout all parts of the country. However, these are not guides and will not give you all the information you need other than the date, time, and place of the shows. Like every other aspect of this business, however, even the best guide has its assets and its liabilities, and you have to learn how to use it properly. Here are a few tips and guidelines.

On the following pages you will find samples of a show guide that we used. It is called the *Crafts Fair Guide* and is published by Lee and Dianne Spiegel of Corte Madera, California. *The Crafts Fair Guide* now has a Web site, too, and the first sample is an application form. At the time we were in business, it was arguably the most-used guide in California, Nevada, Oregon, and Arizona, and we believe it still is. Lee himself was a vendor, and his story is fascinating. It symbolizes and reflects the spirit of the craft world.

Thirty years ago, Lee was selling balloons at craft shows. The craft show industry was in its infancy then and craft shows were of very poor quality. Nobody really made any serious money and craftspeople were always complaining about promoters who lured them to shows that were often dismal financial failures. The next year those promoters would find new suckers to fill their spaces. Attendance was usually poor, and the quality of crafts questionable. There was no type of periodical or magazine that even listed potential shows, much less any information about them—which to apply for and which to avoid. As Lee told me, "I saw a need and I filled it."

Lee started the *Crafts Fair Guide* to meet that need and had only 300 subscribers the first year. While developing his new enterprise, Lee continued to sell balloons to cover the costs of the new business. Today, he still sells balloons from time to time to keep in touch with the customers, craftspeople, and the changing nature of the business. But today he also has 2,500 subscribers who pay $45 a year for his guide. That story represents the true entrepreneurial spirit of America—and, by the way, should give you some idea of the extent of the competition you face in the crafts business. Imagine how many craftspeople are setting up their booths every weekend, all over the country!

Sugarloaf Mountain Works, Inc.
200 Orchard Ridge Drive, Suite 215
Gaithersburg, Maryland 20878

(301) 990-1400 • (800) 210-9900
email: Megan@SugarloafCrafts.com
www.SugarloafCrafts.com

APPLICATION & CONTRACT • SPRING 2007 SHOWS

EXHIBITOR/BUSINESS OWNER NAME _____

Business Name _____ ☐ Corporation ☐ Partnership ☐ Sole Proprietor

Address _____ ☐ Check here if *new* address

City _____ State _____ Zip _____ Telephone ( )_____ Mobile ( )_____

☐ Keep address/phones private *see #34 on reverse side* Email _____ Website _____

MEDIA/CATEGORY - *check only one!*
☐ Leather ☐ Metal ☐ Glass ☐ Photography ☐ Fine Arts/Graphics
☐ Jewelry ☐ Pottery ☐ Textiles ☐ Wood ☐ Miscellaneous

BOOTH SIGN - (limit 30 characters and spaces) ☐☐☐☐☐☐☐☐☐☐☐☐☐☐☐☐☐☐☐☐☐☐☐☐☐☐☐☐☐☐

SALES TAX LICENSES - Please indicate the number for any permanent sales tax licenses you hold.

CT _____ MD _____ MI _____ PA _____

NJ _____ VA _____

IF YOU ARE CHARGING ANY FEES, PLEASE COMPLETE THIS SECTION - *Charges may not be postdated.* Charge to: ☐ MasterCard ☐ Visa

Account Number ☐☐☐☐ - ☐☐☐☐ - ☐☐☐☐ - ☐☐☐☐ Expiration Date ____ /____

Name on Card (Print) _____ Charge Signature _____

GENERAL RELEASE AND ACCEPTANCE OF RULES – This contract covers any and all shows listed below to which exhibitor(s) applies or is accepted. I/we the applicant(s) have read the "Conditions of the Show" printed on the back of this licensing application/contract and agree to abide by said conditions. In addition, I/we, the applicant(s), do expressly release the Producer (Sugarloaf Mountain Works, Inc.) and the Owners of the Show Sites of and from any and all liability for any damage, injury or loss to any person, business or property which may arise from the licensing and occupation of the exhibit space by the applicant(s), and agree to hold and save the Producer and Owners of the Show Sites harmless of any damage, injury or loss by reason thereof. I/we understand that if this licensing application is not accepted, all fees and slides will be returned by mail. If this licensing application is accepted, I/we give permission to use my name, business name, slide descriptions, item prices, slides and any photographs, videotape, or images of me or my items for any and all purposes.

Applicant(s) Signature(s) _____ Title _____ Date _____

SPACE SIZES FOR ALL SHOWS:
Small = 10' aisle x 10' deep (8'deep at Gaithersburg)
Medium = 15' aisle x 10' deep (8'deep at Gaithersburg)
Large = 20' aisle x 10' deep (8'deep at Gaithersburg)
Extra Large = 30' aisle x 10' deep (8'deep at Gaithersburg)

SUGARLOAFER DISCOUNT OFFER – SAVE UP TO $400
Apply to all 8 shows this season and save $50.00 off your fees at every show to which you are accepted!
Note: Application to 8 shows does not guarantee acceptance.

WINTER CHANTILLY, VA • Jan 26, 27, 28, 2007		Fees
☐ Sm. Indoor $595	+ ☐ 300w Elect $70	
☐ Med. Indoor..........$875	+ ☐ 450w Elect $95	
☐ Lg. Indoor $1,150	+ ☐ 600w Elect $120	
☐ XL. Indoor $1,745	+ ☐ 900w Elect $170	
☐ Corner Request........$80		
☐ Applying to all 8 shows discount ($50)	( )	
Total Winter Chantilly, VA Fees Enclosed		
☐ Check Dated _____	☐ Visa	☐ Master Card

WINTER SOMERSET, NJ • Mar 9, 10, 11, 2007		Fees
☐ Sm. Indoor $525	+ ☐ 300w Elect $70	
☐ Med. Indoor..........$750	+ ☐ 450w Elect $95	
☐ Lg. Indoor $995	+ ☐ 600w Elect $120	
☐ XL. Indoor $1495	+ ☐ 900w Elect $170	
☐ Corner Request...........................$80		
☐ Storage Vehicle Parking on site $25		
☐ Applying to all 8 shows discount ($50)	( )	
Total Winter Somerset, NJ Fees Enclosed		
☐ Check Dated _____	☐ Visa	☐ Master Card

SPRING PHILADELPHIA, PA • Mar 16, 17, 18, 2007		Fees
☐ Sm. Indoor $525	+ ☐ 300w Elect $70	
☐ Med. Indoor..........$750	+ ☐ 450w Elect $95	
☐ Lg. Indoor $995	+ ☐ 600w Elect $120	
☐ XL. Indoor $1495	+ ☐ 900w Elect $170	
☐ Corner Request........$80		
☐ Applying to all 8 shows discount ($50)	( )	
Total Spring Philadelphia, PA Fees Enclosed		
☐ Check Dated _____	☐ Visa	☐ Master Card

SPRING HARTFORD, CT • Mar 23, 24, 25, 2007		Fees
☐ Sm. Indoor $450	+ ☐ 300w Elect $70	
☐ Med. Indoor..........$650	+ ☐ 450w Elect $95	
☐ Lg. Indoor $850	+ ☐ 600w Elect $120	
☐ XL. Indoor $1250	+ ☐ 900w Elect $170	
☐ Corner Request........$80		
☐ Applying to all 8 shows discount ($50)	( )	
Total Spring Hartford, CT Fees Enclosed		
☐ Check Dated _____	☐ Visa	☐ Master Card

SPRING GAITHERSBURG, MD • Apr 13, 14, 15, 2007		Fees
☐ Sm. Indoor $525	+ ☐ 300w Elect $40	
☐ Med. Indoor..........$750	+ ☐ 450w Elect $60	
☐ Lg. Indoor $995	+ ☐ 600w Elect $80	
☐ XL. Indoor $1495	+ ☐ 900w Elect $120	
☐ Sm. Barn $495	+ ☐ 100w Elect $30	
☐ Med. Barn $725	+ ☐ 150w Elect $45	
☐ Lg. Barn $950	+ ☐ 200w Elect $60	
☐ XL. Barn $1445	+ ☐ 250w Elect $90	
☐ Med. Outdoor..........$295	+ ☐ 300w Elect $40	
☐ XL. Outdoor..........$545	+ ☐ 600w Elect $80	
☐ Corner Request........$80		
☐ Applying to all 8 shows discount ($50)	( )	
Total Spring Gaithersburg, MD Fees Enclosed		
☐ Check Dated _____	☐ Visa	☐ Master Card

SPRING NOVI, MI • Apr 20, 21, 22, 2007		Fees
☐ Sm. Indoor $525	+ ☐ 300w Elect $70	
☐ Med. Indoor..........$750	+ ☐ 450w Elect $95	
☐ Lg. Indoor $995	+ ☐ 600w Elect $120	
☐ XL. Indoor $1495	+ ☐ 900w Elect $170	
☐ Corner Request........$80		
☐ Applying to all 8 shows discount ($50)	( )	
Total Spring Novi, MI Fees Enclosed		
☐ Check Dated _____	☐ Visa	☐ Master Card

SPRING TIMONIUM, MD • Apr 27, 28, 29, 2007		Fees
☐ Sm. Indoor $525	+ ☐ 300w Elect $40	
☐ Med. Indoor..........$750	+ ☐ 450w Elect $60	
☐ Lg. Indoor $995	+ ☐ 600w Elect $80	
☐ XL. Indoor $1495	+ ☐ 900w Elect $120	
☐ Corner Request........$80		
☐ Applying to all 8 shows discount ($50)	( )	
Total Spring Timonium, MD Fees Enclosed		
☐ Check Dated _____	☐ Visa	☐ Master Card

SPRING CHANTILLY, VA • May 4, 5, 6, 2007		Fees
☐ Sm. Indoor $525	+ ☐ 300w Elect $70	
☐ Med. Indoor..........$750	+ ☐ 450w Elect $95	
☐ Lg. Indoor $995	+ ☐ 600w Elect $120	
☐ XL. Indoor $1495	+ ☐ 900w Elect $170	
☐ Corner Request........$80		
☐ Applying to all 8 shows discount ($50)	( )	
Total Spring Chantilly, VA Fees Enclosed		
☐ Check Dated _____	☐ Visa	☐ Master Card

SPECIAL NEEDS OR REQUESTS • List here or on separate sheet.

Please send a separate check for each show.

CONDITIONS OF THE SHOW

1. The Artist or Craftsperson who designs the work and is a principal of the business MUST be present to show their work. If the craft or art is signed by an individual, they are the person required to be at the show. If the business is named after the artist, that individual must be at the show in person. If more than one person is listed as the Exhibitor on this contract, Sugarloaf Mountain Works, Inc. reserves the right to require proof that both are creators of the work and both are significant principals in the business.

2. No dealers or sales representatives are allowed.

3. All work must be original and completely finished. No imports, kits, items made from kits, items made using commercial patterns or commercial molds, items assembled from pre-manufactured components, unfinished work, items made from elephant or whale ivory, embellished items, commercial T-Shirts, commercial Sweats, or art and craft supplies may be displayed or sold.

4. An application is a commitment to show. No full refunds will be given after the acceptance notice is sent. Partial refunds will be given based on number of days before the opening day of the show we receive your cancellation:

150 days or more notice 80%	90-119 days notice........ 40%	30-59 days notice 10%
120-149 days notice 60%	60-89 days notice.......... 20%	under 30 days notice........ 0

5. A $35.00 fee will be charged on any check returned by Exhibitor's bank. Any foreign check processing fees charged by our bank will be billed to the exhibitor at cost.

6. Exhibitors may only show work typified by slides.

7. All art and craft items displayed must be for sale.

8. Exhibitor's booth must have a suitable backdrop to block the view of walls, storage areas or other Exhibitors' booths. All of Exhibitor's booth and display, including chairs, must be placed within the confines of the space. Nothing is to be placed in the aisles.

9. Corner space requests are not guaranteed. Exhibitors will be notified when they get their specific space assignment whether or not they have received a corner space. Those not receiving corners will have their corner fee returned to them at that time.

10. Sugarloaf Mountain Works, Inc. reserves the right to revoke the license granted by this contract at any time, including at the show, by refunding the space fees paid by the Exhibitor. Sugarloaf Mountain Works, Inc. will not be liable for paying any travel expenses, lost revenue or any other liability whatsoever beyond the space fees paid by the Exhibitor as a result of enforcing this provision.

11. The Exhibitor's booth must be open and staffed during all regular show hours. In many cases, anyone arriving late, leaving before closing or breaking down during show hours may be refused entrance to future shows.

12. Spaces not occupied by 7:30 pm on set-up day may be filled with standby Exhibitors with no refund or allowance whatsoever.

13. All exhibits, goods and materials must be removed by 10 pm of the last day of the show. Failure to have everything off site by this time may result in extra charges.

14. Parking and traffic will not be permitted in the show area or fire lanes from one half hour before show opens until fifteen minutes after the show closes each day. All loading and unloading must be planned around these hours and vehicles are to be removed to the Exhibitor parking lots before the show opens. Vehicles remaining in the show area or fire lanes during these hours may be towed away at the owner's risk and expense.

15. Exhibitors must abide by all fire regulations and/or decisions of the representatives of local fire departments. All booth materials shall be in accordance with local fire regulations.

16. Nothing shall be nailed, stapled or otherwise fixed to the walls, floors or any part of the exhibition rooms.

17. Exhibitor's booth must not interfere with adjacent exhibits in any way.

18. All exhibits are to be in keeping with the overall family-oriented theme of the show.

19. Exhibitors are not to bring pets to the show.

20. All Exhibitors are responsible for keeping their area clean during show hours, including clean-up at end of show. All displays should be neat and clean and tables should be covered on all sides to the floor with a suitable, professional looking cover of flame retardant materials.

21. Exhibitors and their helpers must exhibit professional behavior at all times while on the show site. Sugarloaf Mountain Works, Inc. reserves the right, in its sole discretion, to determine what constitutes professional behavior. Violation of this rule will result in the Exhibitor, their helpers and exhibits being excluded from the show site with no refund or allowance whatsoever. In addition, Exhibitors violating this rule may be removed from future Sugarloaf shows with refunds in accordance with the policy detailed in condition #4 above.

22. All extension cords used at the show must be the heavy-duty, three wire type. No two wire extension cords are allowed.

23. Exhibitors may not display ribbons or awards from other shows.

24. Exhibitors may not sublet or apportion space to anyone else.

25. No open flames are permitted.

26. Sugarloaf Mountain Works, Inc. will not be liable for refunds or any other liabilities whatsoever for the failure to fulfill this contract due to reasons of the enclosure in which the show is to be produced, being, before, or during the show destroyed by fire or other calamity, or by any act of God, public enemy, strikes, statutes, ordinances, or any legal authority, or any cause beyond its control.

27. Insurance, if desired by the Exhibitors, must be obtained by them at their own cost.

28. Exhibitors shall be liable for delivery, handling, erection, and removal of their own displays and materials.

29. Exhibitors found in violation of any of the "Conditions of the Show" may be excluded and have their exhibits removed from the current and/or future shows at the sole discretion of Sugarloaf Mountain Works, Inc. In such cases, refunds will be provided as detailed in condition #4 above. Under no circumstances, including negligence, shall Sugarloaf Mountain Works, Inc. be liable for any direct, indirect, incidental, special or consequential damages resulting from such action.

30. Sugarloaf Mountain Works, Inc. may require the removal of work considered to be in violation of these conditions and reserves the right to make final interpretation of all conditions.

31. If any section, sentence, clause, phrase or portion of this licensing application/contract is, for any reason, held invalid or unconstitutional by any court of competent jurisdiction, such portion shall be deemed a separate, distinct and independent provision and such holding shall not affect the validity of the remaining portions.

32. This contract shall be deemed to have been made in the State of Maryland and shall be interpreted in accordance with the laws of such state. In the event that legal action is required to enforce this contract or any of the terms thereof, such action shall be brought in the Courts of Montgomery County, Maryland, and the Exhibitor expressly consents to the jurisdiction of such courts. The parties agree to accept service of process in such action by ordinary mail sent to their business addresses as set forth in this contract.

33. This contract constitutes the entire agreement between Sugarloaf Mountain Works, Inc., and the Exhibitor and no modification shall be valid unless in writing and signed by the parties or their representatives.

34. **Privacy Policy:** We respect your privacy and will never sell or trade your name, mailing address, or email address. However, we frequently receive requests for exhibitor contact information from the public, and will furnish your phone number, website and and/or email addresses upon such request unless you've indicated your preference to keep your contact information private under "Exhibitor/Business Owner Name" on the reverse side.

Rev. 06/06

A good guide, like Lee's, will give you the location of shows and the weekend they were held *last year*. I have emphasized *last year* because most established promotions book their shows for approximately the same weekend, year after year, just as each show also establishes its yearly tradition. However, dates can never be exactly the same year to year, so until you apply, you will only know the approximate weekend.

Lee's guide and most like it will specify the name of the promoter, the location and date of the show, and where to mail your application. You will not, however, be making your application choices just on that basis. The real bonus of Lee's guide is that you'll find evaluations of every show, by any craftsperson who cared to submit an evaluation, either by handing it in at the end of the show or by mailing the form to the publisher of the guide. That evaluation will be printed in next year's guide and you will receive the guide months prior to your having to apply to any show. Just flipping through the guide will be an eye-opener to you when you realize just how many shows are going on every weekend. An example of the evaluation form submitted by craftspeople is also on the following pages.

Sometimes, perhaps only one artisan may have submitted an evaluation, but more often you will have the opportunity to read the comments of six or eight participants in the show; for the really big shows, as many as fifty people may submit their appraisal of last year's show. So most of the time you will get a pretty fair, objective, and quite varied opinion of the show on which to base your decision as to whether to apply or not.

The information contained in the evaluation form is very specific. Every type of craft is listed under a category designation such as wood, wood and fabric, ceramics, pottery, jewelry, and the like, and each is assigned a letter. When you have chosen your category and letter designation, you just refer to those evaluations that fall within your category.

These evaluations give you a rough idea of what you might expect if you sold at that show. Just remember, though; it is a rough idea. Maybe another person's product isn't made as well as yours or maybe it's better. Perhaps their "wood" is furniture and yours is much less expensive rustic shelves that are in greater demand; or maybe one respondent's customer relations skills are not as polished as yours. Sample pages of typical commentary by craftspeople who participated in a previous year's show are reprinted on the following pages.

Be that as it may, according to their category of craft, the merchants who submit their evaluations will give an approximation of their gross income and an evaluation or description of the setup conditions (long haul, rough terrain, many stairways, no elevators, etc.), nature of the crowd, general weather conditions to be expected, opinion on the promoter, and whatever gripes they may have, real or imagined. They will comment about practically any phase of the show operation, including whether or not there were enough toilet facilities, whatever entertainment was provided, and the quality of the food. Some evaluations are so creative and humorous that we have sometimes wondered if they and we were at the same show. However, most evaluations are devastatingly honest, and only you are in a position to judge how all the information applies to you.

The Crafts Fair Guide
Reviews of Arts & Crafts Fairs
FOR Artists & Craftspeople - BY Artists & Craftspeople
www.craftsfairguide.com   415-225-3259

Crafts Fair Guide

Evaluation Form

Home

About Us

Contact Us

Testimonials

Sample Review

Upcoming Fairs

Artist Showcase

Links

Evaluation Form

Subscribe

City	
Name of Fair	
Date(s) of Fair	What Month / January / February / March — Month [ ] Dates [ ]
Description of Environment	
Description of Public (choose up to three, use ctrl key to select)	Enthusiastic / Disinterested / Well-off / Financially Challenged / Buyers / Lookers / Conservative / Sophisticated / Family / Singles / Retirees
Other Comments on the Crowd	
Describe Weather	
Cost to Exhibit	$[ ] and/or [ ]%
Cost to Public	$[ ]

How do you rate this fair for sales?	Choose Rating
	0 (worst)
	1
	2

Approximate gross, (to the closest $100)	[ ]

How do you rate this fair for enjoyability?	Choose Rating
	0 (worst)
	1
	2

Would you return?	Select One
	Yes
	No
	Maybe

Attendance	Select One
	Low
	Medium
	High

Comments about the Fair in General

Promoter's Name

Promoter's Address

City [ ] State [ ]
Zip [ ]

Promoter's Phone

Comments about the Promoter

Your Craft	Indicate Media
	A-- Paintings
	a--Prints
	B--Basketry
	C--Country Crafts
	D--Florals and Plants
	E--Decorative/Tole

Every three months a FAIR EVALUATION FORM is picked at random in a drawing for a FREE year's subscription to THE CRAFTS FAIR GUIDE. To be eligible, please fill in the following information.

Your Name [ ]

Your Address [   ]

City [   ] State [   ]

Zip [   ]

Your Phone Number [   ]

Your Email [   ]

We will keep all of your information confidential and
will never sell or share it with any other person or company.

[Submit Evaluation]   [Clear Form Entries]

NOTE: **If you receive an error message reading:**
"The form was not submitted for the following reasons:
You are coming from an unauthorized domain. Please use your browser's back button to return to the
form and try again."

This problem is caused by your personal firewall blocking HTTP referrer information which the script checks as a security measure. When that info is blocked by your firewall software, the form returns the error message you received.

To send the form, you can temporarily disable your firewall (which you should be able to do by right-clicking its icon in the system tray* and selecting the option to disable it), and then try submitting the form again. Once you submit the form, go back to the system tray icon and right-click again to turn the firewall back on.

We are sorry for the inconvenience, but in this age of hackers, spammers, and worms, we are trying to protect our site from abuse by spammers or hackers...

IF YOU STILL HAVE PROBLEMS. We have another version of this form which uses your mail program to send the form results to us. Please note that you will probably get a security warning that says you are sending information in an insecure manner, do you want to continue anyway? Just say YES to continue since you are not sending any confidential information.
CLICK HERE TO USE THE BACK UP EVALUATION FORM
(We are sorry, but you will have to fill it out again).

*The system tray is at the bottom right of your PC screen next to the clock. You may need to click the little left-arrow to expand the list. Then you can mouse over each icon and a name tag will pop up. Look for "Norton Internet Security" MacAfee Personal Firewall", "Zonealarm" or whatever firewall you use, and right-click on it to see the menu to disable.

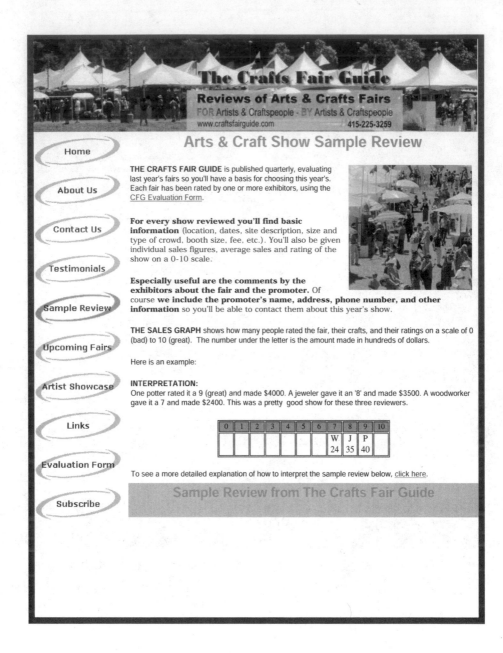

The Crafts Fair Guide
Reviews of Arts & Crafts Fairs
FOR Artists & Craftspeople - BY Artists & Craftspeople
www.craftsfairguide.com   415-225-3259

Arts & Craft Show Sample Review

Home

About Us

Contact Us

Testimonials

Sample Review

Upcoming Fairs

Artist Showcase

Links

Evaluation Form

Subscribe

THE CRAFTS FAIR GUIDE is published quarterly, evaluating last year's fairs so you'll have a basis for choosing this year's. Each fair has been rated by one or more exhibitors, using the CFG Evaluation Form.

For every show reviewed you'll find basic information (location, dates, site description, size and type of crowd, booth size, fee, etc.). You'll also be given individual sales figures, average sales and rating of the show on a 0-10 scale.

Especially useful are the comments by the exhibitors about the fair and the promoter. Of course **we include the promoter's name, address, phone number, and other information** so you'll be able to contact them about this year's show.

THE SALES GRAPH shows how many people rated the fair, their crafts, and their ratings on a scale of 0 (bad) to 10 (great). The number under the letter is the amount made in hundreds of dollars.

Here is an example:

INTERPRETATION:
One potter rated it a 9 (great) and made $4000. A jeweler gave it an '8' and made $3500. A woodworker gave it a 7 and made $2400. This was a pretty good show for these three reviewers.

0	1	2	3	4	5	6	7	8	9	10
							W	J	P	
							24	35	40	

To see a more detailed explanation of how to interpret the sample review below, click here.

Sample Review from The Crafts Fair Guide

CA, OXNARD: California Strawberry Festival
DATE(S): May 14-15, 2005
SETTING: Outside in a large park on the grounds of Oxnard College.
WEATHER: Sunny and warm to hot.
ATTENDANCE: High. "A mixed crowd."
WOULD YOU RETURN? Yes-14 No-3 ?-3
COST: $300 (10x12)   **PUBLIC:** $9
AVERAGE GROSS: $2,707   **RANGE:** $800-$5,800
RATING: 7.2   **SALES / ENJOYABILITY:** 6.6 / 7.7

0	1	2	3	4	5	6	7	8	9	10
		T	A	Y	j	T	W	W	K	X
		8	17	25	19	30	36	29	58	38
				m	Y		H		t	K
				14			20		39	22
				X	z		Z		C	
							16		35	
									m	
									n	

(Numerals = gross sales to the nearest $100 for that vendor.)

COMMENTS ABOUT THE FAIR: "A well-attended show." "I could have sold twice the amount if I'd had more product. I will not make that mistake again. The fair was HUGE! Lots of strawberry food, and so many vendors I don't know how anyone could have seen them all. Setup was a little tough. Bring a cart. I tore down on Monday, but if you don't have that luxury, prepare to be there late on Sunday trying to get out of the parking lot." "Very large crowds. All-day food lines. Good spirit and enthusiasm." "Good music. The craft show is just one aspect of a great show." "Mandatory Friday setup. Lots of dust in the parking areas. Load in and out are somewhat challenging." "Good security and camping. Good cultural mix among attendees." "Good community support. Well-kept grounds." "Great food selection. Activities for the kids. Two stages." "Nice fair in a nice town. Sales were not high, but the show was enjoyable." "Some patrons were annoyed by the entry fee and the high cost of food. There was not much money left over to buy crafts." "With that many people, I should have had much better sales. The lines to buy food were very long. The heat made some buyers cranky and impatient." "One of the hardest setups and breakdowns we have done due to rude vendors wanting to get their vehicles within three feet of their booths." "Sales don't warrant the high entry fee. Dust created a huge clean-up problem. Difficult load in and out." "Well-established annual event with a loyal customer base. Well laid out, but somewhat challenging for vendors on the grassy knolls. There were some mass-produced items and some that would likely qualify as buy-sell or imported." "Great crowd. Huge variety of crafts. Not the place for expensive wearables. Lots of food, rides for kids, and entertainment galore."

COMMENTS ABOUT THE PROMOTER: "Extremely well organized and very friendly." "It was nice to have some 'secret' porta-potties just for the vendors so we wouldn't have to wait in long lines." "Vendor friendly." "Try to accommodate. Solve problems on the spot." "Very professional and fair." "Onsite and accessible all weekend." "Excellent. Always available. Others could learn a lot from her." "Honest, fair, and knowledgeable." "The more fairs I do with them, the more I like them." "Starting to let more buy-and-sell into her shows." "Very nice and well organized." "They do their job. The jurying committee is letting in some buy-and-sell and low-end crafts." "Great people." "Very well organized and helpful."

PROMOTER: Pacific Fine Arts (Dana and Troy Hale-Mounier), P O Box 280, Pine Grove, CA 95665. Contact Bobbie Luiz or Troy Hale-Mounier

Phone: 209-296-1195 Fax: 209-296-4395
Website: www.pacificfinearts.com
Email: pfa@pacificfinearts.com
PRIMARILY FINE ART SHOWS
2006 INFORMATION: May 20-21. Deadline February 15. $350 for 10x12. 308 art & crafts exhibitors. $15 jury fee. $12 to public. All-at-once jurying. Show accepts arts and crafts by the maker only.

How to Interpret the Review

THE CRAFTS CODES: It's not possible to assign a letter for every imaginable craft, so some categories are broader than others.

A -- Paintings	I -- Ceramic	O -- Music
a -- Prints	J -- Jewelry over $100	P -- Pottery
B -- Basketry	j -- Jewelry under $100	R -- Seasonal Crafts
C -- Country Crafts	K -- Kidstuff	S -- Soft Sculpture
D -- Florals and Plants	L -- Leather	T -- Textile
E -- Decorative/Tole	M -- Fiber Arts	t -- Clothing
F -- Photography	m -- Metal Arts	W -- Woodwork
G -- Glass	N -- Packaged Foods	X -- Mixed Media
H -- Sculpture	n -- Food Concessionaires	Y -- No category/hard to define
		Z -- Declined to state

Following the Sales Graph will be crafts peoples' comments about the fair and promoter. The comments are condensed from all reviews received for easy reading and are broken into comments about the fair and comments about the promoter. Select quotes from some of the submitted forms are also included to represent the opinion of all exhibitors who submitted reviews.

Click here to Subscribe to **The Crafts Fair Guide**!

When you are a beginner and trying to use the various guides for the first time, you have very little experience on which to base a judgment. I know that the first year we used them, Judy and I tended to treat the guides as gospel truth. We learned better over the years, for reasons I'll later explain, but as a rough guide, they serve very well.

Particularly, note how much money that the craftspeople in your category say they earned. Then compare it with their evaluations. Note the category for sales and determine whether it squares with the crafters' stated price range and, therefore, whether the evaluators really could have earned what they said they earned. Pay particular attention to whether everyone's sales were generally what you would consider high and what you are aiming to make or whether only specific categories earned high ratings. That can tell you something about buyer taste in that area.

Most evaluators are scrupulously honest. But there are some, as in every walk of life, who for a variety of reasons will misrepresent their earnings at a given show. They may have done poorly for any number of reasons that have nothing to do with the promotion itself. According to the promoters with whom I discussed this subject, if craftspeople do poorly at a show, the first person they will always blame is the promoter. It is just something that promoters learn to live with. In reality, a craftsperson's failure may have had nothing to do with the promoter.

Craftspeople who have spent years in the business may make comments based on prejudices, personal inadequacies, or hidden agendas. In some cases, they may just want to stifle the competition, so they write a poor evaluation of the show. Or, perhaps they made more money than they reported to the promoter, if the show fee also included a percentage of their sales. Then, too, the craftsperson may just be hiding income from the IRS. So all you can do is find those evaluations by someone in the same product category as yours and then decide whether what they say they earned is a figure that satisfies your needs. Of course, that still doesn't guarantee that you will make the same amount of money. Nothing and no one can guarantee that.

Show Guides Online

Some of the available guides and craft show listings are printed below along with their Web site addresses. Certain guides are available only online. The online sites often offer craft event calendars that you can look at without subscribing. For full, in-depth information, however, you usually will have to buy the service.

There are a plethora of available resources online for researching your own locale. Information on almost every area of the country can be found easily. When surfing around the net, you will find that many of the offerings that come up when you search using keywords like "Craft Listings" are really covert advertisements for companies trying to sell commercial services. I found dozens of sites offering to teach crafters how to make $3,000 a month selling crafts. Don't be surprise to discover that researching craft information online can require careful sifting.

www.ABCCraftEvents.com
ABC
PO Box 130
Walland, TN 37886
(800) 678-3566
Contact: Mary Reed

www.Americancraftmarketing.com
American Art Marketing
PO Box 480
Slate Hill, NY 10973
(845) 678-355-2400
E-mail: acm@warwick.net

www.Artfairsourcebook.com
Art Fair Source Book
2003 N.E. 11th Avenue
Portland, OR 97212-4027
(800) 358-2045
Contact: Greg Lawler

www.bobslists.com
Bobslists
159 Brawley Avenue
Salton Sea Beach, CA 92274

www.craftcouncil.org
American Craft Council
72 Spring Street, 6th floor
New York, NY 10012-4019
(800) 836-3470

www.craftsfairguide.com
The Arts Fair Guide
PO Box 688
Corte Madera, CA 94976
(415) 255-3259
Contact: Lee and Dianne Spiegel

www.Craftmasternews.com
Craftmaster News
PO Box 39429
Downey, CA 90239
(562) 869-5882

www.craftshowyellowpages.com
Art and Craft Show Yellow Pages
PO Box 13
Red Hook, NY 12571
(888) 918-1313

www.festivalnet.com
Festival Network Online
PO Box 18839
Asheville, NC 28814
(828) 658-2779

www.grpvne.com
Grapevine Publishing, Inc.
PO Box 1057
Plainfield, IL 60544

www.harrislist.com
The Harris List
PO Box 142
La Veta, CO 81055
(719) 742-3142

www.jolaf.com
Juried Online Arts Festival
Hamlin, WV 25523

www.midwestartscraftsguide.com
The Guide
4251 Hamilton Avenue
Cincinnati, OH 45233
(800) 825-4332

www.SACNewsmonthly.com
2120 S. Columbia Street
Bogalusa, LA 70427
Phone (985) 735-8542
(800) 825-3722

www.SugarloafCrafts.com
Sugarloaf Mountain Works, Inc.
200 Orchard Ridge Drive, #215
Gaithersburg, MD 20878
(800) 210-9900

www.sunshineartist.com
Sunshine Artist
3210 Dade Avenue
Orlando, FL 32804
(800) 597-2573

Many Factors Will Influence Your Show Selection

Ironically, with experience, you may also find yourself choosing not to do some shows that you know are excellent. Perhaps you decide against an outdoor show, where the weather is always poor, when you know of a show that's equally good but is held indoors and you don't have to deal with the weather factor. You also may decide that a show is just too far away, taking up too much travel time or costing too much in travel expenses. Sometimes, making less gross money is better than making more. Do your arithmetic.

Which shows you choose also depends on some simple, practical facts related to your particular life and lifestyle. Only you can determine this. Consider the following: how much cash reserve you have amassed from the preceding year, how hard you are willing to work, the amount of inventory you can afford to produce, and, finally, how far you are willing to travel.

When Judy and I began, we had a young son, Mark. We could take him anywhere. He thought the shows were a real treat, with playgrounds to romp in and new places to see. Missing a few days of school had no effect on his schoolwork, and we always had his teachers send us homework in advance.

As Mark grew older, however, just keeping him amused became a chore. I spent more time entertaining my son than I did selling in the booth. We would tour the show endlessly, go to a movie, do his homework, anything to keep him occupied. Eventually, of course, he could not miss school, and one of us had to stay home while the other did the shows alone—something that we swore we would never do. But now it was big business, and our viewpoint changed.

This put a totally different perspective on the shows. In our case, Judy was the logical choice to do the selling, as she is the better salesperson and could deal best with women—their decorating tastes, color schemes, and so on—and women constituted 98 percent of our customers. This was another forced choice. Furthermore, as our business became more and more successful, I had to stay home in order to produce enough inventory for the next show.

So much capital outlay was now involved that we could only afford to select the best shows where we, from experience, were relatively certain we would gross $3,000 to $6,000 a show. The baskets, therefore, had to be ready for Judy to line and decorate, pack in the truck, and take off to the next show. Where the next shows that we had selected were located presented some major problems. The best shows were very often the farthest away from home and, as a consequence, traveling alone consumed a great deal of Judy's time.

Consider a typical Harvest Festival show. Often the show was in southern California and we lived in northern California. As a result of our show selection, it was necessary to do some 1,200 miles of round-trip driving. Judy would leave on Wednesday and she wouldn't be back until the following Monday. The next Wednesday or, at the latest, the next Thursday morning, she would be back on the road again, off to the next show.

It was a very grueling lifestyle, and after about five years, we just couldn't maintain it any longer. Though we were grossing a great deal of money, when we factored in expenses and time, we found that we could net just as much profit by doing some of the best shows that were closer to us. We came to a point where we passed up many great shows, in spite of our good experience with them or the fine evaluations they received in the Crafts Fair Guide.

Show Fees

If you noted above that we made reference to capital outlay, it is because the subject is especially pertinent to the problem of selecting your shows. We are not referring here to how much money you have invested in equipment and materials to produce your product, though that, of course, is also always a concern. If you don't know this or haven't considered it in depth, you must begin to do so. For it is likely that you will keep money in reserve for the production of your craft and never consider where all the money is going to come from to pay your show fees. Quite possibly, what shows you select will be drastically affected by this question.

The fees that you pay to get into a show cannot be put off and paid the morning you arrive at the show site to set up or after the show is over and you are counting your profit. At the time you mail the promoter your application, a check for her fee must be included. If your application is not accepted and you are rejected, your check will be returned to you. This means that money for perhaps dozens of shows is sitting out there somewhere in the hands of a promoter until she gets around to evaluating your application and sends you notice of acceptance or rejection.

How much money does this amount to? Well, it can easily add up to thousands of dollars. Booth fees for small neighborhood shows occasionally may cost as little as $60, but booth fees for the average show today run between $150 and $200 or more. The really big show promotions cost as much as $750 for a ten-by-ten-foot booth space for three days—and each year those entry fees go up as promoters' expenses increase, just as yours do.

What's more important to you is that the promoter wants your money early in the year and the show may not be until November or December. If you do twenty to thirty shows a year, you must have anywhere from $3,000 to $10,000 in reserve to send out before you have ever sold a dime's worth of your craft work. Even if you receive a rejection a few months after you mailed your fee and your check is returned, that money was in somebody else's possession for those few months. It was not earning anything for you. Of course, you also have no absolute guarantee—other than your past experience—that you are ever going to make this money back when you do all these shows.

Beth Weber, who has many years of promoting experience, points out that the good promoter also has a large capital outlay, well in advance of any show she is promoting. Advertising in magazines and newspapers must be paid, street banners designed, flyers and circulars distributed, application and instruction forms printed and mailed, acceptance replies to craftspeople also mailed, salaries to staff paid, and so on.

As an example, Beth informed me that the parking lot near Kings Beach State Park at Lake Tahoe, which provides space for only seventy booths, costs $3,000 for a weekend. Therefore, the average small promoter's profit margin is not high and, over the years, costs have continually risen. In addition, fees must be paid in advance. Of the five promoters in the business whom we know best or with whom we have the most experience, only one has been extremely financially successful, while the others have simply made a modest living. Excluding the top-level shows—which are, in reality, big corporations—none of the smaller promoters have become independently wealthy.

Another Reality Check

As you contemplate and prepare for all the costs of travel to show sites, food and lodging, and all your other expenses, keep in mind that these expenses should be covered by money that you placed in reserve from your profits the previous year. Everyone who manages a crafts business successfully prepares in this way. You cannot wait and then depend on needed money being derived from earnings and profit from shows you do early in the current year. That profit, if there is much, is usually plowed back into the business and, if you have no other source of income, will be used to pay your ordinary household bills. Your goal is to sell a lot of merchandise at the best shows throughout the year. This should result in a substantial profit by the end of the year.

Once you are committed financially almost a year before the show, you had better make it to that show with a large inventory to sell. After all, you have dedicated your effort, time, and money to that weekend, well in advance, so you must be there. There is no refund on your fee should you fail to show up. The shows you select, then, depend on your having done your financial accounting well.

If you haven't gotten the picture yet, I'll reiterate that the crafts business involves a twelve- to fifteen-hour day, seven days a week, fifty-two weeks a year—and it is an expensive business in which to engage if you are doing it full time and seriously. We don't mean to be discouraging, just realistic. On a full-time basis, you must be prepared to eat, sleep, and even dream about the business, and how and what shows you select is a major part of that business and those dreams.

Your lifestyle will have a carnival or circus atmosphere. Many people believe that craftspeople travel from show to show as a group. There will be times when your business will seem to pervade your daily existence and exclude what most people consider a normal life. Many of our previous friendships were lost because we were simply never available, as we once had been. If we were not so busy in the production of our craft, we were busy planning for the next season. We can't count the family get-togethers we missed, the parties we couldn't attend, the places we couldn't go.

If you're not the kind of person who can adjust to this gypsy style of life and the pressure it creates, don't attempt to go into this business full time—especially your first year or two. Get your feet good and wet before you decide to make that kind of commitment. What we've just said may be the best reason of all for making your show selections carefully. It's hell to be sitting at a rotten show, knowing you missed a friend's wedding or a relative's birthday or anniversary.

Some General Advice

If you are just starting out, keep your travel expenses to a minimum. If possible, put your money in your product and only venture as far away as is absolutely necessary. But don't stick around the neighborhood, as we did. Apply to good shows! Certainly, don't select some local, Sunday-in-the-park show just because it is nearby. A few hundred neighbors won't help you honestly evaluate your product or your sales ability. At good shows, your entry fees will be higher, but so will the attendance. The result is that you will get a truer picture of the marketability of your product.

In summing up this chapter, we would say that in your novice years, your show selection should probably include a smattering of all the types of shows we have discussed, whether you applied to them originally by recommendation, gamble, or research. Little by little, you will discard the failures and reapply to the shows that were successful for you, not successful for someone who told you how great it was "last year." Slowly, you will build an annual schedule that you approach each year with confidence and anticipation. Then you will also come to know the special excitement and sense of accomplishment that comes with the unexpected success and the even greater sense of achievement when you know you have planned your craft season well.

The Plein Air Street Fair

If you live in an urban environment, there are many opportunities to try selling your wares at a variety of street fairs and open air markets. This can be a relatively cheap way to get your work out into the community and create a regular customer base. In New York City, art can legally be sold on the street, provided you observe regulations about where you do this and how much space you take up on the sidewalk. However, as with all else, each of these particular microenvironments has its own set of survival skills that can change abruptly when shifts in the economy (such as a downturn in the stock market) or politics (a new mayor is elected) take place. Your ability to succeed will also depend on how you adjust to a less protective physical environment. Many outdoor urban venues can be grueling. If you are street vending this may mean spending a full day out in the elements without a tent and, in many cases, no easy access to bathroom facilities.

The great advantage the urban open market offers over the ever-shifting venue of craft fairs and street festivals is fixity of location. New York City is very much a city of explorers. The average New Yorker finds endless amusement in simply strolling the streets and checking out what's new in the neighborhood. Outdoor markets offer a perfect post-brunch destination. A well-trafficked venue provides a crafter with the opportunity to build up a regular trade during the year. Customers seeking your product for a holiday gift or a special occasion know where to find you. Permanent outdoor markets in an urban area are often a year-round tourist attraction.

Outdoor craft and gift markets are notoriously attractive to shoppers with a yen to make an impulse purchase. Many vacationers have earmarked spending money for just these kinds of venues, and if you are in a well-placed, high-volume area with the right item, this can be a very lucrative outlet.

For a number of years, I had a booth in just such a weekend market in Lower Manhattan, which attracted high-caliber jewelry and fashion designers. The market, formerly a parking lot, was well known and drew customers from all over the city. The manager of the market extracted "key money," a hefty sum upfront to guarantee the spot, in addition to a monthly rental fee. As care was taken to avoid direct competition between vendors, for many years almost all of the artisans were able to actually make a living doing this market alone. Therefore, everyone had the time to spend the week making new stock, instead of running all over the place trying to find additional sources of income. Over time, however, management grew greedy and became less protective of the rights of individual crafters. A pair of ambitious sisters from England set up shop at opposite ends of the market. Both sisters had millinery aspirations and began to display several hats, which were conspicuously similar in design. Bitter words were exchanged between the sisters, leading ultimately to an actual brawl between the two milliners.

Unfortunately, management refused to interfere. Eventually the problem cleared up, more as a result of the passage of time (the much-disputed hat stopped selling) than diplomatic skills of the parties involved. Management, far from mending its ways, began to allow in direct competitors and more commercial goods. Price wars developed, forcing out the crafters. What was once a flourishing arts market was replaced by a seven-day-a-week "flea" market full of imported bargains, cheap but boring. New York City's loss, but the parking lot owner's gain.

Another urban alternative is the ubiquitous street fair. Throughout the summer and into the early autumn, you can count on at least two or three street fairs to be taking place at the same time, often only several blocks apart. These fairs are well attended and crowded. Originally, each street fair reflected the character of the section of the city it was situated in. Most of the exhibitors had some connection to the actual neighborhood where the fair was taking place.

Unfortunately, the number of fairs in New York City has mushroomed in the last ten years and from what I gather this is true elsewhere. What was once a distinctive annual event limited to a few neighborhoods has blossomed into an industry in itself. These days, whether a fair is in the Italian section of the city or the Ukrainian section, increasingly the flavor of each has become so similar as to be virtually indistinguishable. The same vendors can be found with the same merchandise at all the fairs, alongside the same food stalls.

Despite these downsides, a benefit of fair proliferation is that you can handpick the neighborhood in which you wish to show. In general, the street fair crowd is looking for a relatively inexpensive purchase. This is a venue where people come expecting to buy and they will be disappointed if they come away at the end of the day without a souvenir. If you price yourself within range of the other vendors, you have a good chance of making a profit, as your unique product will stand out from the mass of imported goods surrounding you.

Get to know a street fair intimately before signing up for your booth. Your location has everything to do with your success. Certain street intersections are always at the hub of the action. If you are too far away from these sites, you will see half of the traffic. Try to place yourself next to other crafters and create a little haven of art and tranquility. Early in my career, I decided to take part in one of the most famous street festivals in New York City. I had gone to the fair many times as a participant and enjoyed myself. The promoter genially squeezed me into a prime spot right next to a Ferris wheel, a beer concession, and an Italian sausage stand. I set up my small table with a dainty display of earrings and necklaces and prepared myself for business. As the hour grew later, the throng of late-night revelers swelled. I found myself clinging desperately to my table as weaving bands of slightly drunken pleasure seekers pushed past. My elegant display narrowly escaped complete destruction. There were plenty of customers, just not the customers for me. A few blocks down from me on the same street, another jewelry vendor was making a killing. She had positioned herself next to a booth selling sun dresses and a man taking Victorian photos. I survived that fiasco but learned the lesson on the importance of location the hard way.

Another option for the city crafter seeking retail opportunity is the popular holiday market. In New York City, many of these are outdoors, modeled on the traditional European Christmas markets, with semi-permanent booths. These markets are open only for the four or five principal selling weeks preceding Christmas. They have proved popular with the general public and draw people from the surrounding areas on the weekends. When these markets began around ten years ago, the booth costs were reasonable and many crafters were approached to fill the booths. As the markets became more established the costs rose to an almost prohibitive degree. The current price of about $7,000 dollars for a booth is steep. Although you can pretty much count on doing huge volumes in a brief time (if you have the right product), it is a major commitment of money and inventory. If you are making everything by yourself, you will have to start preparing inventory at least six months in advance.

There are also the usual disadvantages of an outdoor show. The weather at that time of year can be uncooperative. If the weather is extraordinarily cold or inclement, you stand a good chance that foot traffic will slow to a crawl. Real holiday shopping at a retail level does not get going until the last three weeks of December. Many vendors seem to have short-term memory loss on this subject and, as a result, you will often see a miserable set of vendors hunched over their heaters as they wait for business. In the end, these last three weeks will make up for all of your tribulation but the toll on your nerves can be extreme.

It takes a bold and confident crafter to venture into this arena.

—BR

6 The Promoter

IF NOTHING THAT WE have said has discouraged you thus far—and we hope it hasn't—we now will deal with the people who may have more to do with the success of your business, in some ways, than even you yourself. As confident as you now may be that you have a unique and beautiful product—one to which the buying public will respond enthusiastically—without the promoter, the person who produces the craft shows in which you desire to showcase your craft, essentially you have no business. You are completely dependent on the promoter.

Though you may be convinced that you and your product are ready to meet the world of customers who will spend a great deal of money purchasing your craft, you have nowhere to set up your booth and ply your trade until you can convince the promoter of that. So, having considered all the advice you have been given (including ours), having scoured the craft fair guides and decided on the shows that you think are best suited to selling your product, now, all you have to do is apply to those shows, show up on the specified date, and sell. Right? Wrong!

The Process of Applying

As we noted briefly in the previous chapter, whether you are new to the business or one of the thousands of veteran artisans, long established in the bigtime craft arena, if you are applying to shows that you have never done before, you will first have to mail your request for an application to each promoter of every craft show you have selected. While you are waiting for a response, this is a good time to initiate a filing system regarding promoters and their promotions. Make a list of every show for which you requested an application, the date and place of that show, the deadline for applying to the show, and the date you mailed your request. Then check it off when you receive the application back in the mail. That way you don't lose track of the shows to which you have already applied. This is easy to do when you are sending out many such requests. Then be sure to request applications for many more shows than you intend to do. If you want to participate in twenty shows in a given year, send out requests for applications to twenty-five, as you can expect to receive some rejections no matter how long you have been in the business.

It is not at all unusual for a few weeks to pass, sometimes more, before the application you requested arrives in your mailbox. So while you are anxiously waiting, just keep producing your product. Even though you're spending more time and money at this point, and you have no idea whether you will ever be accepted when you do finally apply, that's just another gamble of the business.

If it's any consolation, once you are in the business and have established yourself, you'll be getting applications and invitations automatically. If you're good, almost all doors will be open to you—more shows than you could possibly do. Don't just throw those applications and invitations out. File them away. Next year you may want them. Whether you're new to the business or a veteran, whether the application was sent to you automatically or you had to request it, when you have the application in hand, it is not just a simple matter of filling it out, attaching a check, and sending it right back to the promoter with the expectation that you will be admitted to the show. A laborious process called jurying begins and, no matter how long you are in the business, you will go through this every time you apply to a new show or one staged by a new promoter. Some shows still require you to be juried every year, even if you have been accepted to them before. You will also be required to jury again if you have added any new products to your craft line.

New Application Procedures

In this post-twentieth-century interconnected world, many fairs have their forms available as downloadable PDFs. That means you don't have to wait for the promoter to send you a form, but, of course, you still have to wait for the promoter to receive your materials and review them. Now, in addition to posting application forms, more and more promoters have actually moved the jurying process to the Internet. Artscape, Baltimore's preeminent annual arts festival, has recently made this shift. The Artscape festival is the mid-Atlantic's largest festival of the arts, drawing hundreds of thousands of attendees each year. The Artists' Market showcases 120 arts and craftspeople from across the country. When I asked Kim Domanski, the Artists' Market coordinator for Artscape, to clarify how Zapplication works, she explained:

"This year we have moved to an online application process through Zapplication.org. Many larger festivals also utilize this service. Basically, an artist sets up an artist profile in Zapplication and uploads their images and then applies to any festivals who utilize this service. For us, Zapplication acts as a database for all this information, assembles the images for the jury process, is the system used by our jurors for scoring/acceptance. This is also the database we use for assigning booths."

There is also another commonly used system called Juried Art Services (*www.juriedartservices.com*), which is used by the Smithsonian and the Crafts America shows, among others.　　　—BR

Promoters and the Jury System

The jury system is the process through which you must go in order to convince each promoter that you manufacture a product and can present a booth display that he wants to accept into his show. Promoters are always looking for new products to give their show variety and booth displays that repeat customers have not seen before. There could be 215 to 320 craft booths in the top shows like Harvest Festival or Country Folk Art. Most of the artisans will be among the very best from all over the country, and the jury system is the reason why.

The best promoters are very careful, selective, and discriminating in this regard, as they should be, for your sake as well as theirs. The average promoter depends on booth fees to defray all the costs of promotion and still render a profit. The larger promoters depend on admission fees to cover the expenses that booth fees do not and to produce the necessary profit to remain in business. It is in both their interests and yours to provide the public with a display of crafts that intrigue them and keep them returning to the show, year after year. Rhonda Blakely expressed Country Folk Art's philosophy as follows: "trying to present to the customer a total decorating theme."

This dedication to giving the customers their money's worth is especially true of promotions that charge what seem like especially high booth fees. Such shows as Harvest Festival and Country Folk Art travel nationwide. For years, Country Folk Art had its own magazine with 75,000 subscribers and a circulation of half a million. Yet, as costs of producing the magazine doubled, the publication had to be discontinued. Harvest Festival is produced by Western Exhibitors, who manage craft shows in seven cities on the West Coast (*www.weshows.com*). Obviously, these big promotions have long-standing reputations for quality to maintain, even as they struggle with the same increasing business costs as you do, only on a much larger scale.

Many craftspeople may not believe it—even though it is true—but as one promoter assured me, "Promoters respect their exhibitors and want to help them to continue to be successful." And this is the attitude of good promoters everywhere, for the relationship between craftsperson and promoter is a symbiotic one. Both need each other to be successful and to make a profit. Another promoter put it this way: "I understand their concerns regarding increased expenses, but in order to maintain the level of promotion we all want, we need to stay on top of the markets, and advertise and upgrade our shows as much as we can each season." To do that costs big money. In some markets, Rhonda Blakely informed me, radio advertising now costs as much as television commercials, and the cost of print advertising has doubled.

Other large shows, like the Garlic Festival in California, a once-a-year community endeavor that draws 100,000 people, does not have the substantial budget of corporate promotions. The manager and workers all volunteer their time, and profits from admissions fees are all earmarked for various community projects. As a daytime show, it requires no lights (no electrical bill), and since it is a well-established, well-known show, there is no need for promotion beyond the flyers they send out to craftspeople and local TV and radio to notify them of the date. The entry fee is far less than that charged by big corporate shows with huge budgets to support.

If your application to the Garlic Festival is accepted, you are going to make a bundle of money that one weekend. Just don't count on being accepted. Such annuals as this usually allow no more than eighty to a hundred crafters in the show, primarily to maintain their tradition. These types of traditional shows usually have a nucleus of artists who have shown with them for years, many since the inaugural presentation. Participants often live in the local community and are invited back every year. So they may only accept some fifteen or twenty new craftspeople into their show each year and receive as many as five hundred applications for those few spots. Do not be dismayed if you are not accepted. As profitable as they can be, you should never rely on them as a year-to-year source of income.

We want to advise you, too, that with smaller shows, a promoter may reject you, not because of the quality of your craft, but because he may have already accepted into the show a few craftspeople producing pieces similar to yours. Therefore, there are even fewer booth spaces open to you, no matter how fine your product. So, after a few years of applying to and being rejected by these shows, you may decide it is pointless to keep applying—

particularly if there is a nonrefundable jury fee—whether you are accepted to the show or not. More than a few promotions derive considerable extra profit through this fee.

Whether the promotion is of the average size or one of the big shows, these shows would quickly stop drawing huge crowds of customers, willing to pay admission year after year, if they were not providing the public with a large variety of well-produced crafts. To jury for the vast, top-of-the-line promotions is, therefore, the most difficult, particularly for those of you just entering the business.

What good promoters are looking for can be stated in very simple terms. As Judy and I recognized early in our career, and as described by every promoter I've interviewed, their standards are the same. Promoters seek quality and skill. They examine the raw material that goes into the product, design originality, how the product is embellished that distinguishes it from another craftsperson's similar product, and artistic design. Achieve that and you'll probably be accepted.

Now, of course, as in any other business, there will be those promoters who don't discriminate at all. Just send in your application and if they are not already filled, you're in. As you progress in the craft world and encounter the various promoters, you will find that this is not the attitude of the best promoters or even the majority.

Some promoters really care about craftspeople. Beth Weber, who only promotes shows in the north Lake Tahoe area, is a good example. She sees them as artisans. She is herself a potter and exhibits at every show she promotes. She acknowledges that "Some promoters forget why they are making their money." Beth is discriminating in the craftspeople she selects for her shows and appreciative of each artisan's contribution to the success of her shows.

Unfortunately, Beth is not representative of every promoter you will encounter. You will experience disappointment with shows that operate on that non-discriminating basis. And you will get to know which promoters are concerned only with the money they make. Yet, there will be times that, in spite of this knowledge, you won't be able to avoid doing their shows. Some craft shows, when put on by even the least likable promoters, must be given your consideration because they will make you money!

These are the street fairs that include as many as 500 to 800 other craft booths. These really large street shows are often promoted by people long in the business, contracted year after year to promote the same show. Other than mailing out acceptances, marking booth spaces, and collecting money, they do little real promoting. Every organization in the community is really promoting the show for the promoter, months in advance of the show date. The show draws such huge crowds, representing every economic segment of the population, that the promoter does not have to be at all discerning or discriminating with regard to the quality of crafts presented at the show. These promoters will accept every conceivable kind of craft and quality level of craft until they have no more booth spaces to fill. It's not that the jurying is lax; it's just that even though photographs of your work will be requested, jurying is really nonexistent. Do not regard your acceptance to this type of show as a recognition of your work. However, this is one of the rare times that it doesn't matter. Your craft will be seen by thousands of people who are interested in the market that your craft represents, and exposure is the name of the game.

Handling a Rejection

Many times, regardless of how long you have been in the business and even in seemingly indiscriminate situations such as the above example, you will be rejected, and you will never know exactly why. If a promoter puts on many shows a year, you may be rejected for some and accepted into others. That can be hard to understand. When you are rejected, it is worth your effort to write a courteous letter requesting an explanation from the promoter. Doing so demonstrates your interest, concern, and professionalism. Just the fact that the promoter responds and perhaps gives you a few tips suggests that you have a good chance to get into next year's show or shows, assuming you address the reason you were rejected. Remember, your livelihood depends on the promoter's decision, so it always behooves you to put your best, most genial, and professional foot forward.

The Process of Jurying

Traditionally there were two ways to jury, by mail and in person. In the early 2000s, an electronic variation is gaining in popularity.

Variations on the Mail-In Jury

The first type of jury process is the mail-in submission of photographs of your craft and booth display along with your application and a check for your jurying fee. The second and new Web-driven variation is the digital submission of images and completion of applications online. For many crafters who are somewhat low-tech, the transition to digital applications has proved a challenge. Kim Domanski of Artscape commented that, "Since this is the first year that we are contracting with Zapplication, we are also accepting written applications. This transition has been easy for some artists, and difficult for others. The primary benefits for the artists are that they can save money on slide duplication and postage fees, and they save a great deal of time applying for multiple shows once they have completed their artists' profile. The primary benefits for the festival are that we save administrative time because we don't have thousands of slides to keep track of and return; the artist's information, images and booth assignments are all in ONE database that is begun when the artists first apply, which also cuts down on mistakes on our part; and the reporting capabilities of Zapplication, i.e., our booth assignment roster can be printed directly from Zapplication. And Zapplication advertises our festival to artists who would have otherwise not known about us.

"Having a database of artist's contact information and images also has long-term benefits. I often get telephone calls months after the festival from individuals who visited Artscape and saw someone's work that they really liked or would like to buy for a gift. For any of a number of reasons, this person didn't purchase the work at the festival but would like to now. Often times they only remember what the work looked like and having a database of images allows us to put this person in contact with the artist very easily."

Live and In-Person

The third form of jurying is the in-person jury process. In this case, you will be given a time and place to appear, and you must present your craft to one or more people—on occasion, a whole committee—for their evaluation and approval. Sometimes, they will tell you immediately whether or not you have been accepted and, if not, why. This in-person jurying process can be extremely helpful to you when you are given feedback, but other times, you will just place your craft product on display with many other products, be told when to return to retrieve your merchandise, and be sent your acceptance or rejection in the mail. This form of jurying is less common; most often, you just submit photographs or slides. While in-person jurying may be very inconvenient—since you will have to take time out from the production of your craft to travel to wherever the jury process is taking place—it is to your best advantage and very much worth the expenditure of your time. If you receive comments about your craft—verbally or in writing—positive feedback will tell you what you are doing right and negative appraisal will tell you what you need to improve.

Granted, putting your craft on the line before this type of jury only to be rejected can be ego-shattering and very demoralizing. But, whatever the outcome, this type of jury procedure is an excellent learning experience for you, as it is the most honest critique you will probably ever receive regarding your craft. Friends and neighbors are usually not going to tell you the truth, simply because they don't want to hurt your feelings.

The in-person jury offers a practical, realistic, professional appraisal of your work that can give you a perspective that you never considered, one that you may find very useful as you develop your product line. Remember that even when you jury in person, since you cannot set up your booth for them, the jury will expect to see photographs of your booth display. We will give you more details regarding photographs later in this chapter.

While to jury in this manner presents a good opportunity to have your product evaluated, it also does not mean that every promoter, jury, or committee will evaluate your product the same way. What does not fulfill the needs of one promoter may be exactly to the liking of another. Your product may be excellent, but too similar to other crafts already accepted into the show. Most good promoters try not to have more than two or three of the same category in a normal-size show. Another promoter might not have anything like your work in his show. Then, too, the size of one show may be more limited than another.

Country Folk Art and Harvest Festival both try very hard to find artisans who produce everything themselves, which tells you something about the concerns of these promoters. However, they both acknowledge that maintaining that approach is becoming more difficult. The handmade crafts coming from overseas are not only increasing in quantity, but also improving in quality. Furthermore, customers who once wanted to buy only American are beginning to change their philosophy, if the foreign product is good and is, of course, less expensive. Then, too, some labor-intensive products are now almost entirely relegated to foreign craftspeople. Rhonda Blakely gave me the example of lace or tatted goods. It is now virtually impossible to find anyone who produces this type of product in the United States. All this creates stiffer competition.

Prohibited Products

Embellished products have in the past been subject to a great deal of scrutiny. Many shows will reject any work that comes out of a mold, no matter how well it is cast and how superb the artistic embellishments. Ceramics in particular suffers from this severity. Lorie Walker of Harvest Festival responded that her shows are not entirely averse to mass-produced products provided they are strictly handmade and made in America. She said, "We draw the line at imports. There are plenty of appropriate shows for imported products but they don't belong in a juried American handcraft show. We advertise specifically for the customer to come shop unique products from American artists.

"Our shows have always allowed embellished products. We have potters who make their product from scratch and are wheel thrown or we may have a ceramic artist who buys blank pots to use as a base for

their artwork by painting, adding mosaics work or making it into something entirely different. In our judgement, it comes down to the time
involved in making the product. Vendors with mass-produced handmade products can do more shows than the truly handmade artist.
While it is true that it is more difficult for a one of a kind artist to compete with one who can produce multiples in a shorter time, I haven't
seen any way around this."   —BR

Some promoters specialize in fine arts only, so if your craft is not in that category, you are wasting your time applying. Read the promoter's specifications
carefully. And once you are accepted through this process, it should give you
new confidence in what you are selling and how you are displaying it.

As mentioned above, to jury by photo is the most common practice and
the most convenient. The promoter will want not only photos or slides of
your product, but photos of your booth display as well. Several excellent
examples of beautiful, intriguing, and inviting booths are included in
chapter 7 on Booth Setup and Booth Display, where this subject is discussed in extensive detail. For now, be advised only that if you find yourself applying to shows that do not require such photos, you certainly can
apply as a beginner just for the experience but, for the most part, forget the
show. This promoter is not too interested in the quality of the show or the
quality of your work and so you are apt to find yourself in a flea market
environment. Such shows usually don't last year after year, as customers
today are far more sophisticated than they were years ago. Many enthusiastic, regular attendees of craft shows will show up at a show site, scan it
quickly, get back into their car, and go to another show. They will not
return the following year.

Photographing Your Craft and Your Booth Display

Throughout our years in the business, I can only guess that Judy and I must
have taken hundreds and hundreds of pictures of every kind of basket we
created. We took them outdoors and indoors, in sunlight and in shade, from
every angle possible and ended up throwing away most of them and wasting
a lot of time and money.

The object, as you'd expect, is to take photos that show your product
line to its best advantage. Colors should be vivid and size should be obvious.
The use to which the craft may be put should be demonstrated; that is, dolls
on a bed or in a cradle, shelves on a wall, a sewing basket next to a rocking
chair, pottery on a table, rings on a finger, and so on. That certainly seems

simple enough—if you are a decent photographer. We couldn't believe how difficult taking a simple photograph of our product turned out to be. Hadn't I taken a thousand great pictures of the kids? You bet! Most likely, so have you! Now, think about how many rotten pictures you've thrown away of the children and the family, and the dog. If your answer is the same as ours, unless you are an excellent photographer and have a good camera, hire a professional. This advice comes not just from us, but from promoters like Beth Weber, who told us about the many craftspeople she had to reject throughout the years because the photographs they sent in were poor examples of their work. She added, "If I only had one space and two people's craft work were of equal quality, then the photograph of the booth would define who was accepted." Assuming that both the craft workmanship and the photographs were of equal quality, another promoter told me that the craftsperson's reputation would become the deciding factor. Obviously, if you are a beginner, you have no reputation, so the photographs are all you can rely on to make a good impression.

Judy and I will never know how many rejections we received because of the quality of our photographs. Promoters often told us, when we were finally accepted to their shows, "If I had known how beautiful your work was, I would have accepted you last year." We were told that our photographs lacked clarity and the rich color of the fabrics used in our baskets didn't look true. When we then compared our original pictures with the photographs taken by a professional, we quickly realized that the angle of our pictures was wrong or the colors were washed out. In some cases, the setting in which we placed the basket was more prominent in the picture than the basket itself. In others, the background was wrong or the lighting insufficient or too intense. I'd guess that for every picture that came out well, we threw six or seven away, maybe more. We had better luck photographing our booth display. Even in shooting the booth, sometimes we were too far away and sometimes too close, or the interior was too dark or too light.

Certain crafts magnify the photographic problem even more. Jewelry is an especially good example of a product that is most difficult to photograph. The problems of lighting and particularly reflection misrepresenting and distorting the image are immensely difficult for the amateur photographer to overcome. We wasted $500 on a very good camera and still made mistakes.

It must be said honestly that we've also seen extremely poor photography work by more than one professional but, by and large, it is a lot less expensive in the long run to hire a professional photographer, even though the initial cost is substantial. It is basically a one-time expense until you add new products to your line. Just have enough copies made, select the best carefully, and keep the negatives (or digital files). Then you are ready to send every promoter as many photographs as is required. Those photographs will be returned to you if your application is rejected and, if accepted, the promoter usually returns them at the show. Just remember that photographs are an expense on which you cannot afford to try to save money. The photograph, in most instances, is all that there is to represent you and your work, and the only way the promoter can fully appreciate the quality of that work.

One promoter also pointed out to me that a photograph can also be used to misrepresent the craftsperson's work. It is not uncommon for some craftspeople to send in photographs of one craft item, on which basis they are accepted to the show, and then display numerous other kinds of merchandise that were not juried and that would not have been accepted. Some promoters, for example, will not allow any product that has been manufactured out of the country. For that matter, many customers will leave a show without making a purchase if they observe too many crafts manufactured in foreign countries. If you're discovered doing this, you may be asked to leave the show or the promoter will reject your application to any future shows.

A Contrarian Perspective, from the Digital Age

While it is still true that a professional photographer has much knowledge and finesse that the average person lacks, and would be more likely be able to capture expert shots the first time than would you, the lightning-speed development in the world of digital photography makes it worthwhile to entertain a different point of view.

The cost of digital cameras has come down, while the quality of the pictures they produce has gone up. Many proshooters (if not most) who wouldn't have been caught dead hoisting anything other than a traditional film camera a couple of years ago have become converts. The advantages to the amateur are obvious: the fact that images can be viewed immediately and deleted if they aren't up to scratch, coupled with the fact that the in-camera storage devices are reuseable, mean that the time and money involved in film and film processing is eliminated. In addition, relatively inexpensive digital cameras can shoot under more varied lighting conditions than can moderately priced film cameras of yore and come with lensing abilities that allow the photographer to clearly focus in a wide variety of situations, including when photographing tiny, detailed items.

These advances make DIY photography a more palatable option. The advantage of preparing images yourself is, of course, that you know your own work best and can focus on the aspects of your work you most wish to promote. In order to truly partake of the advantages of digital photography, you will need a computer and image manipulation software. With programs like Photoshop you can take a not-very-good photo and improve many aspects of it: lighting, contrast, background, etc. Although Photoshop is not inexpensive, there are many full-featured graphic programs on the market under $100. Photoshop Elements and Jasc's Paint Shop Pro both come highly recommended and there are many other options out there.

Another piece of equipment that could be useful to you is a flatbed scanner. With this you could take any existing photos or slides and convert them into digital images. Canon, Epson, and Hewlett Packard offer scanners with slide scanning attachments for less than $120.

There is a large learning curve on all graphic software before you are able to produce images acceptable for presentation, so expect to spend some time practicing. Luckily, most people fall in love with the process and, in fact, find it rather addictive.

Acceptance or Rejection Can Be in the Details

We have discussed the jury process and complaints about it with any number of craftsmen and promoters over the years. We came to realize that, in most instances, the reason for rejections was failure to do a few simple things. So we'd like to pass these simple tips along to you.

When discussing show selection, most of the craftspeople we met would tell us that they just filled out the application form, enclosed a few pictures, and mailed the package in. At first, we took that same approach and got routine results, meaning we received some acceptances and some rejections. Then we changed our approach and rarely were rejected thereafter, as long as our application was submitted on time. Here's what we did, and what we suggest that you do.

When submitting photos of your product and booth fully set up, enclose a letter about yourself. Write the letter in a general manner that can pertain to every show to which you will apply, so that you are not rewriting the entire letter every time you apply to a show. Write the letter in such a way as to introduce yourself to the promoter, portraying who you are as an individual. Of course, save the letter on your computer, so that, thereafter, you only have to change the names and addresses of the promoters.

Another way to look at it is to use the letter as a vehicle to promote yourself and your craft. Sell yourself! Tell the promoter about your business history and the quality of products used in the manufacturing of your craft. Include background on your training, expertise, or qualifications in the field and any awards you've received from other promoters.

If you use a mailing list, mention that, too, and explain the extent of your customer following. This is important to the promoter because it means more people will attend the show and, if there is an admission charge, more money will end up in the promoter's pocket. Rich Burleigh informed me that "Many promoters depend a great deal on attendance generated by the mailing lists of applicants to their shows." If you have a store, include that information, and if you've had any press coverage, attach the press clips. This letter or resume sets you apart in the mind of the promoter. Just as name recognition is important in the corporate world, it has its place in the craft world as well.

Nevertheless, you may still receive a rejection letter. If you request an explanation by letter, some promoters will respond to your letter and others will not. The promoters who answer do so because they are impressed with your sincerity, your professionalism, and your obvious interest in their shows. Since their income depends on craftspeople who are willing to pay a substantial fee to enter their shows, if they are really fully professional in the way they run their business, they will find some time to answer your letter. If they do not respond, usually because of a busy schedule, they will generally file the letter away and will probably refer to it and remember you next year, if you apply again. In fact, remind them of the letter or send another updated letter when you apply the following year.

If a show you are considering applying to is in your locale and you have a free day, go to it, evaluate it, and introduce yourself to the promoter—when she is not frantically busy. Try to meet the promoter after you have walked the entire show, talked to other craftspeople, and appraised customer attendance and buying response. When you find the promoter, if you still want to apply to the show, you have something to talk to her about. Perhaps you can pay the promoter some compliment on the show. If your application to the show was rejected, you can express your disappointment and say how much you are hoping to be accepted next year. Probably, she won't remember your application or why it was rejected, but next year, you'll have a better chance of being remembered. The promoter will have a face and a personality to put to the name when going through a stack of applications. Include a picture of yourself outside your booth just to further refresh the promoter's memory. In your letter, remind her of your on-site meeting.

Promoters: Good and Bad

Before we leave the subject of promoters, you should be aware that, as a group, the good promoters all agree that there are certain rules they set for their shows, about which they are very strict and will enforce. Their rules can sometimes seem very annoying, vexing, arbitrary, and trivial, and the promoter knows they are viewed this way. But, like them or not, it is most important that you adhere to them.

When you are accepted to a promoter's show, in your acceptance packet you will receive all the rules pertaining to the show. In some cases, the rules will include the time you are scheduled to arrive and unload your vehicle. Try to be punctual in this regard, as the rule is made because there are not enough unloading areas to allow every vehicle to arrive at the same time. Arrive at the wrong time and you may have to wait hours to unload and set up, and you may not complete the job before the show opens. You also may irritate the promoter who is trying to manage the parking problem and facilitate unloading.

Two other rules that almost all promoters make and enforce relate to closing time, when you may begin to break down your booth, and when you can bring in your vehicle for loading. If you are tempted to tear down your booth early just because the crowd is thinning out and you doubt that you will have any more customers, don't do it. Whether they arrived late to the show or not—and especially if they paid to get in—all customers have the right to expect to see every booth in place with you prepared to sell to them. Should the promoter catch you violating this rule, you may get nothing but a warning or you may not be accepted to any of the promoter's future shows.

You will also be instructed as to where to park your vehicle after you have unloaded it. Usually, you are to park it there throughout the entire show. You can expect that this will be somewhat inconvenient, as sometimes it may be blocks away from the show site. However, there is a very good reason for this: The show is there to serve the customer, not you as the merchant. To whatever extent possible, the rule is there to provide the customers with easy parking and easy access to their vehicles. Oftentimes, purchases can be taken to a vehicle parked close by rather than be carried around all day. This convenience could make the difference in a sale to you and is in your best interests. Customers who cannot walk long distances or find a place to park their cars are not going to stop at the show and they are not going to buy from you. Elderly people and individuals with disabilities need easy access to the show site. They cannot and will not walk blocks and blocks to the show. Just walking the show may be difficult enough.

If you are caught violating this rule, you can again be sure that you will not be invited back by the promoter. Beth Weber told us that getting craftspeople to obey the rules she sets is probably one of the biggest problems that she and every promoter has. When rule violation is flagrant, she and most other promoters will ask the craftsperson to pack up and leave. As Beth sees it, "The rules are made to serve the customers and therefore benefit you."

As in every other aspect of life, promoters cannot be lumped together or stereotyped. It would be wonderful if all promoters were like those quoted thus far. Unfortunately, that is not life. They run the gamut from consummate professionals to absolute sleazeballs. You will like some and despise others. Some promoters you will get to know personally and together celebrate your mutual triumphs. Others you will never meet at all, and still others you will want to stay as far away from as possible—even after you are accepted to their show.

In fact, in some shows, it is not the promoter who juries the applications but a committee you will never know or see. A promoter may have been hired simply to handle publicity and to offer name recognition to those submitting their applications. The committee itself may change its composition from year to year. Consequently, the committee who loved your work one year may be supplanted by another to whom your work does not appeal at all.

We were accepted to a state college campus eight years in a row, while friends with quality crafts would be accepted one year, rejected for the next two years, then be accepted again. When this happens, it can be very devastating to your projected financial expectations for the year. Because you had not anticipated a rejection, you may have to fill in with another show. In this instance, it was just a matter of the personal taste of those students comprising the committee—still another unknown factor in the crafts business. You gamble and you have to accept the results.

Virtually all promoters send you your booth assignment number with your acceptance letter. Big shows may even send you a diagram of the show site from which you may select your spot. A sample diagram can be seen on the following page. My least favorite promoter, however, is one of the few who will not provide you with your booth space in advance. This promoter will also punish you if you don't apply to enough of his shows, keeping you out of his best shows or assigning you an undesirable space.

Here's the way he "planned" some of the events we participated in. On the show date, every craftsperson arrived at 5 A.M. and stood in the dark while names were called, as if we were all in the Army. Next we were each handed space assignments in a sealed envelope, as if it were a military secret. Then, 700 or more craftspeople scrambled to find their assigned spaces in order to set up on time, in a show that covered many city avenues and side streets. They ran to their vehicles, a la Le Mans, and engaged in a road race that resembled the beginning of a demolition derby.

It was a terribly stressful way to begin the day. Thereafter, this promoter was never seen until it was time to pay him his percentage fees at the end of the show. However, this promoter's shows attracted crowds of over 100,000 people each day and, even competing against some 700 other craftspeople, we always made a lot of money. This was the show's saving grace, the bottom line. The bottom line is the reason you are there.

DIRECTIONS:
I-15 East or West, merge onto Hwy 95 going South
Take L.V. Blvd/Cashman Field exit
Turn left on Las Vegas Blvd.

North on 95
Take downtown exit
Turn right Las Vegas Blvd.
Entrances to Cashman Field are right off Las Vegas Blvd.

LAS VEGAS
AUGUST 27-28-29

Cashman Center
850 Las Vegas Blvd. North
Las Vegas, NV 89109
702-386-7100 Fax: 702-386-7126

EXHIBITOR MOVE-IN
Enter off Las Vegas Blvd. at Lot A or East
Washington at Lot C.

No charge for parking on move-in day until
5pm, after which parking cost is $2.00.

*Subject to change.
 Always check onsite with show personnel

LEGEND
★ = CORNER BOOTHS
F = FIRE EXTINGUISHERS
▪ = PILLARS, 4' 6" x 1'6" OR BOXES

MERCHANTS CORNER
LOVERS LANE
KLONDIKE PASS
JAMBOREE LANE
HARVEST HEIGHTS
GOLDRUSH GULCH
FIDDLERS ROW
DERRINGER WAY
CONESTOGA WAY
BANJO STREET
APOTHECARY LANE

PROVIDENCE STREET
NICKELODEON LANE

PARCEL CHECK
LOADING DOOR
EXIT
EXIT
LOADING DOOR
ENTRANCE

WOMEN MEN
CONCESSION
CONCESSION
FOOD SEATING
MEN WOMEN
EXIT

STORAGE

SUNRISE CHILDREN'S HOSPITAL FOUNDATION
SUNRISE FOUNDATION KIDS' CRAFT BOOTH
SUNRISE PROMO

11

The Percentage Show

If you are new to this entire procedure and the craft world, you may not be aware that some shows ask not only a booth fee, but also 10–15 percent of your gross. A lot of cheating goes on with regard to this percentage, as no promoter can monitor the sales taking place in every booth. Basically, a perverted honor system prevails. The truth is that very few craftspeople we knew really paid an honest percentage to the promoter. And the promoter knows—and probably even expects—this.

Some people rationalize ways to pay less, considering it fair to subtract all their expenses from their gross earnings and then pay the promoter's percentage on what remains. They usually express the opinion that the promoter did not earn it in the first place. This may be, but it is beside the point. You knew it was a percentage show when you applied. Others will just not pay it at all, but they can expect a letter from the promoter, as one does sign a contractual agreement to pay that percentage. Do this once, and even if you get away with it, you will never be accepted to that show again. Still others will pay the promoter a larger percentage than they really earned, just to ensure their acceptance into next year's show or to ensure a better booth space the following year. Another craftsperson won't want his actual take "on the record," thereby hiding his true earnings from Uncle Sam.

The upshot of all this is that what you read in a *Crafts Fair Guide* may not be a reflection of what the craftsperson really earned and, perhaps, since money earned is a measure of the shows you select, not a fair way to always evaluate the promoter of those shows or the show itself. Sometimes you just have to do the show to find out for yourself.

Frankly, I've always wished that promoters would simply charge a higher entry fee and do away with the percentage since so much skullduggery goes on. We tried to avoid commission shows when possible, but don't rule them out completely when making your selections. Caution! It will hurt when you do a $4,000 gross show and have to write out a check to the promoter for $400.

Happily, promoters who engage in the negative practices we have described are relatively rare. As detestable as some types of promoters may or may not be to you, if their shows create an arena in which you are financially successful, both our and your personal opinion is irrelevant. It should never affect your decision to do a show—unless you have been accepted to a better show. Because exposure serves your ends best—the more the better—you sometimes can't be too choosy.

Unfortunately, promoters like Beth Weber and Rich Burleigh, who seek to help the individual craftspeople, are becoming more and more rare. According to Beth, "Some promoters seem to be more interested in the money to be made than their interrelationship with the craftspeople who apply to their shows." In the future, that may become part of the reality with which you must learn to live.

One of the nicest promoters, a woman whose shows were called Lady Bug Boutique, helped us a great deal in our early years. Eventually, she went out of business. Saturation of the area by the bigger shows simply took away her customer base. We regretted no longer applying to her shows, but as the show attracted fewer and fewer people, we had no choice. That is the nature of all business, no different than what happened to the mom-and-pop grocery store as supermarkets proliferated. Much of the personal touch was lost.

Remember Your Monetary Goal

Particularly when you're starting out in the business, you must simply ignore your personal likes and dislikes. You must learn to live with your decision for the weekend. You paid money for the privilege, so only what you walk away with at the end of the weekend really counts—unless you are independently wealthy. But, then, why are you doing craft shows at all?

It is nice to apply to and be accepted into shows where the promoters come around from one booth to another, introduce themselves, ask if you need anything, listen patiently to your complaints, try to correct them, and demonstrate sensitive concern about your needs, even inquiring as to whether you are happy and having a successful show. But that is rare. If you are looking for that, you're in the wrong world.

Some promoters like Beth Weber actually do this and have coffee and doughnuts for everybody while they are setting up. But you cannot expect or anticipate this. Just enjoy it when it happens—but bring your own coffee and doughnuts most of the time.

When you are an established success, you can be more selective about promoters, but don't bank on it even then. As an artisan selling your wares, you must always search for new shows, never knowing what you'll encounter. Some of the nicest promoters we knew promoted some of the least profitable shows, and vice versa.

All you have to do to evaluate the potential of a show is to observe the extent of television and newspaper advertising devoted to it and whether there are banners and posters around the town and hung throughout the area well in advance of the show. If that was done properly, then the resulting attendance is the only major factor of concern to you. If the crowds come out, the rest is up to you.

Promotional Costs Are Rising

Since so many craftspeople complain about the increasing cost of booth space from one year to the next, this is a good point to give you some idea of the increasing cost to the promoter. While these figures will not apply to every show to which you are accepted, they represent an accurate account of the top promotions and may not be far off for the average promoter who does a conscientious job of advertising.

I queried Harvest Festival, in business now for more than thirty-four years, concerning the extent to which their cost of operation has gone up over the years. They indicated that the cost of advertising has gone up roughly 10 to 15 percent a year, and the cost of renting facilities in which to present their shows has risen annually as well. That does not take into consideration the continually increasing cost of general overhead and the cost of doing business—things like staff salaries, travel expenses, decorations, and much more. In fact, all the booth fees combined pay only 65 percent of the media advertising expense.

Escalating costs have therefore substantially impacted the crafts business. Just being able to rent the best facilities on the best dates is also becoming a significant problem. There is increasing competition with trade shows and conventions that bring in more people to an area and so acquire priority status. Obviously, then, if promoters of these top shows are to make the profit that they deserve, it must be derived from the number of people they can attract to the show who are willing to pay an admission fee.

Considering those factors, the individual craftsperson should recognize that if the show draws large crowds, the promoter has done his job. You can ask no more! The rest is up to you. Therefore, perhaps this is the proper place to discuss all the reasons, alibis, and excuses that even professionals, long in the business, will use to explain their failure to make money.

Excuses, Alibis, and Blaming the Promoter

Having selected a show and having been accepted, it is best that you learn to accept the conditions under which you are doing business. Then learn from experience and evaluate the show to determine whether you will apply again next year or make another selection for that particular weekend. Do your own quiet analysis and try to come to your own conclusions. This is made difficult by other craftspeople, who can affect your judgment and prejudice your evaluation.

During a show, you will socialize and discuss the status of the show with many of your neighbors. You will see their booth activity and they will see yours. When those in the crafts business are not selling, many will seek any explanation that they can conjure up. They will imagine and explore every avenue of excuse except that theirs is a poor product or one that does not sell in that marketplace.

Craftspeople will blame the miserable heat, extreme cold, the wind and rain, the economy, lack of customer taste, lousy promotion, and even the fact that it is Sunday and everyone is going to church. Heat, cold, rain, and snow may be valid reasons for poor attendance or apathetic buying but, if the people are there, it means the promoter did his job in getting them to the show site in spite of the weather or any other conditions. Given that, you should be getting your share of the business or something is wrong with you!

Many, many times, we had some of our best shows under the worst conditions. More than once, rain or the threat of rain led to a buying frenzy. If a show was good last year, you shouldn't, under most circumstances, let the weather in the area affect your decision to select that show. One of the biggest annual craft shows is in a little town in Nevada. It has a seventy-five-year history and, though it may well snow, you don't bypass this show. We never grossed less than $5,000 during the two-day run of this show, no matter what the weather conditions.

You also don't select shows because they are set in a pretty park or because you can take a swim in the lake or because they have eternal sunshine. Rating the general environment in which a show takes place and how certain conditions may affect sales is legitimate. But, if the crowds are there, the environment cannot be used as an excuse. If many people did go to church, because it happens to be a particularly Godly community, that never stops them from coming out and spending twice as much in the afternoon—if you have what they want to buy. Look to yourself and your product. Don't blame the promoter if the people are there.

Another excuse you will hear frequently relates to the vendors who are your immediate neighbors. On rare occasions, this can be a problem; for example, you may be assigned a space next to a noisy booth, selling raucous music. It may be annoying, but it probably isn't the reason for your lack of sales. The promoter has to put somebody next to that booth. You have to learn to live with these situations. Some shows and some booths are just plain noisier than others, especially at street fairs with rock-and-roll bands. You are going to set up next to all kinds of people, and you may be stuck right near a bandstand.

For years we did a show where our regular booth space was right in front of the stage, and we listened to blaring country western music for three days. To be heard, we had to practically scream at the customers and they to us. That never stopped us from selecting that show and we never asked Rich Burleigh to change our booth space.

Rich, who runs a promotion called Fire on the Mountain, is one of the better small promoters here in California. I say small only because he and his wife only promote three or four shows each year. But those shows are big, traditional events with twenty or more years of history behind them. They draw extremely large crowds; have wonderful, varied, and free entertainment; and keep people at the show all day. If you can't sell and make a profit at Rich's shows, you can't make money anywhere.

Rich was doing us a favor giving us that space I mentioned. He had three buildings filled with crafts and he moved us progressively into the best building and gave us one of the best booth spaces. Everybody with any experience wanted that space. When the bands were playing and the entertainment was taking place, crowds of people stood in front of our booth, the length of the building, to watch—and everybody was looking right at our booth when they did so. Sure, we didn't do much business while the band was playing a set, but we did three times as much when the set was over.

Only a very few shows send you the layout of the show and give you an advance choice as to space location. Most often, you have to be long established with these shows to be given such choice. Try to be happy that you were accepted and realize that your space is the luck of the draw. Try to make it work to your advantage. Often, having the most disreputable-looking booth next to you is a plus. If you have a beautiful booth, you look superbly professional and artistic by comparison.

We were once assigned a space next to a vendor selling children's swings. Another time, it was an ice cream stand. In both cases, mothers didn't want to wait on line or stand there while their children swung back and forth for an hour. Both booths became a noisy babysitter, while the mothers shopped in our booth. Sure, kids came looking for their mother and one or two dropped ice cream in a basket, but it was worth it. Since all our fabrics were Scotch-guarded, they wiped clean easily and if they were soiled we relined the baskets.

The same principle applies should the booth next to you have a similar product. If your product is better, you stand out by comparison. However, if the similar product been two aisles away, the customer might have already made a purchase there before ever seeing what you have to sell. Promoters frequently are castigated for this and they needn't be. We always found that when it happened we benefited. The customer has an obvious choice. If they choose to make a purchase from your competitor next door, put aside your ego, objectively evaluate your competition, and try to determine what it is about the competitor's craft work that the customer found superior to yours. Learn from every experience of this kind.

In none of these instances should you make an excuse for yourself by blaming the promoter and then next year allow it to affect your show selection. While promoters should and usually do try to stagger booths with similar crafts, mistakes can happen. Think positive and make the best of the situation. Next year, you'll be given a different space. If, when you apply the following year, you are absolutely convinced that booth placement caused you a serious problem, explain that in a letter to the promoter and, very often, the mistake will be rectified. Most promoters try to be as accommodating as possible.

Occasionally, you'll run into a problem we touched on earlier—one that is more difficult to assess. Say, every craftsperson with whom you talk has had a successful show, but you've done poorly. You are convinced it is not related to the quality of your product or how well the show was promoted. What is wrong may be the connection between your product and the local market, as in the following scenario.

Our baskets were considered country traditional and so they were simply not a product that would sell well at a San Francisco street show where mostly local citizenry were in attendance. Just thirty miles away on the peninsula, or across the Golden Gate Bridge, we were in sync with the local market. We learned our lesson and thereafter applied to only one show in San Francisco, a big show held in the convention center that drew customers from all over the Bay Area.

When this kind of situation occurs, we did not make excuses for ourselves and our lack of sales. We evaluated the problem in an objective, businesslike manner. It is much like sending a story to a publisher. It is your responsibility to research publishers. Choose the wrong publisher and you receive a rejection, no matter how good your material. Remember! It is your responsibility to research the craft shows that you select and to which you apply. The promoter may like your work very much and just be seeking diversity in the show. The promoter cannot guarantee your marketability.

Be Careful about These Promotions

There are a number of other types of promotions and promoters that fall into special categories and do deserve special attention. Every craftsperson has been lured into these shows at least once, primarily because the promoter does not require you to jury—and could care less about quality. To many in the business, old or new, this kind of show can offer a new experience, a new world, and a new opportunity. When you've received a bunch of rejections and need immediate income, it is easy to apply to and select one of these types of shows, and to fall into the trap. We fell into the trap after fifteen years in the business, simply because we had a free weekend, our inventory was well stocked, and I convinced Judy to gamble a little. I got greedy, and greed can be another trap.

Generally, these shows fall into broad categories: carnival/rodeo promotions, food and gift shows, antique car or antique furniture shows, rod and gun shows, rib or chili or whatever cook-offs, and shows put on by specific private clubs and social organizations. With the exception of shows run by private clubs and organizations, the others all present the same problems and you should generally avoid selecting any of them unless you are financially desperate and in need of picking up even small change, or unless you sell an item like T-shirts that you can adapt to the specific groups of people who attend these shows. Belts and belt buckles and dime-store jewelry may move also, but that's about it.

The reason to avoid these shows is that the promoter is not really interested in quality crafts. Nor is the promoter's reputation based on crafts promotion. This promoter basically puts on big events, often being sponsored by the town who hires the promoter. It may even be a traditional event.

Whatever the case, a big event is being promoted and crafts are merely an addendum, an extra added attraction, often spaced far from the main event, area, or arena where the action is really taking place. The promoter earns a little extra money on booth fees, which is his only real interest.

The customers who attend these shows come with a specific mindset: They are geared to look at cars or furniture or attend the rodeo. Craft quality is usually poor and the crowds in attendance are not there to shop. A full day of entertainment with the kids is on the agenda. All kinds of expensive food is available, there are carnival rides for the children and young adults, and the beer and wine are flowing. Customers have planned their day and their budget to include admission and parking fees, and they plan to spend a bundle of money on food, drink, rides, and the main attraction. They have no money left to buy your product.

Unless your product is food, the food and gift promotion will probably also be a flop for you. This promotion is a showcase for commercial enterprises, specialty shops, and gimmick appliances. You may find yourself sandwiched in between a vendor selling a new carving knife and another demonstrating a blending machine. The promoter has spent a lot of money renting a big convention center and she wants to fill every available inch of space. If you have a craft you can demonstrate, and therefore compete with a tomato slicer on one side and a stereo system on the other, you may survive, but rarely.

Rod and gun shows and antique car shows present the same problems. They are very specific to the customers they are seeking to attract. Of course, they want anyone who will pay an admission fee at the door and so will include crafts as an extra added attraction. Some wives who have no interest in guns, fishing rods, or antique cars will come along with their husbands, and the craft show will keep them occupied, but how much they spend is another matter, as hubby is spending all their money elsewhere at the show. So we suggest you avoid this kind of promotion.

Prime rib and chili cook-offs may be just a Western thing, but similar events involving other kinds of food take place in other parts of the country. We will not speculate on what success you may find elsewhere, but in California and Nevada these shows can be devastatingly poor for craft artists—particularly in Nevada.

Usually a gambling casino hires a promoter to put on a show in the parking lot or out in front of the casino. The promoter has established a long tradition. The show is just another gimmick to draw people into the casino where they'll blow their money. But, those same people won't spend much of that money in your craft booth. The ribs and chili are supposedly in competition, and these food booths attract the hungry who may be competing for some sort of prize. Seemingly potential customers are, in reality, only passersby stopping to fill their face on their way into the casino. We did one such show, made $235 in three days, lost our shirt (even without going into the casino, since we had no money to gamble), and never did a show like that again.

Finally, you have the local club functions and charity events. These can be either highly successful or a real disappointment but are well worth researching. The application fee is usually relatively low—$50 to $75. Oftentimes they have a long-standing, traditional following. Most are just advertised locally, but if they are run by a big church, for example, they are generally well promoted and have a solid tradition behind them. These kinds of shows will usually draw large crowds who are there to buy. Church events can be particularly profitable because the priest, minister, or rabbi has been promoting the show from the pulpit for weeks, and the congregation feels obligated to attend and spend money to support the function.

These can be especially pleasant shows to do because the clientele are always well behaved. The people attending aren't going to get drunk. The promoters are members of the club or church who are volunteering their time and who usually run just this one show a year. The atmosphere is always cordial, friendly, and homespun. They'll provide coffee and doughnuts in the morning, help you set up your booth, offer to fill in for you if you need a break, and serve you lunch if you're there alone. These shows always have a genuine family atmosphere in which socializing with the customer is a pleasure. You should always choose carefully among these promotions, as their warmth and friendliness can't compensate for a lost financial weekend. But when they are great, as was the last show we ever did, these promotions are a genuine joy.

The same can be said for craft shows being put on by service organizations like the Lions Club or the Elks. As we mentioned earlier, most of the time you will find these organizations involved in large, community-promoted shows, but sometimes they will run their own show, particularly in smaller towns. The potential negatives of that kind of show have already been discussed but, once in a while, if you want to or have a need to take a gamble, you will find a "sleeper" that will provide you with sufficient profit to make the trip worthwhile. They are always well supported by the membership and always very pleasant shows in which to take part.

Obviously, a craftsperson's "heaven," the perfect show, would include guaranteed ideal weather conditions and a location where you could drive your truck right up to your booth space to unload and load. Your truck would always be loaded with an excess of inventory, all of which you sell to a large crowd, all of whom were spending their money extravagantly. You would head home with a big two-day profit after saying thank you to the promoters who, given all these heavenly conditions, must have done everything right, including stopping by to introduce themselves, thanking you for participating, and asking if you are happy and content with everything. Occasionally, we found all this but, for the most part, we have to live and die to go to heaven.

7

Booth Setup and Booth Display

THROUGHOUT THIS BOOK, MOST of the emphasis has been placed on subjects involved primarily with your craft—the effort and money management involved in producing it and the means by which you may present it to the world and sell it. Judy and I have tried to share as many of the tricks of the trade regarding these subjects as we can think of, and if you are a beginner and you have sent out those applications and been notified of your acceptance into various shows, you are almost in the crafts business.

If you are a veteran and have gone through the application and exhibition procedure many times, the word beginner still applies to you to some extent if your booth, like so many hundreds we have seen, has not had the benefit of all of your talent, attention, and creativity. Until you sell your craft, you are still creating for art's sake, still engaging in a hobby—albeit one with a new purpose. You can be a veteran in the crafts business, but if you have given absolutely no attention to your booth display, you've been shortchanging yourself and your potential customers.

The Neglected Craft Booth

If, as a longtime craftsperson, all you have done—or think you need to do—is erect a canopy over your head, set up a few tables or pedestals, set out a meager selection of your wares, and hope for the best (and complain about the worst), you are as much a novice as the person who has never sold at all. Booth display, as every good promoter agrees, separates those who are accepted from those who are rejected from their shows. If you have neglected this part of your business or do not apply yourself to it, you have missed or will miss a major opportunity that is open to you. You will remain a novice, or an amateur, until that first day when you put yourself and your craft, professionally displayed, out there on the line to truly compete with everyone else in the business.

If you are ready to so compete, you are also now ready to deal with what we consider the most crucial factor of your business, second only to your product. That factor is the booth from which you are going to sell your merchandise and the method you are going to use to display it.

We don't know why, but we can say with absolute certainty that the following is true: With the exception of those competing at the highest level of the industry, craftspeople sorely neglect the tasks of creating beautiful and yet highly functional booths and setting up inviting displays of crafts in those booths. For some reason, all too often, some of the most beautiful, imaginative, and creative crafts are so poorly displayed that the artistry of their creator is completely lost.

Judy and I have viewed thousands upon thousands of craft booths over the years, and the biggest percentage of them demonstrate a total lack of creativity, imagination, or sensitivity. We have speculated that perhaps it is because some craftspeople develop tunnel vision through which they see only the beauty of their craft—the individual piece of work—but not the totality and surroundings in which they exhibit it. Perhaps it reflects a kind of mental or artistic fatigue, developed after so much energy has gone into creating the craft itself. Or maybe it comes down to just a "take it or leave it" attitude. Whatever it is, the failure to devote creative energy to the presentation of the product is largely responsible for a craftsperson's failure to sell as much as he should. We strongly urge you to spend a great deal of time considering what is explained in this chapter, studying the photographs on the following pages, and then to apply what you read and see to the creation or re-creation of your craft booth.

Your Booth Is Your Store

Every craftsperson should realize that you don't just sell your product. There is a great deal more to consider and accomplish before those exciting days when you actually sell your merchandise. There are many obstacles to face and hurdles to overcome before you set up your booth. Some are practical, others are physical, and many more are aesthetic.

As you begin the process of booth planning and construction, we would suggest that you think of it as creating your own little world, a ten-by-ten-foot shop, an environment into which you are inviting the public and also one in which you will be comfortable and of which you will be proud. We can assure you that the time, effort, and money you put into this project will yield big dividends. For an example of how important Harvest Festival considers booth display, take a look at the promoter's regulations found on the following pages.

Booth Set-up

Here's What We Do For You:

- We provide a curtained 8' back wall, 500 watts of electricity, and 24-hour security.

- Back walls of booths have neutral-toned curtains.

- Standard booth spaces are 10' wide, but *flexibility* is the key! You could end up with part of a pillar or pole in your booth. Some decorator supports have large bases, which you may have to work around. You should design your booths to be 9'6" wide to allow for extra flexibility. Depths vary from 8' to 10'. Refer to the floor plan for information specific to each city.

Here's What We Need From You:

- We require that you provide a minimum of 7' side and back walls—**a maximum of 8'**. Side walls help you and your neighbors present your crafts in your own unique storefront; and make the whole show more attractive to customers. Your front facade can be a maximum of 12' high. Only 50% of the roof can be covered.

- When fully constructed, your booth must be flexible to allow for a 4–6" deviation from the width of the assigned space to allow for pillars and unforeseen floor plan irregularities. Always measure your booth from front to back and side to side **before** you set up.

- Side walls must be opaque hard walls or flameproofed fabric. If you use lattice or grids you must use fabric to cover the backs of the walls.

- Provide carpet or floor covering. We suggest linoleum for food exhibitors.

- We encourage the use of company name signs in your booth. However, **vinyl signs are prohibited**, and the signs must not exceed the 8' side and back wall heights.

- Cash registers may be used, but in keeping with the "handmade" nature of our shows, they should be concealed from the customer's view. Consider building a special area into your booth to house a cash register and your bags. We recommend this for security reasons as well.

- Spreading your product and display into the aisle is prohibited. You must stay completely within the 8x10'or 10x10' space assigned.

> DISPLAY YOUR BOOTH NUMBER. The show directories for customers are useless without visible booth numbers, and you can lose important sales!

- Special sales and discounts will, in most cases, be discouraged as they tend to detract from the overall quality. If you reduce the price of an item during the show replace the price tag instead of crossing out the old price.

- **No K-D canopy or E-Z up type tops.** If you are using the frame of your outdoor set-up, convert it into an indoor set-up. Cover all exposed metal with fabric sleeves or garlands, remove the plastic side and back walls and replace them with attractive flameproofed material.

- No hand-drawn signs are allowed unless it is done by calligraphy.

- Use a tarp or bed sheet to cover the front of your booth at night when you leave.

- Fire Marshals require that all extension cords be heavy duty: 3-pronged/grounded type.

- A 6-outlet power strip is required, which plugs into the electrical outlet provided behind your booth. Turn off the lights by the main power strip's on/off switch.

The above regulations are MANDATORY. Show management reserves the right to enforce them as needed at the exhibitor's expense.

Electrical Notes

500 watts of electricity is **included** in your booth fee. If you require additional electricity, please contact the electrician for your city on the All-City Reference Chart.

- A back drape is provided for you. If you require side walls, uprights, bases, carpet or other equipment, contact the decorators listed on the All-City Reference Chart.

- **For advance payment discount price to apply, payment must be received by the outside contractors with your order by the deadline date.**

1

Creating a Fantastic Booth

We can recite success story after success story to you about artists who re-designed their booths to enhance their crafts. Here are some tips that are easy and effective:

• Use signage! Attractive, colorful signs and banners help people remember who you are and where you're located. Remember, the quality of your signage reflects on the quality of your craft.

• Props—antiques, accent pieces and photos of the craft-making process, for instance— add a nice finishing touch and add flair!

*Remember that free booth evaluations are available one-on-one with Yvonne Chilina at the shows. Sign up sheet is in the Show Office.

Loading & Unloading

Normal set-up is 9AM–8PM Thurs. (Other than exception listed on All-City Reference Chart, no early set-ups are permitted). Load-In closes promptly at 8:00PM. If you break down on the way, please call our office (707-778-6300), get the phone number for our show office, and leave a message there so we can arrange for your late arrival. *If you do not call by 6PM of set-up day, your booth space is subject to cancellation without a refund, please see contract.*

■ As soon as you arrive at the hall, go to the Harvest Festival check-in area located in each hall beginning at 9AM on set-up day. You'll find all the essentials here: updated show information including your booth assignment (be sure to double check this), exhibitor badges, unloading/parking/storage instructions and a warm welcome!

■ Bring a dolly or hand cart! The halls do not provide these for exhibitor use. You will not be able to bring your vehicle into the hall to unload.

■ Loading/unloading procedures differ in each city due to hall access irregularities. To save yourself any frustration, please check with staff before you begin. If you are on the loading dock, please follow this procedure during load-in as a courtesy to your fellow craftspeople:
1. Unload booth and merchandise quickly.

2. Remove your vehicle **immediately** to allow others to have hall access. **Vehicles left unattended are subject to being towed at owner's expense.**
3. Return to construct booth and arrange stock.

■ As you set up, please be courteous to your neighbors— keep aisles clear.

■ **Teardown begins after 6PM closing time Sunday.** (Check the All-City Reference Chart for show hours.) *There are no early tear downs!* Please be considerate of our paying customers and fellow artists by observing this rule.

■ For load-out, simply reverse the procedure!
1. Box your stock.
2. Tear down your booth.
3. Check with Festival show team to see if a loading pass is required.
4. Retrieve your vehicle, load your booth & stock quickly.

■ Load-out must be completed by midnight Sunday night (Monday for Long Beach).

Note: San Diego, San Francisco and San Jose halls all have particularly difficult load-ins. Please be prepared and maintain your patience! You can help others by unloading your vehicle and removing your car or van from the unloading area quickly.

2

One of the many practical problems you face is investing in both an indoor and outdoor setup. This is more complicated than you may imagine. Have you gone to many crafts shows or taken part in many and seen hundreds of booths set up? Have you ever considered the hours and money that are invested in developing a professional-looking booth? Maybe you have and for just that reason have decided not to create one. If so, you've made a serious financial miscalculation. You were being penny wise and dollar foolish.

The types of canopies that will protect you and your merchandise from sun and wind and rain outdoors are quite simple. At outdoor shows, you have probably seen many variations of such protective enclosures. In reality, these structures are as important to the display of your work as the frame is to a painting.

Many such booths are simply four upright and four horizontal plastic or metal pipes, sometimes supporting a tarpaulin stretched across the top for protection against the rain and sun. In other cases, as in the photograph below, the Seydel booth is supporting a vast array of wind chimes and no tarpaulin is used.

Though not in this example, the upright poles are usually set in a can of cement as a way to weight them down against the wind.

These homemade setups, for which you need only purchase piping and corner connectors, are often used by craftspeople who are either not involved in the business at the most professional, weekly level, or, as in the case of the Seydels, it is simply the most expeditious way to present their beautiful wind chimes, a craft that defies almost every other means of being displayed. It serves their needs as no other booth can do but is pretty much out of favor with most craftspeople, since it presents some problems that the Seydels choose to risk.

While a little wind may be advantageous to the sale of chimes, too much wind will destroy the effect. The booth also offers them no protection from sun and rain, and as it is so filled with merchandise, these merchants must find seating somewhere outside the booth. Though the photograph does not make it evident, there are aisles within the booth through which the customer may ramble for better viewing and selection of each chime.

You will also see at outdoor shows a more modern version of a covered booth—a sun canopy that can be purchased in major outlets like K-Mart, Wal-Mart, Home Base, and other such stores. These are semi-pyramid-shaped, with a nylon or acrylic canopy that is stretched across the top and down to the base of each pole. They come in many colors, are easily set up, and homeowners are beginning to use them on their patios and lawns.

On the plus side, these canopies are lightweight and less expensive than the next type we will describe, but they have a number of drawbacks: While they will screen out some sun a good part of a very hot day, they are very unstable, even in a moderate wind, and offer no real protection from the wind and cold and rain. Though they are simple enough to assemble, their assembly actually takes more time than the assembly of any other type of outdoor booth.

Most common nowadays is the fold-up, accordion-fashion, metal booth that tapers to a peak at the top. It spreads out to a ten-by-ten-foot booth and is adjustable in height up to twelve feet, yet the booth collapses into a rectangle, approximately four feet long and a foot square, with the canvas top still attached, making it very portable and compact. You can purchase a canvas carrying case along with four nylon or canvas detachable and zip-up sides that can all be packed into a separate bag. This has to be purchased at special outlets or can be found advertised in many craft magazines. This outdoor booth is quite a bit more expensive than the booths mentioned above (in the $500 range) but is unquestionably your best option.

For our first few years we used the other types, wasted money, suffered the indignities they cause, and finally realized that they did not enhance our product and so were reducing our selling potential. We decided that the expense of this new booth was a worthwhile investment. They are extremely durable: Ours lasted thirteen years and we only had to purchase one new canopy top during those years.

At any outdoor show, you are subject to the elements on any given day. It is to your physical and mental benefit to be properly and completely prepared so that you and your product are as invulnerable as possible. The four upright posts can be staked into the ground or weighted or both. All four canvas sides can either be rolled up or zipped closed and the front canvas even has a zipper doorway. Erecting this booth should take no more than fifteen minutes and will be the easiest part of the entire setup process. You will notice in the photographs that almost every booth that is cited as a good example uses this type of canopy.

Catastrophes, Inconveniences, and Means of Preventing Them

We are spending a lot of time on this aspect of your booth setup, not just to give you the best advice that can be given on types of booths available and in use, but also because we wish to contribute to your own ease and comfort and peace of mind.

Your booth will be your home for ten to twelve hours a day, two or three days each week. On two occasions, we had our earliest booths ripped apart by vicious winds; one was actually blown up in the air and dropped on another craftsperson's booth. More than once I stood in the center of the booth, surrounded by customers seeking shelter from the driving wind and rain, holding the booth down, while Judy tried to sell our baskets.

These are very agonizing experiences, as you can imagine. Those scenarios make for very long, nerve-wracking, and tension-producing days. There is not a moment that you will be able to relax, even if there isn't a customer in your booth or anywhere in sight. It is extremely rare that weather conditions are so bad that a promoter will close down a show, so you will still be there holding down your booth in the storm while most of the customers have gone home.

At another craft show, the wind and driving rain kept blowing our merchandise off the shelves because our booth had no sides. Judy and I spent the day picking up baskets, returning them to the shelves, or trudging to the truck with wet and damaged goods. On one such trip, I also slipped in the mud and severely sprained my ankle, adding to the agony of the weekend. That night we had to dry out every basket at the motel. That same weekend we watched as another person's entire display of stained glass—some $5,000 worth—was blown to smithereens.

Because these kinds of incidents are so common, we strongly recommend the type of canopy we have described. Not only is setup much faster and easier, but there is the speed of teardown in emergencies and the security that this type of booth affords. At many street fairs in which you will take part, you have to take down and set up your booth both days because the street is re-opened to automobile traffic at night. Or even if the street remains closed, it is still open to the public, which means your booth would be vulnerable to thieves and vandalism. This type of booth reduces the time that you have to spend tearing down.

In other instances, the promoter provides security personnel who walk the show site all night long. This very helpful service enables you to leave all your merchandise set up in your booth. You can just zip up the sides and go off to dinner and your motel feeling a sense of security about your property and without having to pack everything up each day.

The open-type canopy also leaves you vulnerable to an overnight rain or snowstorm. There is no worse feeling than sitting in your motel at night, a driving storm outside, knowing that the next morning you will find everything soaking wet and blown over. Much better is the sense of security that all your hard work has not been wasted, your product has not been destroyed, and everything will be intact. The sense of relief you will feel is indescribable when you arrive at the show site on Sunday morning to see other booths literally hanging in the treetops or blown up the street, while yours is sitting there as it was the day before, waiting only for you to open it up, put your money in the cash register, and begin greeting your customers.

Your Display for Outdoor Setup

Depending on your craft, there are probably endless ways that you may choose to design the interior of your booth so that it displays your craft to its best advantage. In considering that, you should simultaneously be conceiving of a way to exhibit and store as much of your inventory as is possible. Since just putting out your stock for display will consume most of your setup time, you want to design the inside of your booth in such a way as to make this activity as simple and non-time-consuming as possible. So, long before you ever drive to the craft show, you should have worked all this out, particularly since you sent a picture of your booth to the promoter, didn't you?

Some merchandise is best displayed on shelves that you will have to either buy or build. Pottery, as displayed in photo on the following page, created by Carol Henschieb, is an excellent example. The shelving is tiered at various levels, which allows each piece to stand alone as an example of her work, her particular artistic technique, and the colors she emphasizes. The simple bamboo backdrop allows her booth to be easily assembled and provides the appropriate color background for her work. Notice that she does not crowd the booth with so much merchandise that nothing is really seen. While this may seem to contradict what was said earlier about providing the customer with a vast selection from which to choose, in this case that advice does not apply because she is emphasizing the uniqueness of each of her pottery items as an artistic piece. Yet she still displays a wide variety of individual pieces and you can be sure that, stored on the shelf covered with bamboo, she has many more pieces.

The top photograph on the opposite page is another excellent example of how shelving can be arranged beautifully and functionally in a small space. Every type of stained glass lampshade and lamp is visible at just a glance into the booth. Take note of the small, stained glass items—primarily night lights—set in the racks on the right-hand side of the booth. These are the less expensive items that Debbie Pirole can depend on selling at shows where the much more expensive merchandise is moving slowly. Notice, too, the simplicity of the shelves on which the merchandise is placed and how much room is left for the customer to roam and browse; yet thousands of dollars worth of Debbie's craft is on display. Though you cannot see it in this photograph, at the rear left is a counter and chair from which she conducts business.

Clothing requires racks and hangers on which to hang the clothing and usually a booth within a booth, where people can try on your dresses or jackets or T-shirts. Nancy Lee Kaufman's booth, bottom photograph opposite page, is a very tasteful and professional clothing booth. Since the clothing she produces does not require privacy in order to try it on, there is no dressing room, and she utilizes the space at the rear left as her business area. There is a mirror in which the customers may view themselves—some-

thing that is necessary for selling this kind of craft. Nancy's booth has a nicely balanced effect: It is not congested with clothing, and there is plenty of room for a number of people to survey what is on each rack, while simultaneously presenting all the designs and fashions in which she specializes.

Artwork, prints, and wall decorations require walls on which they can be displayed. If you are a jeweler, jewelry of fine quality necessitates glass cases and stands on which to put them. A particularly good example of such a booth is that of Maraya, photograph below.

The proprietor's name is prominent, and the credit cards she accepts are displayed in front. The workmanship of the stands and cases alone catches the eye and draws you into her booth. Unfortunately, as I mentioned, photographing jewelry is a real skill, so you will have to take my word that Maraya's is exquisite. We particularly like this booth setup because it combines the ability to view her work from the outside, while inviting the customer into the booth to look further, unlike many jewelry merchants who display only at the front.

Sculpture is usually displayed on pedestals—or should be. To place fine sculpture on crowded, poorly lit shelves would be to lose the essence of the particular work. Jeff Tritel's absolutely superb pieces, the top photograph on the opposite page, is the best example we could find.

Nothing fancy here—that is the nature of Jeff's art. Each piece stands out starkly against a plain white backdrop, and each piece can be viewed from every angle. Whether everyone likes Jeff's sculpture is, of course, a matter of personal taste, but only the most insensitive could fail to appreciate his talent.

The above photograph represents the work of a woman who is new to the crafts business. Judy and I spent a good deal of time conversing with this husband-and-wife team. Her work represents replicas of Native American art and is extremely well done. She appeals to a limited market and is going to have find her niche in the craft world. This booth is representative of someone starting out in the business: She has the beginning of an idea as to how best present her work, but she is not quite there yet. She told us that she was having trouble at this stage producing enough inventory; some pieces were selling very fast and others weren't selling at all. She has a large variety but, because no two were alike, her problem was compounded. She might be better off focusing on producing those pieces that have already proven themselves as desirable, or the business may become too wearing. She has a very unusual product. We wish her well.

The booth of Nancy and Julien Williams, photograph below, is an excellent example of how to handle a special problem encountered by craftspeople who sell handmade dolls, rabbits, bears, and whatever else may be stuffed. All in one booth, Nancy and Julien use tables, hangers, shelves, and furniture (also for sale) on which the rabbits sit. Small items hang from the slatted partitioning and even from the canopy itself. In the back is a counter; behind that is a chair. Yet the booth is clean, neat, and offers the customer plenty of room in which to shop. All in a ten-by-ten-foot space. Underneath and behind them there is also storage space. A booth could not be more compactly designed.

I doubt that we can provide a better example of the ultimate booth than that owned by Jim and Louise Howes, whose business name is Rabbit Run (photo opposite page). This is the small shop referred to earlier. The consum-

mate charm and warmth of this booth is self-evident. Everything in it and on the walls is for sale, yet everything looks as if it were part of a permanent establishment. Creating this effect takes talent, time, and money, but be assured that it contributes immensely to their sales. There isn't a promoter in existence who wouldn't want this booth in his show. That fact is evident in the top photograph on the following page. Here the booth is displayed at a Country Folk Art indoor show. With the canopy removed and the addition of interior lighting, which cannot be seen in the photograph, the top and sides provide further means of displaying an even greater variety of their wood products while enhancing the appearance and overall effectiveness of their booth.

In a category all its own, the bottom photograph on the next page is a good example of a method of selling a craft that is utterly unique. Granted, the craftsperson cannot display a great deal of her merchandise, and usually this type of movable cart is most appropriate at indoor shows and malls. However, it still works fine at quaint, picturesque street fairs, as depicted in the top photograph on page 133, a summer street fair in Nevada City, California.

Finally, the bottom photograph on page 133, "Gatherings," by Rhoda Paul, is very illustrative of a typical outdoor display of floral arrangements. Various pieces are hung, others are distributed about the floor space, readily accessible and easy to observe. The trelliswork—often used with floral displays—is both functional and serves aesthetically to reduce the bland effect of the needed, but boring canopy.

These photographs should give you a good idea of what is recommended for outdoor setups, and you no doubt have seen many such booths in person. Your goal, then, is to devise the best way to display your product, all within a ten-by-ten-foot space—the largest that most craftspeople lease. You will see larger booths, because some craft artists need more room to display all their inventory. Some will pay for two, side-by-side, ten-foot spaces—at double the booth fee, of course.

Double booth space requires that you double your inventory to fully stock two booths and double your shelving or whatever you use to display your craft. Naturally, this usually necessitates a larger vehicle to transport all that equipment and inventory. And it goes without saying that it is necessary to sell that much more of your product to defray the additional cost.

Your Indoor Booth Display

The bottom photograph picturing Weathervane Capital's booth, and the photograph on the opposite page, the booth created by Gable's Country Basket, are good examples of the use of double space at an indoor craft show.

Weathervane Capital takes an interesting and novel approach by creating an outdoor yard display, complete with picket fence. The business counter does not detract from the effectiveness of the craft presentation and, most unusual, in this rare case, there is no need to enter the booth at all. Every weather vane is right out there to be seen by the customer and is

within easy reach. Gable's, while providing a great deal of interior walking room, also presents crafts in total view of the public with easy access. In both cases, the business name selected is also memorable.

Some long-established craftspeople eventually find it necessary and very profitable to expand in this way, but we never were capable of attaining that manufacturing level. We recommend that you should be well into the business before you attempt this larger marketing approach.

Remember, too, that while we said a ten-by-ten-foot space is the standard size booth, that size space can only be relied on at outdoor shows, which accommodate the standard-size canopy. Because your space at some indoor shows may be smaller, you must be able to reduce or expand your booth size as each situation presents itself. Flexibility—on your part and in the design of your booth—is the key. When you have developed and set up your booth, you must remember to allow room for a counter on which to carry out your monetary transactions and at least one chair. Standing on your feet is not an option, particularly after a long drive starting at four in the morning and setup immediately upon arrival.

Yet, now that we've offered this advice, you will notice in the photographs that many do not have such a counter. Some artisans would rather sacrifice their personal comfort for the extra room to display their product or will simply walk in and out of the booth all day, standing to the side when it is crowded, and transact their financial dealings from either a small register placed somewhere in the booth or from a money belt. We don't recommend the latter, but, in the final analysis, it comes down to whatever works for you.

The same applies to what has been said about crafts, like jewelry, that are often displayed only at the front of the booth, primarily to catch the customer's eye. Food booths selling candy, soups, jellies, and jams may offer samples for the customer to taste and buy; craftspeople who are continually demonstrating their product may also follow this setup design. So many choose to display in this manner, rather than opening up the interior of their booth space, because food can be sampled from the aisle as people pass by. So, while it does congest the aisles, everyone has to do what's necessary to make a living. These types of vendors will always have an easier and faster setup than you will. However, for most in the business, that easy a setup is not a viable or even recommended alternative. We suggest that you study the photographs on the pages of this chapter closely. You will have to judge them for yourself and decide which setup styles work for you. As you note the effort and expense that goes into designing and setting up many of these booths, you will realize that creating a new booth or revamping your old one is not a simple task.

If you think you have created a wonderful outdoor booth that is versatile enough to work anywhere—including the great indoors—you will have to reconsider that idea. Most of the time, you will find that your outdoor canopy is not at all suitable for the indoor shows you will do. Very few good indoor shows even allow you to set up your outdoor canopy inside. Your shelving and counter or tables are convertible to your indoor booth, but not the canopy.

If you carefully examine the photographs of indoor booths, you will see that most are enclosed in such a way as to separate them from their neighbors on either side and behind. Old Ranch House Creations, top photograph opposite page, uses the very cabinets being sold as such a divider. Additional cabinets stand against the side of the booth and are stored behind it. The cabinets are made of recycled wood and hardware, and no two are identical. We bought one after taking the picture.

Unlike an outdoor show, an indoor show attempts to create the impression that you are walking up and down a street, looking into individual shops. In fact, Harvest Festival hangs flags at the end of every aisle with street names on them. Many artisans erect wooden paneling with shelving built out from the walls, from which crafts may also be hung.

Others, like Mercantile Store, a booth by Haseford Gifts and Creations, seen in bottom photograph opposite page, use lattice siding, which complements the fine wood decorations the artisans produce.

Notice the business counter at the left front and how well it blends in with everything else in the booth so much so that it might be for sale.

Cottage Crafts, the photo on the following page, another double booth that uses a horizontal lattice to separate the booth from its neighbors, exemplifies one of the most beautiful and elegant uses of space we have seen. Ron and Debbie Uhlack, only three years in the business, have

achieved what some craftspeople never approach in their entire career. Not only is their craftsmanship superior, but the booth has a freshness and sense of openness that just invites people in. Their overhead frame allows for lighting to be attached.

If you cannot build a booth of the above type, or your craft does not lend itself to that style, at the very least you will need to devise a way to hang fire-retardant drapery around your booth, drapery that adds color or background or depth, and so enhances your craft. The name of the booth in the top photograph on the opposite page is Display Excellence by Kris Gibson, and a more appropriate name couldn't have been found. Using simple, white drapery as a background, Kris designed an unusual, staggered-shelving effect that allows the lighting at the top center of the booth to completely illuminate every piece on display.

Since his booth was situated on a corner, he also was able to eliminate drapery on the left side of his booth, allowing customers to view his merchandise from almost every vantage point. On page 140 are instructions for flameproofing.

The effort to create a warm, charming, quaint atmosphere, bottom photograph opposite page, was its own reward for Carol Wickham and Jo Ann Reynolds. Their booth, called My Sister and I, combines their talents. They have created a small shop atmosphere in which the customer feels automatically at home and at ease. This booth contributes to the overall feeling the promoter desires to create.

Some convention centers provide individual enclosures with drapery, but most do not. If you bring your own, you must set up with some sort of portable piping that you can erect and on which you can hang your own drapery or paneling. Lightweight, snap-together sets of such aluminum piping can be purchased out of most craft magazines. The pipes come in different lengths so you can vary the height and width.

Flameproofing Requirements

All booth material must be flame retardant: decorations, drapes, banners, acoustical materials, plastic cloth, etc. Bamboo or straw is not allowed in any hall. Merchandise and any wood thicker than $^1/_{16}$" does not need to be flameproofed. All table coverings, fabric walls, paper, or any decorative material must have a flameproof certificate or tag, and you must attach the tag to the material in a prominent spot in easy view of the Fire Marshal. Flame retardant treatments must be renewed as necessary, and after each cleaning. It is your responsibility to submit proof of this to the Fire Marshal.

Note: The importance of adherence to Fire Marshal codes is obvious. To do otherwise endangers everyone. **If you fail to meet Fire Marshal regulations, we will not be able to allow you to operate your booth, and no refund will be given.** All cities require a Flame Proof Certificate. We strongly urge you to obtain one. If you don't have a certificate, be prepared for a patch test. Refer to the All-City Reference Chart on the inside back cover for the phone number of each city's Fire Marshal.

> To test for flame retardancy, hold a wooden match to a 2" X 4" fabric swatch (the thickest part, such as a hem) for 12 seconds. The flame should go out when the match is removed. If it does not, you will need to re-treat or have it commercially treated.

Permits

The following activities require permits; you must be sure to obtain them from the local fire marshal not less than 30 days in advance of the show:

- Display or operation of any heater, barbecue, heat-producing device, open flame, **candles**, lamp lanterns, torches, etc.
- Display or operation of any electrical, mechanical or chemical device which may be deemed hazardous by the Fire Department.
- Use or storage of flammable liquids, compressed gasses or dangerous chemicals.

It is the exhibitor's responsibility to obtain any special permits required for craft demonstration.

Fabric Flameproofing

We strongly recommend you purchase pre-treated, inherently flameproof fabric. This will save you the time, expense and worry of re-treating and certifying your fabrics after each cleaning. Good sources are:

Flourish Company   Dealers Supply Inc.
501-677-3300   800-524-0576

If you do purchase conventional fabric, keep in mind that the more absorbent a material, the easier it is to treat. Natural fibers are your best bet.

To have your fabrics professionally treated, check the Yellow Pages under "Flame Proofing" or call your local Fire Dept.

You may also treat fabrics yourself after each cleaning, providing you are sure to saturate well and that you test the thickest part of the material carefully after treatment.

Fire retardant spray is available for purchase at the show office.

Commercial fire-retardant is available from:

California Flameproofing and Processing, Inc.
170 North Halstead Street
Pasadena, CA 91107
626-792-6981

Dealers Supply Inc.
800-524-0576

Elaine Martin Company
P.O. Box 674
Deerfield, IL 60015-0674
800-642-1043

4

If you've ever attended a top-of-the-line indoor craft show, you will remember seeing beautifully structured booths with ornate, carved, wooden facades, interior paneling, exquisite drapery, and the like. Every booth in such shows is not as grand as those, but you can bet that those are the ones that attracted the most customers. Such booths require a great deal of advanced planning, skill to construct, space to transport, and more time to erect, but they pay big dividends. Most craftspeople have to find a happy medium between the extremely elegant booth and the serviceable.

At the early stage of your craft career, you may not be ready to become involved in all this. But it is the direction in which you should set your sights if you want to be really successful. Of course, you don't necessarily have to create something quite as artful as we have described. We didn't. The promoter is looking for booths that will enhance the overall attractiveness of the show. The garden variety, flea market setup will not get you into Harvest Festival or any other show of that caliber. Aim for something substantial, functional, and still attractive. You can build the interior of your booth out of wood, metal, plastic, or whatever you may invent that separates and distinguishes you from your neighbors. Here is another place to put your creative ability to work.

Pumpkin Patch, by Dian Hall, photograph below, is a very good example of a creative approach to booth design. Simple piping has been used and then covered with valances that slide on. A light bar in the center illuminates

the booth, which also draws light from the hanging lights of the hall in which the show is taking place. Metal grids strapped together are erected and used to hang the artisan's work. She has used her product hanging on the grids as the divider between her booth and her next-door neighbor's. Throw rugs in the booth set it off nicely, though I would have some concern about people tripping on them. Notice how well Dian has distributed all the various pieces she creates—some hung, some stacked, some sitting in baskets. Her small "boutique" in which the customer can roam and browse is created without great expense.

Booth Design Is a Daunting Task

If you have a lot of talent as a designer and constructor of such things, perhaps you will find building an appropriate booth quite simple. I did not.

During our first five years in the business, I know I built at least five different booths, a new one each year. Finally, I came up with one that really worked for us. Creating an interior setup that could be used both outdoors and indoors and is adjustable to various configurations of space is not a simple task. Just taking into account the changing dimensions required by promoters was asking for more talent than I initially possessed. At times, I was sure I needed a degree in architecture and another in engineering. If you are no more skilled than I, you may have to do it by trial and error, as I did.

One way to help create your desired, finished booth is to establish a theme. Virtually all the booths pictured thus far do this to varying degrees, and that is why they are successful. We explained how ours came about at the beginning of the book. Since some big shows also require you to wear a costume, this may help you in developing your theme. A promoter has the right to refuse to allow you to set up—and may even require you to tear down—if you do not comply with the contract you signed. Once established, a theme can guide how you build the booth, what materials you use to construct it, your choice of color schemes, and whatever decorative effects you select.

Repeat customers look for your booth because it left an impression in their mind. So once you have a booth that suits all your needs, don't change it drastically unless there is some real need to do so. Even then, try to stay within the theme you have established.

That said, it must be acknowledged that for some artists and craftspeople, establishing a theme is particularly difficult, if not impossible. Artists dealing in oils or watercolors, and attempting to display a sufficient number of their paintings, cannot simply set up some walls and hang a few paintings as if their booth were a miniature art gallery. Too many paintings on a wall destroys the effect of each one, while too few amounts to wasted space. The theme has to emerge from the style, school, and medium of the paintings themselves.

Janette Jones, photograph below, solves this problem very nicely by using portable, fold-up screens. These can be opened or closed to any desired degree, then placed in the booth so customers can walk through, as if they were in a gallery, viewing the paintings hung on the screens. Each screen has its own lighting, so Janette is not dependent on the lighting of the building in which she is displaying. Notice that she also offers, on a separate stand, miniatures of her work for people who cannot afford the originals.

Janette does very fine work. However, here is a good example of a problem with the jury process that requires craftspeople to submit their application with photographs. Using an expensive camera that does everything automatically, my wife Judy still could not capture the depth and feeling of Janette's art in this photograph. Some of it seems washed out, which it is not. Until they establish their reputation with promoters, most artists like Janette are much better off jurying in person.

Clothing booths often present a similar problem. Any theme has to be established through the style and design of the clothing itself. Workmanship has to be seen and touched. It simply cannot be adequately photographed. Kathy's Klothes, seen in the photograph on the following page, is a good example.

Kathy once used a very complicated double booth that required customers to enter the booth to appraise her work. She has since designed a very

simple, easy-to-erect booth that allows her to display her products through the use of open space, with strategically placed lighting. Most important, she can set it up alone! The type of hangers she uses enables her to present more merchandise, more easily viewed, rather than crowding everything on traditional closetlike racks. Smaller accessories, such as detachable collars and cuffs, are placed in wire trays that can be transported without having to remove every item from every tray. Drapery on two sides serves as a backdrop for many of her unique styles. Overall, there is a sense of openness and easy accessibility. When using draperies as an enclosure for your booth, keep in mind that they are almost always required to be fire retardant. You can buy such draperies from convention center suppliers.

Finally, the photograph on the opposite page is an excellent example of how to best display floral arrangements. This booth, known as California Victorian, uses grid paneling extensively, along with tables on which vases with floral arrangements are displayed. This is either a double booth or a booth and a half but can easily be rearranged to conform to any size space available.

We particularly liked this booth because the proprietors have not attempted to cram their booth so full of floral arrangements that the customer cannot distinguish one from another. Each piece has its place of prominence and can be seen for what it is. We wish the rich colors and fresh appeal of these freeze-dried flowers could be truly captured on film.

Loading and Packing Your Vehicle

It may seem mundane at this point, and even irrelevant to the subject of setup and display, but setting up in a smooth and relaxed fashion—as opposed to setting up in an atmosphere of confusion and tension—may be directly related to how you pack your truck and what you do or do not bring with you. The following advice may seem to be nothing more than common sense; yet, when you find yourself in a hurry to be off to a show, some of these pointers are quite easy to forget.

Always pack your vehicle so that what you need first—your collapsible canopy or whatever rigging you use to enclose your booth—can be taken out first. The same applies to every other piece of equipment you need for setup. There is nothing more aggravating than having to unload your entire vehicle, just to retrieve what you need first and then having to tiptoe through and around everything while you are trying to set up. So remember: Your product should be the last thing you remove from your vehicle. Using the following suggestions, make yourself a checklist and use it when loading and unloading your vehicle so you forget nothing. In a rush to leave early in the morning, we would often forget a road map or money. Anxious to get on the road after the show, amid all the chaos taking place, we left many an item behind, like a shelf or a chair or a tool that we needed at the next show. Remember the rule: First In, Last Out. Last In, First Out. This rule applies to major items only and depends on the capacity of your vehicle; how you load your booth, merchandise, and accessories; and the arrangement of the space available to you. Like all women, my wife could always find another nook or cranny in which to put something.

All merchandise, which usually takes up the most space, should be loaded first, since it will be last out of the vehicle. Your collapsible canopy with all the paraphernalia to set it up—canvas sides, weights, shims, piping, tarps, everything for the booth—should be loaded last, so it can be taken out first. Keep your dolly or hand truck readily accessible so that you can use it to transport your booth setup materials and your merchandise. Display tables, pedestals, shelving, racks, and chairs should be loaded so as to be next out of the truck. The cash register, charge machine, and cellular phone and counter on which to place them should come out of the truck next. They should be set up immediately, since, at outdoor shows, many customers arrive while you are still setting up. A toolbox and all tools necessary to erecting your booth need to be available for almost immediate use. A spare tire and jack should be easily accessible, if needed, without having to empty half your truck to get to it. Always carry a first aid kit and all the medication that you require, perhaps under your seat. Include sun block. Keep an ice chest with food and drink handy. This not only saves you money, but at many early morning setups, there is no place to get anything to eat or drink until the show opens. Always carry a broom, a shovel, and, sometimes, a rake, umbrellas, sun hat and sunglasses, rain gear and extra shoes, rags or towels, extra plastic tarp, and duct tape. Make yourself a small kit with such office supplies as pens, pencils, Scotch tape, extra price tags, business cards, paper clips, rubber bands, and the like.

We found that the above items were essential for outdoor shows. The following are the major items for indoor shows, in addition to most of the above. Pack your fire-retardant drapery or whatever you use as siding for you booth so that you can set it up first. Lighting equipment, power strips, and extra light bulbs, along with a 100-foot extension cord are often needed immediately. Your indoor frame from which to hang drapery or siding should be accessible first. Don't forget your carpet, cut to the size of your booth. We often forgot this, since it wasn't used for outdoor shows. Take along a small vacuum or broom to clean the booth. A small stool or a small ladder to adjust lights and hang drapery is always necessary.

This list is just a starter for you. No doubt, you will add many things to it as a result of the unique product and booth you have created and your own personal needs. And if you're wondering how you get all this into your truck or van, you have two options: Either learn to pack your vehicle better than you have in the past or buy a bigger truck. That is not meant sarcastically. Judy and I began our career carrying everything in the back of our

Suburu station wagon. After buying two trucks—the second bigger than the first—we ended up with a twelve-passenger Dodge van that we gutted to fit all the items described above.

Setting Up and Show Site Conditions

Setup is very physically and emotionally demanding. More than 95 percent of the time, setup is done on the same day the show opens. Allowing at least three to five hours to set up, depending on the show site, you can then look forward to selling your product for the next nine to twelve hours, depending on the show. The first day of a show, therefore, is always a very long, exhausting, and either frustrating or exhilarating day, depending on how financially successful it turns out to be.

Yes, you've arrived enthusiastically at the show, but your spirits may be quickly dampened by many of the problems you will encounter. Booth spaces may be poorly marked. Somebody may have erroneously begun setting up in your space. It may be raining or even snowing. You may arrive late at the show site and the street is jammed with vehicles being unloaded, so you are unable to drive up to your booth space. You then must wait nervously until you can unload or park your vehicle, perhaps blocks away, and transport everything by hand to your booth space.

At many convention centers, due to few spaces at the loading dock, you will be given a time to arrive and you must be on time. Even then, you may find a line of vehicles in front of you and have to wait an hour before moving up to the loading dock. You can bet that your space will be a long way from the loading dock and you may have to make twenty to thirty trips to dolly everything to your space, perhaps in and out of an elevator or climbing stairs to do so. Once you've unloaded, you must move your vehicle as soon as you can to allow another vendor to move in. This means that you will have to pile your entire setup and inventory into your ten square feet and into the aisles commingled with your neighbors, all in the same predicament. Often at convention centers, you will find large metal plates on the floor, making that area of the floor uneven. The electrical connections may be fifty or more feet away from your booth. When you set up your booth, it may bump into an overhead air duct or some other architectural obstruction.

The litany of problems spelled out above is just a small sample of the frustrations you may encounter. In essence, perfect setup conditions are the exception, not the rule. As a result, Judy and I probably had more debates, discussions, and flat-out arguments concerning the various configurations in which the shelving could be arranged than about any other subject related to the business. Every show site presents you with different challenges.

At an outdoor show, you'll find yourself at five in the morning, when it's still pitch black outside, trying to set up in the cold or even rain with a flashlight. If the show is in a park, you may not be allowed to drive your vehicle up to your booth space because the town wants to preserve the grass. Thousands of people will trample that grass into oblivion for the next two days, but you still can't drive on it. Would you guess that was one of my pet peeves? You can't find your booth space because the chalked-in numbers have been erased or because, as one idiot did, the spaces have been marked with green powdered chalk on green grass.

Eventually, you do find your space and somebody else is setting up in it. Now you hunt for the promoter to correct the error and spend half an hour finding her. Maybe you've never seen the promoter before and have no idea who you are even looking for. Nobody you talk to has a clue as to what she looks like, much less where she can be found.

You finally find the promoter, the space assignment is straightened out, and you are setting up your canopy when you discover that there's a big hump in the street, right in the middle of your space, or a sewer into which dirty water will be running all day or an oil slick you have to clean up. The wind may be whipping through your booth, but the show must go on, so you continue to work frantically until the show opens. And while you are doing this, you will often be doing it with early rising customers looking over your merchandise and engaging in friendly conversation, ready to pounce on something they want the second you have your cash register set up. In fact, we have made a lot of money this way at seven in the morning, selling directly out of the truck to anxious buyers, while setting up at the same time.

If the show is in a park, your site may be on an uneven slope or the ground may be rocky or you may be stuck in the mud or there may be a tree in your way. Since you had to preserve the damn grass to pacify those in the community who didn't want the show there in the first place, you'll be trudging through high grass, mud, or sand, or over concrete abutments. I won't mention the gross and disgusting problems you'll encounter. Just use your imagination.

There is simply no end to them. No matter how long you are in the business, there is always a new problem for which you didn't prepare. Once again, just try to be as flexible and nonchalant as possible. Since you can tell from the way I am writing this exactly how I usually reacted to these situations, do as I say and not as I did. Try to retain your sense of humor. Nobody can prepare for every possible contingency.

To this end, we have some more tips and suggestions, but we will not attempt to provide you with a checklist on how to conduct and control yourself. If you're the calm, laid-back type of individual, the kind who smiles through adversity, you don't need my help and I couldn't give it because I don't understand people like you. But, if you're like me, after numerous expletives cursing fate, go take a walk in the park. Some personality factors do deserve special attention and consideration.

Learn Your Role

If you're part of a team, after the first few shows it will become obvious which of you tends to get agitated easily or needs only a few minor setbacks to lose his patience. We suggest that the more easily flustered one become the "gofer." He lugs everything out of the truck; assists in setting up the booth, tables, and shelves; does the heavy grunt work; helps solve all the major problems; and then disappears somewhere. Since Judy was the patient one, I made the coffee run when we reached this stage, then hunted for a friend, and stayed out of sight until Judy had everything beautifully arranged and we were ready to do business. By then, I was again ready to smile at my customers.

It took a few years of debating to eventually decide that this was the best way to conduct our business, so we suggest that you sit down and discuss it with your partner early in your craft show journey. In our case it meant that we had to agree that Judy was going to do more of the work. I agreed readily; Judy more reluctantly.

It may be that you and your partner work well together through every stage of setup. Some partners do, but most do not. Frankly, I just found myself in Judy's way as her way of arranging the booth was almost always more practical, artistic, and easier than mine. So why engage in a futile squabble that will set a negative tone for the day? Find your role and stick with it.

Indoors or outdoors, the mental strain is the same. So you have to learn how to accommodate yourself—both to the conditions in which you find yourself and to each other. Under this stress, it is too easy to make mistakes, break things, and blame everything and everybody but yourself. You are better able to evaluate your entire situation under calm conditions. Then—and only then—if you've tried to solve every possible problem and there is something that just cannot be tolerated or to which it is impossible to adjust, go to the promoter with your dilemma. Most promoters will try to help you solve your problems, if they are solvable and not of your own making.

Back to the Checklist

As I typed out the suggestions for developing your own checklist, and my mind wandered through all those upsetting catastrophes that occurred early in the morning when my patience was thin, I realized that many things on the list seem to have no apparent reason for being there. So some explanation seems in order. It constantly boggled our minds, and more often left me highly frustrated, when we discovered that we had not brought something essential to the show, which we, of course, found ourselves desperately in need of. Usually, that meant that one of us had to stop everything to go make a purchase—or beg someone else to lend us the item. The gofer is good for that, but you still lose time. So make yourself a tool kit with all the items necessary to your special circumstances.

It seems redundant to suggest that the driver carry a map of where you are going. Every driver has a map case. And we did too. But do you know how many times we had every map except the one we needed to get where we were going? It really hurts when you are late for setup and can't get to your booth. Judy and I agreed that she was the copilot in charge of directions. I just turned right or left on her instruction. Of course, the next time we went to the same show site, I never remembered how to get there and was reminded of my forgetfulness, but I lived with it.

If your vehicle doesn't have a real spare tire (not the skimpy, modern kind that takes you all of five miles), buy one. When you get a flat tire, the gas station is always more than five miles away. I know! When you are traveling long distances and you get a flat, you may be out in the middle of nowhere. We were there. So were many other craftspeople, who have even missed the first day of a show or arrived extremely late due to a simple problem of this kind. That kind of error costs money that you can't recover.

Always carry shims for leveling. In a park or even on the street, you will never be on a flat surface. My neighbor always seemed to have the flat spot. There are countless uses for duct tape, a spare plastic tarp, rope, extension cords, light bulbs, extra weights to hold the canopy down in the wind, stakes to stake it to the ground, and the all important bungees for multiple purposes. There isn't a thing that has been mentioned that we didn't need at one time or another—and more than once, in spite of our experience. When you do as many shows as we did, some are going to fall on the wrong time of the month. Need I say more? It is very embarrassing to have to hunt around looking for another craftsperson from whom you can borrow what you need. It is like wearing a big sign saying rookie.

I didn't check our space assignment at one of our first indoor shows, loaded all our longest shelves in the truck and found myself borrowing a saw and cutting two feet off all my shelving when I found the booth space was eight-by-ten feet instead of the standard ten-by-ten feet. I think it was on that day—and a hundred days like it—that I asked myself how I got into the business. Judy always reminded me of my prophetic words. Of course, when we got home, I had to buy the necessary material to make an entirely new set of shelving. A very time-consuming and expensive error on my part. That is why we stress this aspect of the business.

To recap, here are some of the things that you should include on your checklist:

- ❏ Collapsible canopy
- ❏ Canvas sides for canopy
- ❏ Weights
- ❏ Tarps
- ❏ Dolly
- ❏ Display tables or shelving
- ❏ Cash register
- ❏ Charge machine
- ❏ Cellular phone
- ❏ Cash counter
- ❏ Toolbox
- ❏ Spare tire and jack
- ❏ First aid kit
- ❏ Personal medication
- ❏ Sunscreen
- ❏ Ice chest
- ❏ Broom or vacuum
- ❏ Rake for outdoor shows
- ❏ Umbrella
- ❏ Sun hat
- ❏ Sunglasses
- ❏ Rain gear
- ❏ Rags
- ❏ Duct tape
- ❏ Maps
- ❏ Rope
- ❏ Extension cords
- ❏ Light bulbs
- ❏ Bungees
- ❏ MONEY!

How to Best Display Your Product

One way or another, you will get your booth set up. However, for some reason, many craftspeople fail to design and set up their booth in a way that displays their product to its best advantage and enhances their product's beauty and salability. Some just don't seem to know how to present their work in the best light; some simply have no artistic sense; others just don't bother to pay attention to this crucial aspect of the business. Given what we all see and experience every day when we go to the shopping mall or watch television commercials, correct presentation of your product—your creation—should be the primary concern and first priority of every craftsperson. Yet, oftentimes, it isn't.

Far too many merchants with good products fail to make big money because they fall short in this area. That is why we included so many photographs of booth setup. Because of this, Judy and I started a consulting firm, called Fresh Perspectives, specifically to conduct on-site evaluation of craft booth setup and display. Because the problems craftspeople encounter are unique to each booth and the product being displayed, we can only spell out some general guidelines.

Create a Warm, Friendly, Colorful, and Inviting Atmosphere

As you become more experienced in your observation of potential customers, you will notice that many people don't like to step over what they perceive as an imaginary line across the front of your booth. At an indoor show, it isn't even imaginary, since you should have a carpet laid across your entire booth space and this clearly defines the aisle in which the customers are walking and the entrance to your booth.

Observing this phenomenon, Judy and I eventually came to the conclusion that, for some people, stepping across that line seems to represent a statement of financial commitment. This is especially true during the early hours of the show, when the aisles are not crowded and people have more time to look, think, and consider. To a large extent, I have no doubt that it is psychological, but it exists nonetheless. It is your job to entice customers over that line.

One way is to keep your loss leader up front, just inside your booth. Just in front of the booth would be better, but you can't block the aisles with your merchandise. The loss leader will at least cause potential customers to pause, at which time you should greet them and engage them in some conversation. At that point, they will usually step across that line and you've made a beginning. After that, use your judgment to decide how much conversation to employ.

Illuminating Your Booth

At outdoor shows, lighting your booth is rarely, if ever, a problem. Find yourself facing the rising sun in the morning or the hot setting sun at night, and you'll have more light than you ever want or need. Indoor shows, on the other hand, present you with numerous lighting problems and challenges that must be overcome.

Your object is to illuminate your booth and your merchandise as well as possible, while maintaining a warm atmosphere and avoiding glaring lights that disturb the customer. Some people are particularly light sensitive and will leave the booth if a light is glaring in their eyes. Other people have trouble reading price tags, especially if the lighting is poor, and will leave the booth rather than ask the price. Refer again to the photographs to see how various booths have solved the lighting problem. For your convenience, a reference sheet, "Lighting Your Space" appears on the next page. It was provided to us by the Harvest Festival promoters and is part of their Hands-on Show Guide.

Lighting Your Space

Overhead hall lights are dimmed or turned off at Harvest Festivals, so it is vitally important for you to create a direct lighting system within your booth to enhance your craft. Your lights should shine directly on your craft. After set-up, stand outside your booth to check your lighting from the customer's point-of-view.

Four or five spotlights should provide ample lighting for your booth. We provide 500 watts of electricity free-of-charge for each 8'x10' or 10'x10' booth; 750 watts is provided in a 15' booth and 1000 watts is provided in a 20'

booth. If you need more wattage, contact the show electrician to order it prior to your arrival (see All-City Reference Chart for name & phone).

Helpful Hint: Small halogen lights throw off 1.5 times more light than a traditional bulb, i.e. a regular 50-watt bulb puts out 50 watts of light, a 50-watt halogen bulb will throw off the equivalent of 75 watts while using only 50 watts of electricity. The halogen lights are a little more expensive but in the end you get more light for your money.

Backlighting:

Lighting from behind used in conjunction with primary accent lighting from the front. Adds depth to a three-dimensional object. Creates silhouettes. Makes volume of object more apparent and separates it from the background.

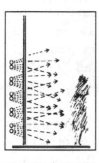

Floodlighting:

Downlighting with flood lamps to illuminate areas or walls. Appropriate when high levels of light are needed, such as to spotlight a large piece of equipment. Could also establish an upbeat, upscale mood by making the booth a flood of light on a dark show floor.

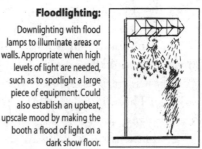

Wall Lighting:

Subtle form of floodlighting. Uses lamps mounted closely to the wall at a very shallow angle. When projected from the bottom up, makes the wall appear taller. From the bottom down, makes the wall seem firmly attached to the ground. Also accentuates textures, makes the wall appear to glow.

Spotlighting:

Accent lighting using a narrow beam lighting. The form of downlighting most used in exhibitry. Should be used sparingly to illuminate featured items 3-10 times more brightly than their surroundings. Attracts visitors & provides subdued drama.

Uplighting:

Lights are pointed upward to reflect off the ceiling, an awning or ceiling drape. Provides even light with little glare. Also known as indirect or bounce lighting. Provides cheery, bright & shadowless atmosphere, but may flatten or wash out an exhibit. Best if used with accent lighting.

Color Wash:

Using gels or filters to add color to establish contrast on a wall or floor. Presents strong visual cues to establish an atmosphere or theme.

3

Most indoor facilities have overhead lighting, but these lights are rarely sufficient. Oftentimes, they err in the opposite direction: They're so glaring that they detract from the show's ambiance. This is particularly true if the craft show is in a large convention hall or an arena where the lighting is seventy-five feet or more over your head. You can see this in some of the photographs. The hall will have light, but it's not the kind of light that enhances your merchandise, brings out the color of your work, or shows your products to the best advantage.

Because the situation described above is so common, you need to invest in some kind of track lighting that you can focus from directly above your booth or attach to the sides or shelves. This will enable you to spotlight every area of the booth without shining light into your customers' eyes. Such fixtures can be purchased in any good lighting store along with the proper bulbs.

You should also purchase a few electric power strips and the 100-foot extension cord we mentioned. Most indoor facilities have outlets all over the floor, but your booth may not be close enough to one of them to plug the strip in directly. It would be a good idea if you went to a few big indoor craft shows to observe the various lighting systems used by the craftspeople with long experience. This will help you determine which system would best suit your needs. In some cases, a few small lamps, placed strategically in your booth, may also do the trick. Obviously, craftspeople who sell lamps have it made.

In order to achieve the proper effect, we set up our entire booth—complete with merchandise—at home in our living room at night. In a completely dark room, we were able to experiment with every possible variation of lighting until we found what combination worked the best for us. Harvest Festival's Show Planning Checklist, seen on the opposite page, recommends this strategy as well, along with many other good tips.

You may find, for example, that foot lighting—lights pointed from the floor upwards—or side lighting best brings out the qualities you most wish to showcase in your product. Experiment with every possible placement of the lights until you find the arrangement that works best to achieve your desired effect. Some photographs we have included in this chapter may help a bit, but not much, as no nonprofessional photograph—particularly in black and white—can capture the real effect of lighting. You should note, however, the various placement of lights. They may give you some ideas with which to experiment. Since no two booths are exactly alike, each craftsperson must find her own solution.

Other Lighting Problems

In some convention centers, the management turns off the overhead lights when the show starts, either to save on the electric bill or to highlight the

Show Planning
CHECKLIST

Long-term planning:

- ☐ Make sure ALL items to be sold have been juried
- ☐ Order Exhibitor Discount Cards from the Harvest Festival to pass out and mail to your customers
- ☐ Make arrangements for shipment of your booth and inventory
- ☐ Obtain current seller's permits (as required) for each show city (see All-City-Reference Chart)
- ☐ Report your permit numbers to the Harvest Festival Customer Service Department
- ☐ Flame-proof all fabric and obtain a Flame Proof Certificate
- ☐ Plan your costume; be sure you comply with Harvest Festival dress code!
- ☐ Are you exhibiting in November or December? Remember to highlight your dress and decorations with Christmas accents
- ☐ Make your hotel (and air) or RV park reservations; note the cut-off date for Harvest Festival rooms
- ☐ Order pipe & drape & electrical for each show, as needed

Before You Leave Home:

- ☐ Test your booth set-up: set it up, check the lighting, and take a photo!
- ☐ Check the All-City Reference Chart for set-up, tear-down, & show hours
- ☐ Tune-up and winterize your vehicle.
- ☐ Check your booth size for each show.

Bring to the Show:

- ☐ Your Seller's Permits and display them at each show
- ☐ Your exhibitor badges to each show
- ☐ Your Show Guide for reference…don't leave home without it!
- ☐ Your Flame Proof Certificate
- ☐ Your most recent invoice

show in a more professional manner—most often the latter. Sometimes, too, the overhead power goes out and the only light you may have is that in your booth. After all the work and effort you have put into producing your product, you want the customer to see it.

Incidentally, or maybe not so incidentally, you are paying for your electricity. Some promoters include it in the total cost of your booth space; others charge for it separately. If the charge is separate, you can choose not to hook up to an electric source, thereby saving $30 or $40, but this would be a foolish way to save money. Don't forget that many shows run until nine or ten o'clock at night. You could find yourself without any lighting at all.

Without sufficient light, many people who are partially color-blind (like me) cannot distinguish colors, especially dark colors like black or navy blue or subtle shades of blue and green. Such subtleties may be the quality that most expresses the uniqueness of your product. This was the case with our baskets, as it is with all fine jewelry. Color contributes immensely to the impression made by fine pottery, where glaze and depth of pigment and paint can be so important.

So, too, with products made of glass, and especially any product involving the use of stained glass or miniaturization. At one of our last shows, there was an older woman who did the most exquisite miniature painting we had ever seen. Nobody was buying from her because, first, she should have provided a means of magnification; second, her pieces were not at eye level; and third, she did not provide any lighting. So pay close attention to this aspect of your display. Don't just throw up a bunch of lights and think that is all there is to it.

Arranging Your Merchandise

For most craftspeople, arranging merchandise on shelves is the job that consumes more time than any other part of the setup ritual. If you're a potter, it may mean removing hundreds of pieces of pottery from their packing crates, unwrapping each piece of work, and finding the proper place for it on your shelves.

A jeweler will spend hours pinning every earring to a board and setting each ring in a case. A booth featuring what we earlier referred to as Foo-Foo may literally involve 500 to 1,000 odds and ends—bits of craft work of every conceivable size. Every floral display must be hung to its best advantage. We—I shouldn't say we—Judy would spend three or fours hours before every show, arranging our baskets, while I disappeared or stood around looking ineffectual.

There's a critical reason why this part of setup takes so much time: how you display your craft can drastically effect how much you sell. Little decorative touches that enhance the customer's visual pleasure and help to entice customers into the booth can make a big difference in your sales. You'll see abundant examples of these kinds of touches in the photographs. Where you strategically place your merchandise is even more important.

To maximize the advertising and selling potential of your booth, your most attractive big sellers should generally be at eye level or below. In that position, customers not only see your craft at close range and from the best vantage point, but they can touch it and pick it up. That tactile possibility inspires customer desire. Eye level or below also enables shorter people to view your craft without having to reach for it. At the same time, women often like to rummage. Some customers are always looking for things that are out of the way, treasures that everybody else missed. With some exceptions, as noted in a few of the photographs, most often a fully stocked booth caters to this customer tendency.

Storage Space

The question of a fully stocked booth leads to the question of just where do you put all this merchandise in so small a space? With the only exception I can think of being jewelers, who can carry $50,000 worth of merchandise in three or four suitcases, the rest of us have to strategically work this problem out.

If you are very clever at arranging space and your particular craft makes it possible, set all your merchandise for your customers to see. However, it may be necessary to set aside some space—preferably out of sight, behind you, or under tables—where you can keep your extra inventory handy in order to replace stock as it sells. If you are a solo act, as Judy often was, on a busy day you will not have time to leave the booth and go back to your truck, where more merchandise may be stored.

Remember that you want the customer to feel that she has every possible choice. If potential buyers don't see something that is exactly right, you can reach into that handy storehouse and show them something else that may be just what they wanted. Booths using display tables have it easy: Space under the table itself allows for convenient storage. In every photograph in which there is a table, particularly one covered by a tablecloth, you can be sure something is stored underneath. If use of a table is not appropriate to your craft, you will have to find another method of storage.

At most outdoor shows, storage of extra merchandise is rarely a problem. There is usually a good deal of room behind you, and sometimes you'll be able to park your vehicle right behind your booth. At indoor shows, the promoter usually sets aside a large portion of floor space where everybody can store merchandise and quickly retrieve it, as needed. But don't count on it everywhere.

The Advantage of an Open Booth

The presentation of most craft products is best served by providing customers with entry to your booth, so they can come in and browse. Tables or even very narrow entryways generally present a barrier between you and potential buyers and hamper the customer's view of merchandise displayed at the back of the booth or behind you. If the aisles are crowded, a potential customer may barely glance into your booth. A few customers standing in front of the table can also block the aisles, making it almost impossible for people to clearly view your product. A booth arranged in this fashion discourages would-be customers. They usually don't want to have to fight to see or enter a booth. Sometimes, when the aisles are jammed as at Christmas shows, the customer will be jostled and shoved right past your booth—like rush hour on the subway—without ever seeing anything.

The scenario above applies to the normal show but, ironically, the opposite effect can occur and work in your favor during the holiday season. If your booth is jammed with people, it often prompts others to check out what all the fuss is about. Human nature being what it is, when people see a large crowd gazing at, examining, and buying your product, they can't help but be intrigued. They will then squeeze, push, and shove their way into the booth to see what they are missing out on and buy something, just because so many others are buying. So spend as much time as is necessary to create a booth arrangement that attracts lots of customers into the booth and then assists you in keeping them there until they buy something.

This is also a time when the height of your booth and shelving is important. If the inventory is moving out fast and the booth is crowded with people, instead of keeping things at eye level, you may find that high shelving works better, because it allows you to stock more inventory. High shelving may pose a problem because some people can't reach products high up without assistance. On the other hand, some people are always intrigued by what is furthest away and hardest to reach. Human nature, I guess.

Price All Your Merchandise

Every item in your booth should have a price tag on it that is easy to see and read. People do not like to ask you how much a particular item costs. For many people, asking the price is embarrassing. Asking how much something costs automatically implies that you may not be able to afford it. Lack of a price tag, therefore, can cost you a sale.

In addition, when the booth is crowded, the customer may not have the time to wait in line just to ask a price. More important to the psychology of selling is the fact that when people are shopping they are uncomfortable admitting to you, or even to themselves, that they cannot afford something.

Certainly the customer is aware of her finances and her budget—that's why she's looking at the price tag—but she doesn't want to discuss it with you. Absence of a price tag forces her to do so.

Sometimes the absence of a price tag encourages dickering over the price and attempts by the customer to bargain. You should never bargain with the customer.

Demonstrate Your Product

We aren't suggesting that you become a pitchman, modeling yourself after a salesman for a new vegetable slicer or a miracle stain remover. We're still talking about booth arrangement and how to allow the space to make the most of your wares.

Some products speak for themselves: A kite is a kite; a bowl is a bowl. But the uses of other crafts—like our baskets—may be less apparent and may need to be demonstrated. Less traditional products often confuse people. Rather than ask what a product is for and risk appearing stupid or ignorant, they may simply leave the booth.

We realized that this could happen when we fielded repeated questions like, "This is a beautiful basket, but what do I do with it?" Sometimes I was tempted to tell them. But, I remained professional—particularly if my wife was standing next to me. One day, however, I couldn't resist. We had made a basket we called a bird basket because it resembled a traditional birdhouse without a roof. We displayed delicate soaps and small towels in it. Still, a woman asked me the question, "What do I do with it?" So I told her to hang it in a tree. Judy didn't think that was very funny. Neither did the lady. I disappeared and Judy mollified her and sold her another basket. I didn't hear the end of that for a while.

Since each of our baskets was designed for a different purpose, they were placed on the shelves with something in them—napkins in a napkin holder, a bottle of wine in a picnic basket, toilet paper in another small basket. Nevertheless, some people were oblivious to the obvious and still asked the question. The bird basket incident happened the last year we were in business, so I guess my patience had run out and it was time to retire.

If your craft is strictly decorative, give it a background that enhances it and shows it off. If it is a hands-on item—a ceramic mixing bowl, perhaps—place it in the customer's hand. Let her touch it and feel it. Encourage the customer to develop an attachment to it. Try to help the customer relate to the product by discussing her home and where she wants to put it in her home. Point out or refer the customer to those pictures in your album that creatively depict how you use it in your home or yard, or wherever the craft is appropriate.

Learn to play your booth space. The entire booth can be considered an artistic medium or environment in which you work and ply every aspect of your trade. Use your booth space to take your customer on a shopping tour. Get out of your chair and mingle with people. Take things off the shelf and hand them to the customer. "Did you see this? Is this the color you're looking for? Maybe this suits your needs better?" Or just restock and rearrange your merchandise from time to time. By doing that—a seemingly simple, innocent act—you can make customers in your booth take notice, look at your craft more closely, ask questions, and buy. As difficult as it may be, no question a customer asks should ever be ignored or treated as stupid, my occasional sarcasm notwithstanding. Instead, as Beth Weber, craftsperson and promoter, said, "Remind them that they have creative talents that you don't have." And, I'll add, even if it isn't true.

Most customers enjoy getting to know you. Quite a few, particularly the elderly, attend craft shows out of loneliness. The craft show is their opportunity to get out of the house, be with people, and still feel that they are safe. Many, many of the craftspeople we have met in the business have never considered this factor—most likely because they live in a world only of crafts. They forget that most people do not have the talent or imagination to do what they are doing.

Customers admire and even envy your creative ability; occasionally, they even express those feelings with a comment like, "Oh! I could never do this." That is the time to say what Beth said, reminding them that they probably have talents you do not have. A little flattery goes a long way when selling a product. At the same time, you want—in a modest way, while thanking them for their appreciation of your art—to take advantage of the customer's perspective of you as an artist. In the vernacular, this is called "working the crowd."

Advertise Yourself

At first reading, you are apt to think that there is no way to advertise yourself at a show, and, admittedly, what we are suggesting is subtler than what is traditionally thought of as advertising. We are not recommending that you walk the aisles or stand in the entrance, hawking your wares like a carnival barker. Yet there are many ways to self-advertise without upsetting the promoter, irritating customers, or drawing complaints from other craftspeople.

One of the most important ways to advertise is to create a large banner with your business name and logo on it. Many large promotions require such a banner. Hang the banner at the front of your booth, from the top of it, at an angle out over the aisle. Most experienced artisans display such a banner at every show—indoor and outdoor—but particularly at indoor shows. In large shows, crowded with customers, the banner enables the customer to look down long rows of craft booths and spot your booth.

Some top-of-the-line shows like the Harvest Festival may post a directory with a map of the entire floor layout and the name of every craft booth on the map. This is another form of advertising, and it is a real help to customers who are looking for your booth among 500 or 600 competitors. Other promoters, such as Fire on the Mountain, will request that you contribute a piece of your work to be displayed in showcases at the entrance to the show. This is usually optional, but you should definitely take advantage of this form of advertising. Every customer who walks in is going to see a sample of your work without walking up and down the long aisles.

Another technique was one we learned by accident. The technique could be classified as selling, but it was also a form of displaying. At one of our earliest shows, our booth space was way off in the back of the show and very few customers were coming our way. I had reason to return a large picnic basket to our truck and was walking through the show, only to have a number of women stop me and ask where I had purchased it. They later showed up at the booth. Thereafter, whenever the buying action seemed slow, or our booth space seemed out of the flow of the crowd, either Judy or I or our young son would amble casually around with a picnic basket in our hand. This won't work for all crafts, but if yours fits the bill, I recommend the technique.

The Perils of Tearing Down

In spite of the chapter title, we would be remiss if we didn't include a few words about teardown—that time when you pack up all your inventory, break down your booth, load it in your truck, and head for home. This can often be the most exasperating and tedious time of the entire show—the most frustrating and absolutely aggravating. Well, you can tell how much I enjoyed it. Judy always displayed the self-control and patience of a saint, while all I wanted to do was get home.

Because you are approaching the closing hour, the time drags. Most of the customers (except a few who think they can find a bargain) have headed home. You would like to follow in their tire tracks and you would like to start clearing the shelves, beginning the sweaty process of leaving the show behind you. After two or three days, you are tired, bedraggled, and want only to shower, sit in your favorite and most comfortable chair, and sip a martini or a brandy or whatever happens to be your beverage preference. However, regardless of what you want, the promoter's rules say closing time is five o'clock or when the beer and wine stops flowing. As we explained, those rules you must follow.

It is at this time that a craft show most resembles a traveling circus and the mood can be summed up as "every man for himself." Maybe a few hundred vehicles are getting ready to line up for a relatively few parking spots. If you're at the end of the line, you may be two to three hours getting out of the show and you realize that, in that time, you could have been home—if you'd been first in line. In every direction you will see other craftspeople heading for their cars and, if you're like me, you want to also. If you are by yourself, you have no choice in the matter, which for me is even more frustrating. It was in that situation that Judy learned self-control. I never did.

This situation provokes a lot of anxiety, and that is why we're taking the time to describe it. At this point, there is a strong temptation to cheat a bit on the promoter's rules on parking or packing up early, and sometimes you may get away with it. I know, because I was always tempted and often tried. Beth Weber always gave us a booth space right across from her—I think, in part, to prevent me from doing it. She let us into the show because she liked Judy and she knew that Judy would restrain me. It's a good thing she did. The end of the show is not the time to clash with the promoter. That promoter will remember you next year and may well reject your application. So be patient—as much as it kills you.

If you are by yourself, use the time to do an inventory. Cash out your register and put your money away safely. That means having a money belt secured tightly around your waist. Then, when it is closing time, take down your booth and wait until it is either possible to pull your truck up to your booth space or you can leisurely begin hauling everything to wherever your vehicle is parked.

Take your time and don't allow yourself to become frustrated. You'll find the drive home more relaxed and a lot safer. We've seen a lot of accidents because frustrated craftspeople were too anxious to get home. Judy backed into one. This is not the way to end a show.

8
Dealing with Customers

THE READER MAY WONDER why we are devoting a chapter to this. After all, don't you just collect the money and allow your product to sell itself? The answer is yes, and no, but mostly no. As we have stressed in the previous chapters, the crafts business is a business just like any other. True enough, you may not have a store in which potential customers shop on a regular basis, but for the two or three days that you are doing a craft show, your booth is a store and you should regard it as such. It is very much like owning a chain of stores in a variety of places.

As must be clear by now, I personally am not the salesman type; Judy is. However, I'm not referring to the stereotypical, high-pressure salesman you find in a used car lot. I'm discussing people who genuinely enjoy people and can spend ten hours a day dealing with them. Judy is that kind of person. Being an optimist, she took the approach that every show would be a great show, even though she knew better. She greeted people from the standpoint that most people are good people and that if you treat them nicely, they will respond in kind. Most of the time she was right.

I tend to be a pessimist, probably because of my background in law enforcement. After the uniqueness of the business wore off, I had to come to terms with the truth that I just didn't enjoy selling—even our creations—for any extended period of time. Judy took pleasure in it. That is why we were so successful.

Be Honest with Each Other and Yourself

As we mentioned in the previous chapter, if you have a partner, you should divide the tasks of the business based on each person's abilities. You will have to decide who is best suited to spend the most time in the booth—based on

163

both knowledge of the product and sales ability. If you are a solo act and selling does not come naturally to you, you'll have to develop a rapport with people, learning to accept each individual for what and who he is, for those few minutes that he spends in your booth. If you are unable to do that, you probably won't make a lot of money and may not be in business long. Making money, no matter how good your product, depends a great deal on how well you relate to the public. However, you don't need special training in salesmanship. What you do need is to apply some common sense to each new situation in which you find yourself.

Spend some time evaluating your own personality and discuss the subject with your partner. If you have a temper, learn to control it. If you tend to be sarcastic, as I do, remember that many people do not appreciate that kind of humor and will react to it as to an insult. If you are the more serious and somber type, learn to smile and expose your personality and sense of humor a little more.

More than anything, keep in mind that people are not in your booth to engage in intellectual dialogue. Some want to chitchat, others are strictly business. Try to learn to recognize the type of individual with whom you are dealing. When the booth is very crowded, it probably won't make a difference, because neither you nor the customer has time for idle conversation. But when customers are scarce, if you are not the kind of person who easily engages in light, pass-the-time-of-day conversation, practice and develop the ability. Just talk a little more, let yourself go. If you tend to talk too much and overwhelm people, learn to listen. More than anything else, be sensitive to the customer. It may mean the difference between keeping a customer in your booth or watching her leave it empty-handed, the difference between a sale and no sale.

Some Absolute Nos and Nevers

Here's a very good example of what we are concerned with here. A young man had the booth next to ours at one of our last Christmas shows. Having watched him for some hours, we noted that he (1) had a very presentable look, and as I learned after having to force some conversation, (2) was quite intelligent, with an a easygoing personality, when he used it. The wood product he was displaying was of a superior quality. Anyone seeking the product he was offering would have been proud to display his chessboards and other game accessories, but very few potential customers purchased anything from him. Most walked into the booth, took note of his aloof attitude, and walked right out again.

From the moment the show opened Saturday morning until it closed Sunday night, this young man never got out of his chair to greet a customer and he never stopped reading his book. If asked a question, he looked up from his book, perfunctorily answered the question, and returned to his reading. He finished the book by the end of the show, but he made very little money.

Regrettably, it is not uncommon to see many craftspeople doing the same thing at almost any craft show that you attend. If they are not reading a book or doing a crossword puzzle, they are reading the morning newspaper. Would you like or expect to walk into a shopping mall, walk up to the register to make a purchase and find a newspaper acting as a barrier between you and the clerk?

Then there is the craftsperson (sometimes even a friend) who, when things seem slow, comes to your booth, stands in front of the counter, and talks endlessly. Dealing with this can be especially difficult and most experienced craftspeople know better. Maybe it is slow in his booth, but that doesn't mean it is slow in yours. If another merchant is engaging you this way and you see it is interfering with your ability to deal with your customers, just excuse yourself and walk over to a customer. That is a quick way to terminate the conversation and should be understood by any craftsperson with any savvy.

Sure, it is boring to sit in your booth like a caged animal when there are few or no customers. After lunch hours or before closing, patronage is always slow and time does drag. But reading a book is not the way to attract anyone into your booth. With your head in a book, you have no idea who has walked by, or even who may have stepped inside the booth, stepped out again, and continued down the aisle to buy in another booth or from your competitor. There were other chessboards in that show I mentioned.

Judy and I learned along the way that oftentimes the person selling in the next booth is not the person who actually produced the product. I later found out that the dour young man at the Christmas show did not produce the chessboards he was selling; rather, he had been hired by the artisan to sell for him. Sometimes, for personal or business reasons (to be discussed in chapter 9), the craft artists will hire people to go out on the road and sell their products. The young man was a poor example of this. On salary, he had nothing to lose by reading his book. That craftsperson had no idea of how much money he was losing as a result of this man's supercilious attitude and lack of sales ability. That can be a lesson to you if you ever consider hiring someone to do your shows.

For the big craft operations, hiring sales help is no doubt profitable and convenient. Maybe some craftspeople have little to lose, but we don't recommend hiring someone else to sell your craft. There is just too much profit to be lost.

More than once, we agreed to mind a booth for what we believed were fellow craftspeople, only to find out when they returned, hours later, that they were hired personnel who had no emotional or financial investment in the craft. On a straight salary, no commission, these hired hands could care less about tending to business. If for some reason you should have to hire someone, hire carefully and firmly set your rules.

Even sending out family members to sell your merchandise does not guarantee a profitable show. As conscientious and personable as our daughter and son-in-law were when we tried this one year, we found that they just never sold as much as we had sold at the same show for years in the past. If it had happened at only one show, we would have chalked it up to a bad year, but since it occurred at every show they did, we had to attribute it to some intangible personality factors and just plain experience. Perhaps nobody can have the same devotion to a product as the person who has sweated blood to produce and perfect it.

Yet, on rare occasions and under special circumstances, assisting a fellow craftsperson can be rewarding. One day, a neighboring craftswoman, whom Judy had never met before, had vehicle problems that had to be resolved if she was to get home. This required her to leave the booth for more than three hours. Judy hung a sign on her booth referring customers to our booth and managed both. Sales in both booths were excellent and the woman gave Judy a very nice gift from her best wares. We have developed a close friendship since that day. That was a rare occurrence and we still don't recommend doing this very often.

There is a tendency among craftspeople—usually when business is slow—to leave their booths unattended and walk the show themselves, stopping to talk to a dozen friends along the way, generally about how bad the show is. How would they know why it was bad, when they were never in their booth to improve their sales?

On many occasions, we have been next to merchants who had the nerve to ask us to "mind their booth for a moment" and then were gone for hours. We learned to never, never be talked into this, unless there were very extenuating circumstances. Certainly help out if a neighbor has to make a rush call to the bathroom or wants to quickly get something to drink, but you don't want to be stuck trying to conduct their business as well as your own, keeping track of money transactions for them while tending to your own. In that case, your business will inevitably suffer. You must focus on and be concerned about the people entering your booth; you can't be distracted by what is happening in the unattended booth next to you. Customers know that they can walk down the aisle and find something they like someplace else.

That doesn't mean that you attack the customer like a vulture on a rabbit. All that is required is that you look as interested in the customer as you want her to be in your product—and you have to be in the booth to do that. Have a smile on your face. Acknowledge the customer with some sort of a greeting. You might ask if she needs any help, but we caution you that there is some risk in opening a conversation with that old refrain. If the customer says no, and she often will, you are left out on a non-conversational limb. So try to be versatile. Skip clichés like, "Oh, what a beautiful morning." Maybe ask if she's enjoying the show. That's more general and less apparently pushy. Most of all, keep your mind fixed on the fact that this is now your livelihood and no longer a hobby.

We couldn't guess at how much money we have seen lost because a craftsperson had a haughty attitude or conducted business in the absentee manner described above. Hundreds of times we told a neighbor, "You had a customer who said they'd be back." Well, you know about the "Be-Back Family." Guess how many ever returned? You shouldn't have to concern yourself with the potential customers entering another booth.

The Positive Approach and Techniques You Can Use

When customers have stepped across that imaginary line we spoke of earlier, most of them are in the booth because they are considering spending their money on your product. It is at that moment that you should remember that you are dependent on them, not the other way around. If you are truly financially independent of the customer, I don't know why you would be out working in this marketplace at all.

Most craftspeople are sensitive to people, and with some experience, you will find that you can sense what approach is needed. Some people want absolutely no conversation, while others would stand at your counter and talk all day. To customers who don't want to chitchat, just explain your product and let them do the rest. With very talkative customers, if you are not busy, indulge them. If you are getting busy, develop a way of cutting short your conversation without being impolite. Excuse yourself and explain that another customer needs you. This I found easy and Judy found more difficult.

If the customer seems to be in a dilemma and you suspect she is concerned about price, subtly, without ever mentioning cost, show her something less expensive. Basically, just engage her in the same sort of normal, friendly conversation you would a person in any other circumstance. Try to exude enthusiasm and pride in your product. That generates interest and appreciation, which, in turn, generates sales.

Judy was very adept at complimenting people and she did it genuinely. She would observe them and instinctively find some nice, friendly way to greet them. She might comment on a woman's blouse or earrings or sweater or hair. If the woman was pregnant, she would ask when she was expecting. If children were brought into the booth, she reacted to them positively.

When it came to children strolling around our booth, especially if their parents didn't have them on a leash, I usually worried a lot. Watching a child poke into every basket, I'd sit there fretting about when the kid was going to drop ice cream or a Slurpee or a hot dog into one of them. Since this type of accident only happened once in seventeen years, obviously, I was worrying about a remote possibility. I just had more difficulty adjusting to potentially adverse circumstances. Through the years, my concerns about the prospect of children wreaking havoc on our booth abated, particularly as I noted that more than one child—especially little girls who are learning to shop—showed their mother an item that the mother later purchased.

Occasionally, you'll get some breakage and damage may be done, but that happens to every store owner. It is part of the business, so learn to accept it; otherwise, you'll become a nervous wreck, as I was in the beginning and for quite a few years thereafter. You can purchase liability insurance, but insurance companies who handle this business are hard to find and unless you are dealing in very expensive and easily breakable merchandise, the cost may not be worth it. Because an underwriter's estimate of cost would vary so drastically, depending on your product and the expense involved in developing your booth, you will need to investigate this and make a decision that is relevant to your unique product and circumstances.

Stand Behind Your Product

How many times in your life have you made a purchase, brought it home, and found that it was defective? And how many times have you found that, for a variety of reasons, you either could not return it to the store from which it was purchased or you could not get your money back or a replacement? If this has happened to you, you know that you probably never purchased anything from that store again.

As a merchant and as an artist, you must be always ready to stand behind your product if you want to maintain good customer relations and a repeat customer business. In our case, if a customer found a minor defect in a basket but still wanted to purchase it, we would discount the price. If the customer wanted that particular style of basket with identical fabric and we didn't have one in stock at the show, we would make another especially for her without adding the shipping cost. On the rare occasion that something a customer purchased broke when she got it home, we asked no questions and simply sent her another basket. Sure, maybe once or twice it was a flim-flam job, but far more often, the customer respected our integrity and came back to buy many times in the future.

Appeal to the Customer's Senses and Sense of Self-Importance

Suppose you notice a customer ogling your product, but the customer seems wary about touching it. Put it in her hand. As a promoter said to me when discussing the jury process, "Handmade crafts and original art needs to be seen, touched, and, in some cases, even the fragrance needs to be experienced." Psychologically, it's harder for a customer to resist buying something after she has applied her senses to it. Then, while she is holding it, help her picture it on her or in her home or wherever your product is appropriate. If you're selling something wearable, wear it yourself. If it is decorative, tell customers where you place it in your home.

If it's important to selling your craft, have a mirror in your booth. That small album hanging in your booth, with photographs of the product in various settings, is also helpful. And, if you don't have what the customer really wants, be honest about it and refer her to some other craft booth where she may find it. I can't tell you how many times just exhibiting that little bit of honesty later brought the customer back to our booth.

Don't assume that every person has the ability to envision your product in use, or in the appropriate setting. Ask whether the customer is buying for herself or someone else. Is it a gift? What's the special occasion? If it is a gift, refresh her memory as to her friend's favorite colors or help her mentally reconstruct her friend's house or even her personality. Some people have great imaginations; others don't. Taking the time and effort to give the customer this kind of personal attention lets her know that you feel she is important and that you appreciate her interest in your product. We all like that feeling when we walk into a store. One of my biggest gripes is walking all over a department store, unable to find anyone who cares enough about my business to answer a question or help me find what I am looking for.

Though I wasn't at ease with this approach at first, I did learn to do these things and found that I began to enjoy the response I received. I never could get myself to say "What a beautiful baby" when the kid was ugly, but if you want to keep some mother in your booth while she is shopping and trying to manage three kids at the same time, be ready and prepared to help her out. We kept some candy in the booth for children. Before you give candy to their kids, always ask the parents for their permission first. Buy a string of stamps and put one on a child's hand. Engage them in conversation about it.

Maybe you can keep the children amused. Have some small games in the booth or children's reading material or coloring books. If you have room in back of your booth, as at some outdoor shows, invite the children to sit down back there while their mother shops (always checking with the mother first, of course). If the mother is pushing a stroller, invite her to roll it to the back of your booth so it doesn't block all your booth space. We had triplets in the booth one day and that stroller left no room for anybody else.

The main point is that each potential customer is really just a new person you are meeting for the first time. If meeting people isn't natural to you, you'll find that it becomes more natural after a number of shows. Any initial reticence or shyness or sense that you're being phony disappears with experience. Maybe it is as simple as "Do unto others." The rest will come naturally. Your customers will feel important and respected.

Keep in mind that the customer coming to a craft show is there for a good time. It is an event to which she was looking forward. You're simply part of that event and it is your job to help her have as good a time as possible. Maybe she won't buy from you that moment and you'll think you've wasted your time, but you'll be surprised to find how many come back a few hours later and purchase from you just because you made her time in your booth pleasurable. I was stunned at how many of our longtime customers came over to us, gave us a big hug at our last show, and told us how much they were going to miss us.

People come to craft shows for many reasons. Some are looking for entertainment or people around them. Others want to get out of the house for the day, to give their kids and the dog a walk, and so on. You'll see a lot of people just out for a bicycle ride. Compared to other forms of entertainment, the craft show is an inexpensive outing. The more enjoyable you make it for them, the more money you are also likely to make for yourself. This may seem like nothing more than common sense, but putting it into action isn't always easy.

As a probation officer, by nature and training I was a pretty cynical person. The kind of interpersonal skills necessary to sell are hardly the same ones needed in dealing with criminals. Yet, little by little, as I relaxed, I also began to like people more. We suggest that you try to cultivate this type of people-friendly attitude if you want to be a success. If I could do it, anybody can.

Men at a Craft Show

There is one group of people with whom you will deal regularly who require a few words that may seem to contradict everything that has been advised up to this point. Men—particularly husbands—can pose the biggest threat to your sales. A husband can take more business away than your fiercest competitor. No one we know ever really solved this problem.

Long before I got into the crafts business, I was a typical husband. Judy had to drag me to a craft show. You'll see countless men in this position. The husband does not want to be at the show and is simply patronizing and indulging his wife. This husband takes the kids along and pretends it's a family day out, but he really wants to be home watching the football game and is not inclined to spend money on crafts.

Since it may not be fair to apply what I just said to all men, I'll modify my opinion to this extent: Some promoters have noticed an increasing number of men attending craft shows held in new markets. It is speculated that this may be the result of the increasing number of women now in the workplace and on different work schedules. As a result, perhaps the craft show is beginning to truly represent an entertaining day out with the family.

Having stated this caveat, I'm still not convinced that this trend represents the majority of men, dutifully tagging along behind their wives at craft shows. What I observed for seventeen years was that as the wife enters your booth, the husband gently eases her out. Every item she picks up, he finds fault with. "We don't need it. What are you going to do with it? Where can you possibly put it? I can make it myself." That verbal reaction is almost as predictable as the sun rising. This is why Saturdays are generally better financially than Sundays. On Saturday, most women attend a craft fair alone or with a female friend, and they are there to shop and buy.

On most Sundays, particularly during the summer months, the show is crowded with young people who have no money or husbands who have no interest in being there. Ironically, let a husband who truly wants to buy his wife something enter the booth, and inevitably she'll talk him out of the purchase. She is going to demonstrate her frugality. Dare I say, that is typically female, or am I engaging in stereotyping or male chauvinism?

Whatever! That's life, I guess. Conversely, the nice young couples who stroll by and who are either engaged to be married or have just begun dating act quite differently. The young man wants to make an impression. He is always ready to open his wallet. The love of his life at the moment can have almost anything that she wants. That is certainly typically male and I'd bet no woman objects to that kind of stereotyping.

We found that the best response to the husband's negativity is to be as cordial as possible and even agree with his negative attitude. I would commiserate with him and tell him about how I once felt about craft shows before I got into the business. I'd talk sports with him or politics or anything to distract him from his wife's involvement with our baskets. Meanwhile, Judy would be engaging the wife in craft conversation, showing her various baskets, their uses, and differing prices.

Sometimes reverse psychology generates a sale. Be truthful and admit that you know they don't "need" your product. In reality, there is nothing for sale at a craft show that any of us can't live without. Acknowledge that your product is an extravagance that not everyone can afford. Husbands don't like to admit that they can't afford something. Depending on how I sized up the man, I might also suggest how sometimes it is necessary to indulge a wife, pointing out how it is better than having her upset. Then, when he realized that his wife really wanted a basket, he usually opened his wallet, if not truly his heart.

One good selling technique is to point out that only at craft shows can such items be found at such a reasonable price. On the side, I would suggest to the husband that if his wife really wanted a basket, he might be better off buying it at a craft show than have her buying it at Macy's. If the man had remarked that he could make it himself, I would engage him in a conversation about woodworking, ask about how much he did, what kind of equipment he had, and how much time and money he thought it would require to make just one basket. Most often, that would discourage him and he'd approve of his wife spending $48.

However, if none of that worked, we'd thank them for their interest and I'd wish the man luck making the basket. Many times, an hour or so later, the wife would come back and purchase the basket with the words, "He'll never make me the damn basket." Beyond that, just graciously thank them for stopping by and looking. You've done all you can and the purchase is up to them. Remember the adage, "The customer is always right." Without customers, you have no business.

Controlling Your Feelings

As in other endeavors, there will be days when you don't want to be at a craft show. Some days you may not feel well; other days you're just not in the mood; still other days, you may have other problems distracting your attention. On days when everything irritates you, you really won't want to see another human being, much less talk to one. I had a lot of days like that and, when I did, Judy gave me the signal to disappear. There will be days when any of the foibles and weaknesses to which we are all prone will be affecting you. When that happens, remember how you feel and what you expect when you enter any store as a buyer. The customer is not interested in your problems; she has enough of her own. So, on those bad days, just dig down deep and get through the day. The show must go on.

Creating a Following in a Craft Show Environment

As I was reading Phil's comments about customers, with an eye toward updating the material for the second edition, I found myself agreeing with just about everything he said. It's a timeless truth; you have to be interested in people if you want to sell to them—or, at least, you have to be able to do a credible job of feigning. Actually, if you don't have a genuine interest, you probably shouldn't be in this business, because you have to be willing to invest yourself in "the people part" if you want to build a loyal customer base.

Which brings me to Joann Amitrano, a Brooklyn-based wire-work artist who, through hard work, a sincere regard for people, and an innate sense of design, makes her customers feel like they are shopping in an exclusive boutique. A human dynamo, she is the mother of two lively little girls, devoting herself in equal measure to running a household and the creation of one-of-a-kind wearable art. She is a people magnet and whether she is pushing a stroller down the sidewalk or shopping in the supermarket, she is often stopped by people who ask her where she bought her jewelry. She is happy to tell people that it is her own work and invite them to her next show.

Joann has been creating jewelry since she was fifteen and has a large Brooklyn and Florida fan base. She maintains a large mailing list, which she updates as often as she can. (Look to the final section of this chapter for more about mailing lists.) She instinctively provides the specialized customer service that is offered by the finest high-end retailers in the land. I recall reading an article in the *Times* a couple of years ago about Prada and the way the expert sales force there caters to its wealthy clients by remembering their tastes and special needs. Joann's clients may have met her on a street or at a church bazaar, but they receive no less care. Before every show, she sends out a personalized card to each one of her customers with photographs of new pieces that she knows will appeal specifically to that particular customer. She keeps notes on customer purchases, helping to refresh her memory of their individual color and style preferences. As a result, at many of her shows she is often one of the few vendors who does a steady business.

She pays great attention to her display, varying her props and backgrounds according to the season and coloration of her current collections. Her pieces have an organic quality, which she skillfully underlines through her choice of display. Many of her props are culled from nature, an unusual gnarled branch will be selected as a base to drape a series of bracelets or a large conch shell she found on the beach will set off a pair of semiprecious earrings to best advantage. She also makes extensive use of professional store displays. An old-fashioned dress mannequin in the center of her booth, draped with her latest creations, serves to promote a high-end ambience and allows her to present more expensive items. By adopting this method of combining natural objects with commercial displays as a means of exhibiting her work, she creates an atmosphere that stirs the customer's imagination and at the same time ensures that her customers consider her higher price points justified.

Joann says, "If you are not an extrovert, work on it. If you are shy or are uncomfortable in crowds, the customers will feel you don't like people. You must entertain them in order to sell to them. Pay attention to each customer and try to pick out what is attractive to them, but be quick to pull back if they are indicating that they are not ready to buy. Acknowledge their indeicision and invite them to return. Try to get them to sign a mailing list. More than anything, I love people and I love to make people feel good."   —BR

Establish a Mailing List

By asking customers to sign a book or mailing list or by taking contact information from checks or customers' IDs, you can, with the customer's permission, establish a mailing list. We would suggest doing this, starting at your very first show. If you don't do it, you're missing a great sales opportunity. A simple way to begin such a list is to hang up or display on a table a clipboard with name and address forms. We suggest you do not refer to it as a "mailing list," since people don't want a lot of junk mail. Just tell the customers that if they fill it out, you'll mail them your show schedule next year.

If a customer pays by check, take her name and address from the check before you deposit it. Should the customer use a credit card, have preprinted index cards available on which she can provide you with mailing information. Or if the customer pays cash, ask her for her address, explaining that you intend to mail her a yearly notice of your craft show schedule. If she does not wish to give her address to you (perhaps she considers it an invasion of privacy or does not desire more "junk mail"), politely accept her reason.

Over the years, this list will grow quite large. At today's postage rates, this can be expensive, particularly since a certain percentage will be returned as "No longer at this address." This does add up and can seem like a waste of money, time, and effort. However, it is a legitimate business expense for tax purposes and well worth the hours, the labor, and the expense. Also, these days you may be able to build an e-mail list in addition to a snail-mail list. Doing this can put a lot of dollars in your pocket instead of Uncle Sam's because of the savings on postage.

Of course, you don't want to spend any more money than necessary, so to minimize your snail-mail cost you may choose to devise some personal method of paring down the list. Based on thirty-two years of experience, Jim and Fran Seeley recommend winnowing your mailing list every three years. Depending on the size of the mailing list, you may also want to purchase any one of a number of good mailing-list computer programs that print out addressed labels, once you input the data. This is a big time and effort saver, as opposed to writing out envelopes or postcards by hand.

As to those returned as "No longer at this address," just erase the name from your list and accept those that are returned as part of the cost of doing business. After your first year in business, notifying customers from the previous year that you will be in their town again and providing them with your entire schedule for the year is well worth the cost. It is also a deductible business expense, as are the computer programs. If you are dubious about this form of advertising and business expense, we can assure you that we found that, even if a customer doesn't make a purchase at your booth, she often comes by to thank you for notifying her that the show is taking place. As with any of us on a hectic schedule, she may not have known about the craft show, forgotten the date, or forgotten the show altogether. She'll tell you that she didn't want to miss the show and appreciates your kindness in mailing her a notification. This pays dividends in your customer relations. She will be back when she wants what you have to sell.

Jim and Fran ran the statistics on their use of a mailing list, having kept accurate records of repeat customers who purchased from them as a result of mailed notification. They found that customers they had personally invited to a show accounted for 40 to 45 percent of their sales, and these sales, because these customers spent more than their uninvited customers, accounted for 60 percent of their gross sales.

Providing your customers with your schedule is good public relations and good advertising, regardless of whether or not they make a purchase from you. From the advertising perspective, you've reminded them of you, your product, and your business. If they don't buy today, they'll often buy another day, as long as you have a good product.

It takes a few years to develop a substantial list. Naturally, you only mail notices to people who live within the general area of the show and are likely to attend. Judy and I never did a statistical breakdown, but Jim and Fran did and computed that if you spend $1,000 on mailing and gross $50,000 that year, it translates to spending two cents to generate each dollar. We had a smaller mailing list and found that profit earned from purchases made by about ten customers to whom we mailed show notification paid for all our mailing expense; everybody else was a bonus. If you use your computer to accomplish this task, it is, over time, much cheaper than ordering at a print shop and less time consuming than mailing by hand.

In the final analysis, this whole process is just another important form of promoting yourself and your product for which Jim and Fran gave me a little jingle: Early to bed, early to rise, Work like hell and advertise.

E-mail and Your Customer Base

Hoping to swell the ranks of your next trunk show? Want to introduce your latest dragonfly collection to a clamorous public? E-mail marketing is your ticket to reaching more customers than ever before and at lower costs. The best e-mail list that you will ever have is the one where people voluntarily give you their e-mail address. This list will be composed of customers who have purchased your product, have expressed an interest in your product, or would like to be alerted about where you are showing your work next. What is more, if you request your customers' e-mail addresses as part of your normal spiel, you can easily grow your list. When asking your customers for their address, give them a reason to get on your e-mail list. Tell them exactly what you are going to be showing them. "I would like to send you pictures of my new work as it comes out," or "I would like to update you when I am showing next." Let them know that you will be only e-mailing them when an exciting event is taking place or when you have a particularly pertinent piece of information.

If your list is small, you probably can send your e-mails through your normal e-mail account. Generally speaking, you should not do this with more than fifty e-mails at a time. The benefit of this approach is that it is free and there will be no advertisements in your e-mail. If your e-mail list expands to a few hundred names, there are a number of services that, for fifty bucks a month or so allow you to send large numbers of e-mails to your list, without advertisements in them. There are also services that will insert ads into your e-mail but allow you to send it for free.

When you send out e-mails, send them out to your entire list as bcc (blind carbon copy). No one wants their e-mail address shared with the world. In order to avoid being identified as a spammer, be careful to get the permission of each recipient of your intended e-mail. A Web site that is set up to gather e-mails should contain a check box that, when checked, gives you the go ahead to send e-mail. There should also be an opt-out option for those who wish to be taken off the list.

Your e-mail address should be easily recognizable so that people won't think it is spam and delete it. CraftsbyBrauna@yahoo.com works well as an immediately recognizable address, whereas Brauna2173@yahoo.com would likely be deleted as spam. When considering the composition of your e-mail letter, it is your subject line that should get the most attention. Probably only 30 percent of legitimate commercial e-mail ever gets opened or read. The subject line must explain why someone should open the e-mail. Give a sense of the urgency or the relevance of the contents of the message in your title. "Latest Spring Designs," or "Picture of my dragonfly design collection" are better titles than "New Designs." You are reminding people of a preexisting desire to buy and preparing them psychologically for the new season. If you can tap into something that is topical and hot and give them a reason to read, so much the better. While using words such as *free* and *sale* will get you a higher open rate, they do not highlight the quality of what you are doing. I recommend against it. In addition, subject lines need to be short. Anything more than four or five words is too long.

Content of your e-mail will vary according to your product. Try to strike a tone that is representative of the nature of your work. Remember to give a clear instruction on what action you want your customers to do next. Do you want them to buy something, go to your upcoming show, or visit your Web site? Whatever the desired action, make sure to indicate it straightforwardly in your e-mail. Don't be shy. Lastly, when putting together your message, it is essential to make your contact information visible and easy to access.

In your excitement at reaching an ever larger number of new customers, don't overlook the fact that one of the greatest uses of e-mail is as a means to keep in touch with your best customers. If someone buys something, send them a note to ask them if they liked it. E-mail is an effortless way to build relationships without being too obtrusive. The creation of a new piece that you know a special customer will love is the perfect opportunity to send a picture and a brief note.

While I grant this is a lot of work, it is a worthwhile investment of your time. Twenty percent of your best customers bring in eighty percent of your business. —BR

9

An Overview of the Crafts Business— and Beyond

As Phil wrote in the first edition of this book, there are "numerous aspects of the crafts business that did not fit into any categories we had previously covered." He felt that it would be important to mention them, as it would impact on the reader's business and future. As the craft market has become ever more competitive, having an expanded awareness of the craft business is even more important in the twenty-first century than it was at the end of the twentieth century. Here, we will include aspects of this "cottage industry" that were covered in the last edition, updating where necessary, and take a look at other prospects—including the growing Internet market—as well.   —BR

Renting Floor Space in a Shop

You may be confronted with a proposal from a store owner who will rent you floor space, space in which you will set up a permanent booth to display your craft. This arrangement seemed intriguing, so Judy and I did it twice and encountered every negative this business arrangement presents.

In reality, the proprietor is simply creating a perpetual craft show, a mini-fair. Your rental fees are more than paying all the proprietor's bills. Furthermore, he expects to receive perhaps 10 percent of your gross sales each month, adding to his profit and subtracting from yours. That may require you to raise your price to compensate and may therefore render your craft less attractive to customers.

In these situations, nothing is provided but the floor space. You incur the expense of creating an attractive mini-booth and keeping it well stocked each month. That means additional travel or shipping expense. The proprietor only has to sit by the cash register and collect the money. You price tag each item, so there is no commingling of funds and you must keep an accurate record of inventory that is now out of your control, sitting in one or more shops. It also behooves you to verify what and how much was sold, how much money you are owed, and what you have to replace. Meanwhile, that unsold inventory, sitting in that boutique, is not accessible to you should you need it at a show.

As the manufacturer, you may now be adding substantially to your production volume, while much of your merchandise is not generating any income. As the months pass, you will discover the inevitable: The shop exists as a fixed part of the community. It does not have the customer volume of a craft show. The local citizenry who shop there view it as a gift shop. Initially, you'll sell well when your product is new. Later, sales will diminish drastically when regular customers have seen all your merchandise.

Most contracts of this kind are for a minimum of three months. During the holiday season, if you have the right product, this arrangement might be very profitable. But, overall, the proprietor has no personal investment in your craft and knows nothing about its manufacturer. At shows, you are interacting with the customer, discussing your product. Not so in such shops! Your craft is just another drawing card and has to sell itself. The owner wants your craft to sell well so he earns a greater percentage, but he cannot be selling your product and manning the cash register at the same time. Yours is just one of many booths and yours may go a-begging. Eventually, you'll find yourself removing your booth and severing ties with the shop owner, who now has to induce another gullible person to proceed with this arrangement, which pays the proprietor's bills.

Selling on Consignment

We suffered this business arrangement and its consequences when we accepted an invitation to place our picnic baskets on consignment in an exclusive gift shop in Carmel, California. The proprietor convinced us that he could sell them at double the price, which at that time meant a price tag of $90. In this case, again, the shop owner was not risking his own money. We were invited to use some of the floor and shelf space in the shop. The owner took a percentage of the price we put on the product. His suggested price was just too tempting to refuse.

On an agreed-on date, we delivered six picnic baskets to the shop. The owner then arranged them on a beautiful oak table, set in a huge French window, open to public view. We left enthralled. Five months later, a total of one basket had been sold. When we drove 200 miles to the shop to retrieve the remaining five, we found them not in the shop's window, but on the floor at the back of the store. Naturally, we terminated the agreement, picked up our baskets, and sold them that weekend at our next show. Even in Carmel, California, the price was too high.

Yet, we again succumbed to temptation and agreed to place our baskets with another boutique owner who also graciously agreed to display our craft on consignment. This was not the mini-fair-type store I described earlier, or the small, exclusive shop. This was a very large, elegant, and beautifully appointed boutique. It was charming, warm, colorful, and especially inviting to women. Like so many boutiques of its kind, it was owned by a woman who had always wanted to own a boutique.

When you agree to this type of deal, you have no input as to where or how your product will be displayed. The proprietor attempts to create a hodgepodge of every conceivable craft through which customers can roam and spend a few hours, if they choose. This proprietor accepts only a small quantity of your merchandise to add to the mix. It will be scattered everywhere around the store. You don't pay for the space. You do set the price. Every negative specified above applies to this arrangement, plus many more.

With apologies to the majority who run such businesses in a professional manner, those who don't can cause you many problems. They also have no personal investment in your craft. Their goal is to fill their floor space to overflowing. If they don't sell your merchandise, they'll sell somebody else's.

Under these conditions, inexperienced proprietors really don't know what and whose inventory they have at any given moment. They have even less idea of how to keep track of it. From delivery time to the store until the next time you drop by, your merchandise will have been handled, manhandled, and moved all over the shop. Visit the store a week later and you may have difficulty even finding your merchandise. Most often, it won't be displayed to the product's best advantage. I'd find our baskets in some corner where a customer had left them or filled to overflowing with some other craft product. Frequently, merchandise was damaged.

Worst of all, some proprietors have absolutely no business sense. A boutique can be as much a hobby, or avocation, as anything else. When it is time to send you your monthly check, you may get a phone call informing you that expenses were really high last month and the payment will be delayed. In one instance, the proprietor didn't even know what she had sold or how much she owed us.

That said, it is not our intention to demean businesses of this type that operate efficiently. Most do! If you wish to market your craft in this manner, as many craftspeople do, you may earn a fairly good living. Just be aware of the problems involved, particularly if you are also trying to keep up with a full craft show schedule.

Starting Your Own Store

In the last section, above, Phil mentioned (rather disparagingly, perhaps), that the boutique that "was owned by a woman who always wanted to own a boutique." While making consignment arrangements with inexperienced retailers can be very frustrating, there are plenty of crafters who would like to lay claim to a piece of permanent real estate themselves. For many artists, tired of the wear and tear of the craft show circuit, the fantasy of opening a small retail studio is a galvanizing concept. The idea of being able to both work and sell in a single environment without directly competing with other vendors seems infinitely appealing.

A store offers you the opportunity to have complete power over your work and how it is displayed. You are indeed king or queen in your own little world. However, unlike the craft show circuit in which you can choose the number of shows and their scheduling, you must expect to be tied to your store in the beginning at least six days a week and sometimes seven. You will eat, sleep, and breathe "store" for the first few years. This is not a path for the faint of heart. Unless you are absolutely obsessed with the idea of owning your own store, leave it a pipe dream. If you are determined to forge ahead, take care to do due diligence and do your research. The choice of where and when you open your business is crucial.

Katie Cleaver is an example of a crafter who chose well. Katie Cleaver has a little jewel of a shop on the main street of a small town in Vermont in an area where changes come slow and the customers are loyal. She has been doing business in the same spot for around thirty years. Originally from the Midwest, she dropped out of college and apprenticed herself to Philip Morton, a well-known jeweler. "He was quite a character," reminisces Katie fondly. "He had a store from which he sold his work. In the morning, the apprentices were allowed to do their own work; in the afternoon they did his production under his supervision."

She acquired her first retail experience selling in his shop and got a taste of how a craft business is run, maintaining his ledgers. After trying one craft show, she knew immediately that she was not cut out for a life of craft shows. She didn't enjoy the traveling or the packing and setting up. She wanted to settle in and get down to the real work. When she first started searching for an area to set up shop, she drove around all of New England and eventually returned to Bennington, where she is to this day. She had been advised by colleagues to stand on the street and count the passing heads in order to see how many people traveled it. She chose a building on a well-trafficked, central street where she could live above the store. She knew she would have to keep her overhead low, particularly in the beginning.

Originally, Katie was under the impression that Bennington was a craft town. It had that reputation, as there was another well-established jewelry artist in the area, Ed Levin, and the renowned Bennington Pottery was right in town. She soon discovered that despite the presence of these highly reputed artisans, the tourist trade in Bennington could not be counted on to bring in steady business. Fortunately, Katie was prepared to court the local population and surmised that over time the students of a nearby women's college might be enticed to buy her jewelry. She decided to take in repairs and accept special orders in order to bring in additional income. This early strategy proved successful. Within a few years, she had established herself and was able to discontinue her repair service. She works in the back half of her store at a well-worn bench she and her father constructed at the beginning of her tenure. Several upended log stumps with polished surfaces serve as additional worktables. The walls are covered with inspirational photos and works of art, some of jewelry, some of other crafts, the drawings of her children. It is a cozy, much-lived-in environment.

Sitting in her shop one snowy Saturday, trying to interview her, I noticed the earmarks of the successful small crafter with an established clientele. Although a blizzard made driving conditions tricky and Katie had not anticipated much business, there was a steady stream of regulars queuing up in the tiny front room to buy, pick up, or place a new order. She is a friendly person with an extroverted personality. She is comfortable in her own skin and people are comfortable spending time with her. Always curious about the lives of her customers, she remembers every one, if not by name, definitely by face, and she remembers what they bought, the history of the piece, knows somehow whether they wear it often and how it suits their lifestyle.

"One thing I like about Katie is that she never makes the same thing twice," one woman tells me as she mulls over the contents of a display case. She is wearing a necklace and a bracelet, clearly intended as a set, and is there to add to her collection. Meanwhile, Katie is busily making adjustments on a finished piece that another customer has come to pick up. She drapes the necklace around the woman's neck and stands her before a mirror to adjust the length.

"Isn't that kind of cute?" Katie beams and her customer beams back. The room full of customers nods in satisfaction.

Katie is a stand-out against modern technology, and she can afford to be. She is not online nor does she accept credit cards. Her prices are very affordable by contemporary standards. In fact, she has been told by many of her customers that she ought to raise her prices. "I am not out to fleece my customer, I know I could charge more but I am out to make a living, not to become rich. I guess you could say it is part of my philosophy of life." Clearly, her customers support that philosophy and her work. They keep coming back for more.

For every Katie, however, there is another craft retailer who has been forced to close his doors due to insufficient traffic in the area where he set up shop or an unwillingness to pay the sticker price on handcrafted American goods. If you are considering opening a store, thoroughly research the area that you interested in. You will need to look at the stores in the vicinity and see how many of them have been able to survive and flourish beyond the five-year mark. You must analyze the types of stores that have managed to put down long roots. Few areas will provide enough clientele for a store selling a single craft item. While handmade jewelry or Adirondack-style furniture may be a good bet, glass chandeliers (let's say) could be tougher. It generally takes as many as three to five years for a retail store to really get established. If you already have a flourishing craft show business and are able to draw some of your established clientele to trunk shows or events at your new venue, this can be a great help in the difficult first years when you are trying to attract a steady flow of customers.   —BR

The Cooperative Craft Gallery

Many crafters are drawn to the idea of a cooperative craft gallery. Each member is envisioned as an equal member with an equal amount of responsibility. The selling week split between all the members should permit the gallery to stay open every day of the week without eating up anyone's personal work week. Although this would seem to be an ideal solution, as with anything else, you need to procede with caution. Usually, one person with more highly developed business skills will find himself saddled with much of the administrative responsibility. It often happens as well that one crafter will be more successful than the rest and the others can become resentful of having to pay their portion of the bills. It is not unusual for infighting to develop and a gradual blurring of the lines of what one artist is allowed to sell and another, not. Despite these reservations, the right store for the right mix of artisans can be a very satisfying business venture.

Selling by Catalog

For those seeking to expand their sales venue, two other areas deserve consideration. The first, the catalog, has existed since the printing press. Selling by catalog can produce an income, but placing your products in someone else's catalog is costly, and if you have a large variety of wares, it is difficult and expensive to display them all. Some catalog producers will accept your photos; others include photographing your product as part of the primary contract. You then must ship your product to the company so that professional product photographers do the work.

The major problem with selling through a catalog is that you never know what will be ordered, when, and how much. Some catalogs are published semi-annually, some only annually. If you decide to try this, we suggest that you select one or two of the most outstanding catalogs and be prepared to produce and ship in volume. Again, this can shift the emphasis in your crafts business to manufacturing only, with no time to spend at craft shows. Therefore, some people produce for this market only. The cost of advertising and photography is probably a great deal less than the money invested in producing for shows. We can give you no firsthand advice regarding this enterprise. So if this option is one you think you might prefer, look into the possibilities. Like everything else in the business, it is a gamble and it depends on just how much profit you can live with.

One disadvantage is obvious. You cannot estimate your potential income for the coming year, since you cannot predict the marketability of your product. Crafts are a luxury, often influenced by seasonal changes. How reliable a source of income they may be in this marketplace is questionable. The few people we have met who tried this market gave it up. Even if you're successful, you run into the same pitfalls as you do in dealing with a sales representative.

The Television Market

Anyone who spends time watching television, and has cable or satellite capability, has some idea about how many shopping networks are on television today. This is a huge marketplace with a jury system far removed from the craft show jury. We know one person who tried the Home Shopping Network and, for her, it was a mixed blessing. Her story is worth telling, should you wish to market your crafts this way.

A few years ago, Rosie Lamar, who produces a line of unique stuffed bears, decided to sell her bears through the Home Shopping Network. To do so, she first had to travel to Florida to jury her bears in person. The process was simple. The Home Shopping Network officials liked Rosie's bear. Their experts appraised it and determined that they would have to price the bear at $199. They ordered 250 bears and took 60 percent of the retail price. As a general rule, because of the volume of merchandise they sell and the time element essential to their financial success, they must sell $6,000 worth of merchandise a minute.

Since she was paid for all 250 bears, whether the Home Shopping Network sold them or not, it would seem that Rosie did well, making $79.60 on every bear. However, Rosie had to incur the expense of making a video about how she manufactured the bear. Then she had to hire people to help her complete the order. Rosie had already scheduled her shows. So she now had the added pressure of completing the Home Shopping Network order on time while trying to conduct her normal, craft show routine. Of course, her craft show schedule suffered a loss of profits.

From her share of the profit, Rosie also bore a number of expenses: She had to cover the cost of purchasing the prescribed stuffing for the bears and the cost of designing boxes to exact specifications to ship the bears. She had to order special shrink-wrap packaging in which to place each bear. All 250 bears had to be shipped to the Home Shopping Network in one shipment, so she had to have special wooden palates constructed—so many boxes to a palate—to add to her cost of shipping. She made some profit but considered the entire experience a disaster. And remember! It was a one-time-only deal, since the Home Shopping Network doesn't often repeat its items.

This cautionary tale doesn't mean that selling via TV isn't a viable and profitable way to market your product. No doubt it is, or so many thousands of products wouldn't be sold in this manner. We can only tell you what Rosie experienced selling her stuffed bears using this marketing venue. Part of the problem was that she did not know what to expect ahead of time. She may go through the whole process again with a new design. This time with her eyes wide open!

The Internet

Today you only have to go online and type in "crafter" or "crafting" or variations such as "craft worlds," followed by the name of your state. You could spend a week researching the responses. The number of individuals, shops, and crafts at your fingertips for viewing and purchasing seems endless. Here are a couple of random entries that came up among the 200 million possibilities I got when I Googled:

The Crafters Den, *www.craftersden.com*, is an actual store and coffee shop based in Hudson, New York. The store's Web site features dolls, country art, jewelry, baskets, and carpets. An order form can be downloaded, you can order directly over the Net, or you can order through a toll-free telephone number. Then there is *www.springvalleysigns.com*, a company selling hand-carved wooden signs for stores, businesses, and name signs for your house. You'll see somebody carving out this type of sign at many outdoor craft shows. From the illustrations provided, you can order to your specific design requirements. Red Dog and Company, *www.reddogchairs.com*, is a Kentucky-based manufacturer of handcrafted mule ear furniture. The owner, Mike Angel, a Kentucky native, has developed a thriving business using the skills of members of the local rural community. Customers can view his full range of chairs and stools in an online gallery.

In all three instances cited above, these companies are catering to customers who, in the past, sought and found these items exclusively at craft shows.

If you do not have a Web site, chances are you have been looking at the various craft related sites and wondering if you were relegating yourself to the back shelf by not having your own site. In the not too distant past, around the time that the first edition of this book was being written, it was not uncommon to watch fellow crafters and designers jumping on the Internet bandwagon, lavishing their time and money to construct sites on the principle "Build it and they will come." Those who viewed this mass lemming-like leap into the new medium with skepticism often found that their doubts were well merited. They witnessed the early adopters lose their enthusiasm and allow their sites to lapse, eventually confessing that they had taken their sites off line. These early sites were often slow to load, confusing, and poorly conceived. Everyone knew they needed to get online but no one had a notion of how to begin. Of course, crafters were not the only people infected with wild Internet enthusiasm, followed by crashing disappointment. Can you say "dot bomb"? The entire medium needed a course correction.

Despite this discouraging beginning, the last five years have had a great sea change. Increasingly, real business is being done on the Net. Consumers, particularly younger buyers, have become accustomed to shopping online. Access to twenty-four-hour-a-day shopping without having to leave home is gradually luring customers away from strict brick-and-mortar retail. Comparison shopping can be done with the click of a mouse and orders shipped the same day. The urge for instant shopping gratification, which used to be only satisfied by perusing the shopping malls, can now be achieved in the comfort of your own living room.

The convenience, product selection, and lower prices available online have contributed to greater contentment on the part of online buyers. The steady rise of sales can also be attributed to higher confidence in on-time deliveries during the height of the holiday season. Jewelry and apparel designers report a huge increase in the last few years in business through their Web sites. The Neilson/Net Rating e-commerce reported a 113 percent growth from 2003 to 2004 in jewelry sales. One jewelry smith confided that she earns at least 60 percent of her revenue from online purchases. It is hard to know whether this scale of growth can be expected to translate into similar growth for other trades in the craft industry, although there are many who are confident that this will happen.

As a result, the need to have some sort of presence online is no longer felt to be optional. Most younger crafters and designers have at least a portfolio site with their current work posted. Many are experimenting with online stores, malls, and galleries. While this has not always brought immediate financial success, a general mood of optimism prevails.

The cost of having a professional construct your Web site can vary dramatically. A simple portfolio site that operates as an online display case for images of your work with links to your show schedule and contact information can cost as little as $ 400. A more expensive setup with a shopping cart enabling customers to place an order directly online and make payment in one streamlined operation can be as much as $2,500. You will need as well to register a domain name and find a hosting service for your site. Once your site is launched, of course, you will want to ensure that the public is aware of your presence on the Internet.

Getting Noticed Online

One of the most obvious methods of promoting your site is to submit it to search engines. Search engines utilize automated programs known as spiders to track keywords on the Internet and return a list of documents where these keywords were found. Documents with relevant information will be included in their index inventories.

Although there are large number of search engines, there are only three that have the potential to attract a great quantity of people to your site. These are MSN, Google, and Yahoo. While search engines will eventually find your site on their own if other sites link to yours, a passive approach is pretty much guaranteed to relegate your site to the dust heap. Rather than waiting to be discovered, I recommend taking the initiative. Google is generally agreed to be the search engine of choice. More searches get done on Google than any other search engine and as Google is the only search engine that offers a free listing, it is an easy place to start. However, don't expect your listing to show up for at least six months. To get a high ranking when you search you will need a goodly amount of inbound links, correct keywords, and metatags and appropriate content on the page. In order to gain immediate visibility, one route is to submit your site to the Yahoo sponsor directory, which costs around three hundred dollars a year. This can save months of waiting for your site to be included in Yahoo search results.

The key to online success is singling out a particular market niche that a billion other people have not already focused on. "Unless you have several hundred thousand dollars, you are not going to be able to build a brand online. For small advertisers, it is all about provoking a direct response to your product," states Marc Prosser, chief marketing officer of FXCM, an online currency trading firm. "The advantage the small company has online over a large one is that the bigger companies are required to be consistent in what they say about their product. They have to constantly reinforce their central message. They need to appear consistent, stressing the quality of their merchandise and services."

"As a small company, you are free to concentrate on all that is unusual about your product. Interesting content will help sustain customer interest and keep them on your site. Equally significant, the more precise the information on your page is, the better your chances of showing up when a specific search request is made."

Let's say your specialty is onyx rings. Onyx rings do not constitute a niche. It is important to understand that it is not the fact that you create onyx rings that is the draw. It is the fact that the consumer can come directly to you for this specific item that they cannot get anywhere else. If your ring is great for special events, you might want to show nontraditional onyx wedding rings. A search for onyx wedding rings will have a good chance of pulling up your site. There may be many types of onyx but if your onyx comes from Ireland and you have content describing the particularities of Irish onyx, you are more likely to show up on a search request for Irish onyx wedding rings. Your site should offer content that stresses all the exceptional advantages you alone provide. As a small Internet entrepreneur, your goal is to make your site stand out in a crowd. Rather than drawing a thousand window shoppers to loiter briefly on your site, you are hoping to pinpoint ten carefully targeted customers and motivate them enough to buy your work. If they are already looking for your specific product, they are much more likely to make a purchase.

"Another essential element of online marketing to remember is that your online image is really based on who you are rather than what your particular product is," explains Prosser. "A small company is never going to have the cache of a Tiffany. No one is going to say, 'Ooh, aah!' simply at the sight of your box, because you don't have a brand. What you do have to offer is a story. At a craft show you are under constant pressure to sell as much as possible. There is never enough time to provide the complete picture. Online, you have all the time in the world."

In this day and age the realistic crafter knows that he is going up against large commercial forces. Target and Wal-Mart have endless financial resources to bring to bear, which you will never have in your wildest dreams. You are not going to be able to muscle out these larger players. In the real world, many customers are never going to make it to your door. Online you have the opportunity to even the playing field a bit. By attaching emotion and meaning to your product, you can woo your customers.

Design Matters

Clearly, Web site design is subject matter that requires more than a few paragraphs, but several principles seem to be generally agreed upon by all. Clean design is essential. A consistent presentation with well-organized content divisions is necessary to ensure that it is easy for your visitor to navigate from one segment to the next. As your customer surfs the net, you often have only one chance to capture his attention. If you drive him away, it is unlikely you will be given a second opportunity. Online speed is of the essence. Your site must download within eight seconds if you do not wish to stretch the patience limit of the average Internet customer. Avoid as well any element that would tend to distract or annoy the viewer such as light text on a dark background or flashing text. Take into consideration various browser differences, as this will affect how your site will appear on the screen. For example, placing a form on the right side of a page when there is content on the left can lead to the possibility that your form will be partially obscured on some viewers' monitors. Streamline your text and try to minimize the length of your paragraphs.

There is a widespread notion that anyone can design a useable Web site. It is tempting to turn to friends and relatives to erect your Web site as an economical first step. While this approach has worked for some, many have come to regret this decision. So, before making your first move, educate yourself. Examine the sites of your competitors, particularly those working in a similar craft. You will notice there is a great range in style and ease of navigation. Try to get a handle on what attracts you and what annoys you. The distinctions will blur as you search through the wealth of information, so keep notes. You may not be able to afford to do the fanciest site, nor is that necessarily what will work best for you. Remember also that you will probably be managing and maintaining your own site. You will need to be able to update your site regularly, by yourself. A site with the air of dusty neglect will not generate much excitement. New work needs to be posted. A calendar of upcoming shows, press clippings and testimonials from valued customers must be kept current.

There are many Web site designers who will offer you a great-looking site that includes dazzling special effects such as animation and music. However, when it comes to the day-to-day operations that affect your ability to change prices or switch out old inventory, you will find yourself reliant on the Web designer to institute the modifications. Dependency on the services of a Web designer can be costly and can affect your bottom line. Whether you are attempting to build your own site or hiring a Web designer, it is best to keep it simple. In the beginning, functionality and the ability to control content is more important than appearance.

Testing out the waters on an inexpensive site will allow you to experiment and make mistakes without doing major damage to your pocketbook. A Google search for "web hosts" will provide you a list of about ten reasonable possibilities. After reviewing them, you should be able to pick out one that offers a complete package for what you want to do. Basic Web sites can cost as little as $5.95 a month through services such as *www.GoDaddy.com*. While this format can have a generic, commercial appearance at odds with the individualistic look of your work, it is a great way to be up and running on the Internet with very little capital outlay.

Many novices opt not to use a cart and have customers e-mail, fax, or call in their orders (or even send in orders by mail). You can accept MasterCard and Visa transactions through your credit card machine. Remember that you can always go back later and add features to your site.

Be warned, however, that even the most basic Web site setup demands a great deal of your time, and like most craft people, you are probably already wondering how to find an extra hour in the day to get everything done. Be prepared to invest many hours in getting up and running even if you start with a simple Web page. If you are to be the Master of Your Own Site (and your own destiny), you're going to have to learn how to operate the software, at least at the most basic level. The learning curve can be steep for beginners.

Rather than thinking of a Web site as a way to get rich quick, you should consider it a part of your marketing strategy. The primary function of your site is to promote yourself and your art. If you have built up your other, more traditional promotional tools, you have a good head start in the direction you need to go. You will want to ensure that these tools interface seamlessly with your site. Include the Web address on business cards, stationery, packaging, your booth, and even your artwork. All your promotional materials, both real and virtual, including your letterhead, invoice, purchase order, and brochure, your business card, as well as your Web site, should share a look that will contribute to the overall impression of quality, creditability, and artistry of your business. The colors and font you select must represent you effectively and make you memorable. These same elements should be consistent in appearance both on and offline.

I must caution you, though, that the Internet is still a new market for craft products. Most of the craft people I have interviewed have spoken positively of the benefits of the Internet but very few have reported doing the majority of their business online. At best, it is a wonderful opportunity to promote oneself at relatively low cost. Personally, I do not think that the Internet will ever supercede craft shows entirely. The appeal of handling a craft object and getting to know it personally can't be replicated electronically. Most Internet sales seem to be the direct result of the buyer having had exposure to the artist and her work at a show.

10

Wholesaling
Your Product

AS YOU CONDUCT YOUR business, you may be approached in person at a show or by telephone by people inviting you to display your merchandise in their boutique. They may offer to buy your product—at a wholesale price—for sale in their shop.

As you consider this proposition, the natural inclination is to consider the offer a wonderful opportunity to sell more of your craft and make more money. There is good money to be made in these markets. Many craftspeople manufacture their craft exclusively for this kind of market. Others supplement their show income through this kind of outlet. But before making a quick decision about wholesaling your craft, many factors should be seriously considered.

Manufacturing for such marketplaces and maintaining your production schedule become exceptionally labor intensive and pressure packed, particularly with a heavy show lineup. This fact is often forgotten when the offer is particularly tempting. You can easily jump to the conclusion that you've discovered a quick source of additional income. For exactly those reasons, we succumbed to these invitations early in our career. We learned—not quickly enough—that all too frequently our profits dwindled and the enterprise became more trouble, work, and aggravation than it was worth.

Your first wholesale customer might be a shop owner who has noticed your work at a show. The shop owner wants a wholesale price and intends to purchase some specified quantity of your product. This shop owner's intent is to double the price in his store. He wants a wholesale price from you that will allow him to generate a substantial profit without having to charge a price that discourages customers. Because he is ordering in volume, the owner will try to convince you that he deserves this hefty discount.

However, depending on how you have decided to price your craft, you may already be selling at a wholesale price. What you must determine before you accept this proposition is at what price you can safely sell your product and still be compensated for the materials and labor. You must be able to at least double all your costs when selling wholesale and triple it when you are selling retail. If your retail price is already rock bottom, you will not be able to offer any further discounts and survive. On the other hand, wholesale is a viable option if you are able to sell your work for half of what you sell it for at a retail show. You will want to give careful consideration to whether you want to do both wholesale and retail. Selling at wholesale requires volume sales to be profitable and you must set minimums when you take orders. A positive benefit to nurturing wholesale customers is that they frequently become repeat customers and will increase the size of their orders if your work sells well. If you are confident that you can profitably keep up with this addition to your workload, make the deal. When you do, get the order in writing and set a delivery date. Payment for a first order is usually COD or charged to a credit card. While it would be nice to receive some money in advance, this is rarely done.

Making a wholesale agreement with a shop or boutique owner can, however, involve a few problems. The proprietor may request that you refrain from doing a show in the vicinity of his store. The shop may be open during the craft show, so the owner is not happy about the competition. From the owner's standpoint, his shelf price for your product is going to be much higher than your price at the craft show. Thus, in doing a show in the owner's community, you are underselling your own product at that store and undermining the shop owner's price. Under these circumstances, you will have to raise your retail price to match his if you wish to maintain the account or honor his request if there is a certainty of substantial ongoing business.

Although Phil cautioned wisely against the pitfalls of wholesaling, in updating this material, I would like to offer a different perspective. In the remainder of this chapter, I will offer tips on what to think about if you decide that you do want to sell wholesale, as I have found that to be a rewarding, if difficult, part of the business.   —BR

Selling to Small Stores

If you decide you want to attempt the wholesale route, you do not have to wait for merchants to request your product; you could approach a few small shops and boutiques. You will want to case the various stores in a neighborhood and analyze which one will best suit your product. The stores you choose to target will need to showcase your work to your advantage. You want a clean, professional environment with a clientele that is suited to your line. While some managers and owners are open to a direct approach without preamble, most prefer to be contacted by phone and to set an appointment.

A professional presentation requires a portfolio and a few lose samples for the first visit. Some owners will buy outright from stock if your packaging is attractive and store-ready, but many will ask you to return with an order at a later date. Certain times of the year are slower than others and you do not want to make your first appearance during a "dead period." During the seasons when brisk business is taking place, the buyer is more likely to be open to new, unsolicited merchandise. Appearing too close to season can also be a deterrent to getting an order. Many novice crafters descend on buyers just a few weeks before Christmas, figuring to cash in on the major holiday, only to be told that the buying has been completed for the season. Most small store buyers will consider new merchandise for the holiday in September. Many boutiques do their Christmas buying in August at the trade shows and will know how their store will be stocked for the months all the way through February. If you approach her in early fall, you may persuade a buyer to test out your product and then place a second order for Christmas.

While you may not walk away with an order or sale in hand on your first store appointment, do not allow yourself to get discouraged. It takes quite a bit of pounding the pavement to establish yourself. A good first impression always helps, however, and if a buyer likes your work she will keep your brochure or card on file and you may get a call at a later date. For your meeting, dress with panache and have all of your presentation materials in good order. You are really there to sell yourself, and the buyer will remember you as well as your product. Well-designed, informative promotional material gets saved in the buyer's filing system and boring, unrepresentative material gets thrown into the waste bin as soon as you leave. The fruits of your appointment may not show up until two months later when the buyer is leafing through her file and digs up your brochure. You never know.

Wholesale Shows

After experimenting with small-scale wholesaling, some crafters decide to make a complete transition from the world of juried arts and craft shows to that of international trade and gift shows. These shows are strictly wholesale and to some degree require a shift in perspective. The craft person has to add yet another hat to his many other hats, that of the designer. As one crafter-turned-designer explains the difference,

"The artist and artisan create with the desire to express his inner vision. The designer creates with the desire to express the inner desire of the customer." Of course, you do not need to leave your artistic principles at the door of the trade center, but the more you move toward a commercial market, the more you will need to take into account what is already selling and what are the current trends in your media. Although this is true to some extent at the craft shows, it is even truer at a trade show.

As a way to meet many potential customers face to face in a short period of time, trade shows can't be beat. The best outlets for handcrafted goods in the trade show circuit are often to be found in the juried handmade section of gift shows. While it is possible to get a booth in the non-handmade section in these shows, you will be surrounded by inexpensive merchandise and customers will probably only find you by sheer luck. Getting into the handmade section is very competitive, particularly in New York. At times, the waiting list can be as long as seven years. Don't let this intimidate you. Many vendors drop out every year and others do not renew their status on the waiting lists. Perseverance is essential in this arena as in all others.

Boston Gift Show *www.bostongiftshow.com* (800) 272-SHOW
California Gift Show *www.californiagiftshow.com*
New York International Gift Fair *www.nyigf.com*
San Francisco International Gift Fair *www.sfigf.com*
The Seattle Gift Fair *www.seattlegift.com*
Washington Gift Show *www.washingtongiftshow.com*
Alberta Gift Show *www.albertagiftshow.com* (866) 721-4403
Montreal Gift Show *www.montrealgiftshow.com*
Toronto International Gift Show *www.torontointernationalgiftfair.com*
Vancouver Gift Show *www.vancouvergiftshow.com*

There are also many other venues for wholesale craft marketing. *Niche* magazine and *The Crafts Report* are both excellent source for wholesale market listings. You can also find online listings on trade show Web sites.

www.biztradeshows.com
http://Tradeshow.GlobalSources.com
www.ustyleit.com
www.tsnn.com
www.nichemag.com

Not all tradeshows will be appropriate for the handcrafter. It is important to select only the shows that feature small businesses and are targeted for your specific customer.

A successful trade show can bring in a flood of orders and you may be confronted with the need to produce many pieces in a short time. Before you even apply for your first trade show you will have to take a good hard look at how you make your product. Even if you are accustomed to making a large quantity of inventory in advance for your retail shows, you will find that an order-taking show brings with it different demands. While you can try to anticipate which items will be the best sellers and prepare ready stock, you will often discover that you are surprised by your orders. You must be prepared to fill these orders from scratch.

For most artists, it is hard to make the move from making one-of-a-kind pieces to production. Certainly, we all find that there are times when we find ourselves remaking a best-selling item for the umpteenth time and promise ourselves that this the very last one we will ever put together. Usually, the challenge involved in tackling a slightly different color scheme or attempting to apply a fresh technique to an old favorite manages to keep our juices running.

In production, you must tackle the problem from the opposite end of the stick and figure out how to best repeat and capture the spirit of your piece as many times as possible, with the least amount of wasted time. You can't afford to reinvent the wheel each time you sit down at your worktable. As you work, pay attention to how long it takes to produce each style, how long you need to allow for baking or drying, which parts of the process are the most labor intensive, and what quantity of supplies you need for a certain amount of inventory. Try to break your process down into a series of simple steps that you would be comfortable repeating either by yourself or with help. Time yourself. Many crafters are so close to their work that they have never really looked at what goes into making their pieces. They create as they go along, never considering the individual skills and procedures involved in producing the final product. Once you are no longer making one piece at a time, you will inevitably begin to see your work through different eyes. Time and experience will help you streamline your production cycle. You will learn as you go along how to translate your work process into steps that lead to maximum efficiency.

Designing a Production Line

Although preparing for a retail craft show demands discipline and preparation in order to have sufficient inventory and range of merchandise, in the end you can always pack up the car with what you have and let the chips fall where they may. In wholesale, the investment is of a larger magnitude. The cost of the shows is greater. The upfront preparation and cash outlay feels more speculative. There is something comforting about watching your pieces sell one by one and your stash of money swell in a retail show. A wholesale show has a different rhythm to it. You may experience a rush on the booth early on and have the pleasure of rifling through a wad of purchase orders in the morning of the first day. On the other hand, you may not get a nibble until late in the afternoon and then suddenly, for no apparent reason, you are madly writing orders. Whatever the shape of your first shows, there are many things you can do to ensure that you are as prepared as possible both to pull in the customers and keep their interest. The very first on the list is to take time to design your line.

Unlike a retail customer who has only to please herself when she is shopping, a wholesale buyer for a store or a gallery is searching for a product that will appeal to as many of her clientele as possible. Often, in fact, you will discover after speaking with a retailer that her own personal taste is vastly at odds with her customer base. The buyer must consider not only the item itself, but whether it will fit in with the rest of her incoming merchandise for the season and how it can be best displayed. If she is a seasoned buyer she will have already taken into consideration which categories she intends to buy and how much money there is to spend in this category. Your job is to convince her that your work coincides with her plan and budget and that you have enough variety for her to place a good-sized order. The best way to do this is to think in terms of "stories."

Usually when we speak of stories we are thinking of narrative fiction and, in a way, this is not really far off from what you will be trying to do. The trick is to try to create groupings of work that relate to and complement each other. This can be done through color, size, and theme similarities. Related materials can suggest connections as well. A nice collection can be created through presenting the same shape in vastly contrasting sizes or many different shapes in the same size.

By juxtaposing these elements you will be suggesting to the buyer how they can be presented in her store environment. It is key to have sufficient variety in each collection so that a satisfactory selection can be put together for an effective display.

One jewelry designer took this principle quite literally. He created a line of geometric earrings based on four basic shapes, a square, a circle, a rectangle, and a triangle. Each shape was offered in small, medium, and large in silver, gold, and copper. He then designed longer earrings, which consisted of each shape doubled and tripled. (Two triangles linked together on a simple ear wire and then a version made out of three triangles.) These, too, were offered in silver, gold, and copper. Lastly, he made a series in which he intermixed all the three shapes and produced them in three size groups. By playing with shapes, sizes, and metals he was able to devise a collection that used a consistent vocabulary. He called his collection "Basics," which appealed to clothing buyers who felt this approach would speak to classic dressers. Cleverly displayed, his collection had a great impact and sold well.

Try to design with a variety of price points in mind. You do not want to scare away the buyer who might be interested in purchasing your less expensive pieces in quantity. At the same time, you want a higher end buyer to consider placing an order for a few of your more exquisite and expensive products. A solitary piece, no matter how beautiful, is difficult to sell, so make sure to create in variables of three at the very least. Once you have designed your line with this narrative approach, it becomes much easier for you to draw your buyer through your entire booth. As you draw the buyer's attention to thematic highlights, you can use the opportunity to bring up fine points of your process and the quality of your unique product. The more you are able to suggest connections between one item and another, the more likely you are to interest the buyer in your overall collection. A careful examination of your work, your enthusiasm, and rapport with the buyer should result in a large order in the end.

As trade shows are a commercial market, you will find that they are subject to trends. It is important to keep abreast of the current colors, shapes, and styles and allow at least part of your line to reflect these elements. Subscribe to trade magazines and pay attention to what is happening on the street and in the media. While you do not want to be a slave to trends and lose your own personal identity, you do not want to be completely out there on your own unless you have a very strong feel for what you are doing. This can be a bit of a dance. Most buyers are looking for a fresh voice or look. Yet, at the same time, few are willing to invest heavily in an area they are uncertain they can sell. There are always a few ahead of the herd, the rest run comfortably with the flock.

One year I had the strong feeling that the time was right to make the transition from minimal jewelry. I thought women were ready to return to large, statement pieces. I hung boldly enameled flower pendants from chunky strands of raw coral or turquoise beads. Many buyers were enthralled and quite a few returned to my booth several times, but in the end I only received two or three orders. The following year on vacation in Italy, I was gratified to see almost every major fashion store prominently exhibiting a necklace of similar design.

It is important to establish a clear-cut identity for each collection. The pieces should seem to belong together. If it is a set of dinnerware, for example, the plates need to coordinate with the bowls and cups. If you are offering this collection in three colors, your code number should start with the color, then add the number for the style. A large green dinner plate might be GR10 and the matching salad plate, GR11. The red collection in this style would similarly be R10 for the dinner plate and R11 for the salad plate. A coherent style code lends authority to your line and makes it much easier for a buyer to place an order. It helps as well to give each collection a name. A customer may not remember a code number after he walks away from the booth but he will recall an evocative collection title. You might consider "Moss" and "Brick" if the color is the more important element or "Gauguin" and "Gypsy" if you are trying to tell a more specific story.

Writing a Purchase Order

A well-written purchase order should not need any additional handwritten notes to convey information. If you have tightly constructed your line, you will be able to write directly from your item tags. In the heat of the show, special instructions may seem quite straightforward, but a week later in the quiet of your home it often translates as gibberish.

Believe it or not, one of the key factors to having a successful wholesale show is a carefully written purchase order. Failure to get the proper information can cause great difficulties later. Before you start taking an order, you must obtain the full billing and shipping information. Make sure to issue a P.O. number, establish terms, and set a shipping date. Get a contact telephone number and the name of the buyer. If a buyer is in a hurry, he will often hurry you through this process and you will discover later that you are missing a crucial piece of information. Remember to bring enough purchase orders to last the whole day. It is very frustrating to be in the middle of a show and suddenly realize you have run out of forms. Save regulation blanks in your show kit. Buyers like to carry a copy of the order home with them, and lack of a purchase order can mean that you won't be entered into their inventory system. In extreme cases, your order can be refused upon delivery because there is no record of it. A three-part purchase order allows you to give a copy to the customer, keep a copy for production use, and have a copy for your permanent order log.

Taking Custom Orders

When your business is small and the orders are small, taking a custom order can be a great way to add to your volume. Keep in mind, however, that what is simple to accomplish in small amounts can become a nightmare if the numbers are large and the specifications complex. Listen to the proposition all the way through before responding. Consider carefully requests for volume discounts and the customizing details before agreeing to do the order. Take notes and questions and suggest a meeting or phone call after the show is over. Under no circumstance should you allow yourself to be pushed into making an on-the-spot decision. A real order in good faith will not slip through your fingers because you took the time to think it all the way through. You need to resolve for yourself whether you can meet a deadline or earn enough money to make it worthwhile. You cannot compete with a factory. I myself have been very fortunate on this score, but over the years have heard many horror stories of novice designers taking out loans, investing all of their resources to complete a large order, only to deliver a few days late and have their entire order refused. These stories did not have happy endings.

Do your best to accommodate a good customer, but remember you are not doing yourself any favors if you are forced to drop all your other orders to push this big one through. Of course, you want the big fish, the prestigious accounts; every one does, but never forget that it is the small galleries and shops who are loyal and may stay with you through the years. The little country boutique owner who loves your work, feels a personal pride in having discovered you, and counts himself your friend will be there through the ups and downs of the economy. The needs of the larger stores can change quickly due to pressures you may not be aware of. Buyers for big chains come and go. Some have large personalities and will make promises they can't keep or seem not to remember. You cannot rely on them exclusively when you are starting out.

It is important to bear in mind that one custom order is a simple affair. Thirty or forty custom orders with precise little details needing to be cranked out under a deadline can be far more daunting. While it may be easy to change the length of a piece or add a different closure, any change that is agreed upon verbally sight unseen adds an element of danger. Unless you have a long-standing relationship with your customer, do not attempt to take on a large order with many changes without submitting a sample for approval. Make sure to consider any cost differential if you are upgrading the quality of your materials or additional time it will take to make a special detail before quoting a price. If in doubt, write up the order and mark in bold writing on the purchase order "to be quoted." Color code these special orders with a sticker and when you are sorting through after the show, address these issues immediately. Too many unconsidered promises and mistaken quotations can turn what appeared to be a great show into a quagmire. You may even discover that you have lost money.

Meeting Shipping Deadlines

Some of the decisions you make before the show will influence the success of your show after it ends. Shipping dates is one of these. You want to ensure that your orders will be ready to be shipped out complete and on time. On every purchase order is a space for the expected ship date. It is common to start a show by quoting four to six week delivery. If the show exceeds expectations, you can gradually extend your delivery dates another few weeks. It is a good idea to avoid promising early shipping unless you have ready stock available or are certain that you are able to slip in a special order without putting the rest in jeopardy. At the beginning of a show it is tempting to try to meet all requests just to get the ball rolling, but as your orders accumulate you may find you have seriously overextended yourself. What seemed a matter of little consequence becomes a big pain in the ass once you multiply all the little exceptions. In the end you will find that you succeed in pleasing one customer and angering a great many more.

If you can stick to your promised ship date, you will please most. In the end it is not when you ship, but that you ship when you said you would. One well-known jewelry designer ships four months later than all the rest. She tells her customers her precise shipping schedule as they place their orders. She is booked solid through the year despite the fact that her customers must wait an extra two months before they receive her goods. Her customers will wait because she ships when she promises and they know they will get the quality they expect.

If you are running late, you must call your customers and apologize in advance, letting them know when you will be sending out their order. Remember to include an invoice in your shipments. An invoice differs from a purchase order in that it is the completed order. Your invoice should list only the merchandise you have shipped. If you have been unable to fully complete the original order, bill only for what is contained in your shipment and shipping costs. You can back order any items you were not able to finish and, in most cases, you can ship the remainder of the order later with an agreement from your customer. Your invoice should include the same information you received on the purchase order, including the original purchase order number so that the customer can match up the invoice to the original order. If you mail your invoice separately, make sure to enclose a packing slip with prices so that the store will be able to put your merchandise out.

Getting Paid

In the wholesale industry, payment terms fall into several categories. C.O.D., or cash on delivery; pro forma, in which the customer pays upfront; or terms that include Net 15, Net 30, Net 60, or even Net 90, which means you will receive payment in fifteen, thirty, sixty, or even ninety days after you ship your goods. Many stores will give you their credit card information, which you can charge at the appropriate time. Much business is still paid for by check, however, and established businesses will submit credit sheets with bank information and references. You must make a point of checking these references before you start your production. This is a tedious task, but doing it well advance can spare you the heartache of shipping to an uncollectible account later on.

When shipping to a large department store you may need to set yourself up to handle barcoding and special shipping instructions such as multiple drop shipments (shipping to multiple destinations). Department stores will often have stringent shipping instructions, and failure to follow the letter of the law can result in penalties and deductions. These mammoths are used to mainly dealing with large entities and can be less than understanding about the personal circumstances of a small crafter. A significant order from one of these prestigious stores can either be your golden opportunity or the direct route to crash and burn.

Do your research on the credit history even if the word of mouth is excellent. You want to enter into this kind of investment of money and energy with your eyes wide open. You will also want to take a close look at the consequences of laying out the necessary amount of capital and whether you have enough to survive until you receive payment.

Melinda Billings, a painter who specializes in hand-painted silk scarves, was approached at the New York Gift Show by a much admired chain store. They placed a substantial order to be delivered three months after the show. For three months, Melinda labored literally day and night to prepare the order. She hand-painted each silk scarf, steamed it to set the dyes properly, and hand sewed in her labels. She painstakingly prepared the forty shipping boxes, lining them end to end in the dining room, wrapping each scarf individually, and then putting sets of four into plastic bags. She meticulously followed the shipping instructions, placing the packing slips on the outside of the boxes and marking the sides of the boxes with P.O. numbers, ship dates, store department name. The shipping alone took her several days to complete, but she shipped on time. The scarves sold well and there were no returns or complaints.

After thirty days, the expected check did not arrive. Messages to the buyer and accounting department received no reply. Being a stubborn woman, Melinda called the accounts department every day for eight months without ever reaching an actual human. It was through sheer happenstance that one afternoon the phone was answered by an accountant who had been expecting a call from his wife. He was persuaded to fork over a check once she explained that she was an artisan with no other source of income than her craft and the rent was due. She was lucky. The other crafters who had fulfilled their orders from that show never received a dime. This kind of horror story is not a common occurrence, but it is an important reminder that you have to be sharp and self-protective if you decide to play with the big boys.

Smaller stores for the most part are working hard to build their clientele and reputation. They are loyal customers and pay their bills just as you do. Nonetheless, it pays to lay the groundwork and train your customers to pay on time. On the fifteenth and thirtieth of each month, bring out the folder with all of your unpaid receivables and take a look at what is outstanding. If payments are behind, send out a notice the same day. It is never a bad idea to send out a reminder invoice after fifteen days to your Net 30 customers. The squeaky wheel gets paid first. If you follow these procedures, you will notice very quickly when an account has gotten behind. You must start making calls once they are thirty days late. If possible, try to find out whether they are undergoing a slow period or, worse, are in danger of failing, and set up a payment plan. When you are working with an account to help them get back on track, you must always let them know that you are sympathetic to their plight but do not allow them to end the conversation without extracting a promise to pay some small amount against their balance. See if they can see their way clear to pay fifty dollars a week. If not fifty, ask for twenty-five dollars—even ten dollars a week can add up. Let them know that you shipped them in good faith and you expect them to make a reciprocal gesture. If you work with your customers, they will work with you. Your instincts will serve you best in these situations. After you have been dealing with the public for awhile you will find that your initial intuitions were almost always correct and you would have saved yourself a lot of grief by paying attention to that nagging sensation in the pit of your stomach.

Cottage Industry in the United States

At a certain point in the growth of your wholesale business, you will discover that it is no longer possible to physically keep up with the demand. You may be working around the clock seven days a week but find that you are falling behind your shipping deadlines and a new show is looming just around the corner. When and if you run into this scenario, your choices are three. You can work yourself into a mental frenzy and maybe into a hospital; you can cut back on the number of shows you are doing; or you can hire assistance. In the beginning, one of the easiest ways to approach this is to bring in someone to handle the packing and shipping or an administrative assistant to prepare invoices and answer phones.

Next, many craftspeople take on apprentices. Students will often work for free or low wages if they can learn the trade as they go. If you enjoy teaching, this can be an agreeable way to pass on your hard earned knowledge and bring in cheap help at the same time. Students, however, are often not content for long with simply doing repetitious grunt work, and this is primarily what you are seeking. When interviewing job applicants, avoid hiring artistic types unless you are willing to accept that this may only be a step on the way to the creation of their own business. They are probably going to stay with you for a brief time while they learn new skills and then set out on their own. There is also the danger that they will copy your designs. While imitation is the sincerest form of flattery, you must take these considerations into account when searching for quality help.

The best hire is the person who loves to work with his hands and is seeking a form of employment that will allow him to do so. Too many home craft businesses, in their anxiety about keeping their costs low, refuse to look at the bigger picture. I have seen excellent workers let go over the small matter of a dollar or two in hourly wages, while poorer, cheaper workers who were kept on slowed production down and then left in the end. Remember that your end goal is to create a stable and productive work environment for everyone. It will result in growth for the company and steady employment for all involved.

The use of contractors is another option. This arrangement can be beneficial for both parties. You have the advantage of sending the work out of your house and the individual contractor has the opportunity to function as a self-employed, one-person company. Whether or not you are able to retain your best contractors will depend in part on how sustainable your business is. If you are strictly a seasonal craft, there can be a crunch during the most important times of the year. Be careful not to grow beyond your state of financial readiness. It is very stressful to try to keep people on your payroll when you are struggling to keep your head above water.

On one end of this spectrum, Randy Johnson, a jewelry designer in the Catskills, has chosen to outsource his jewelry to local workers within easy driving distance of his home. Although he considers himself a designer, he is a master of many different techniques, translating craft into fashion with an astonishing versatility. His first collections were born out of his love of macramé and branched out into other "soft accessories" that were both unique and wearable. Randy trains his workers in his home, demonstrating the crucial finishing touches that make the difference between mere hobbyist and stunning creations. He is a natural teacher and a stickler for detail, a combination that results in the finely crafted and innovative products he is known for in the industry. After he is certain that the worker has understood all of the requirements of the job, the worker is sent home with a box containing samples, a checklist of the expected work with due dates, and a checklist of materials included in the box (this allows unused parts to be re-entered into inventory if they are not needed and avoids loss or mislaying of materials).

On the other end, Brooklyn designer Pam Meyers, of Alchemy, produces her signature architecturally inspired jewelry in a front-room studio attached to her apartment. In order to ensure the quality of workmanship, Pam prefers to work directly with her assistants. She feels it is essential to supervise and inspect each phase of the production. A highly organized individual with a wicked sense of humor and the ability to write a keen business letter, she epitomizes the ideal blend of craft sensibility with the business acumen necessary for success in the wholesale craft market.

Through the ups and downs of a tempestuous craft marketplace, she has managed to maintain a modest-sized, home-based business. At times, she has a staff of four or more, including administrative and shipping help. When difficult times enforce a bit of extra stringency, she tightens her belt and burns the midnight oil, producing the work herself. As a result, the spirit and quality of her jewelry never suffer. A night person, Pam goes through her orders every evening and sets up the next day's work. When the staff arrive in the morning, everyone sets immediately to work. Listening to music, as they labor through the day's production requirements, periodically someone will consult with Pam when a problem arises.

These two crafters have made decisions that reflect their individual personalities and needs. Not everyone is comfortable turning his or her home into a place of work. For some, the idea of hiring and supervising is stressful. For others, the intrusion of employees into their home oversteps the boundaries of privacy. Taking your own work style and personality into account as you expand your business is crucial for your long-term success.

The obvious advantage of hiring contractors is that you are free to work during the day without the continuous interruptions and questions from staff. The disadvantage is that you may have to allot extra time to inspect the work when it comes in and fix the inevitable problems that arise without on-the-spot supervision. If you have a large pool of skilled handworkers in your area, you may well wish to go in this direction, as word of mouth will send willing, competent workers your way.

If you are leaning in the direction of bringing hired help into a pre-existing workplace, take some time to organize your studio rationally. This will allow workers to find what they need and return it when they are done without having to constantly interrupt you to ask for trivial items. Workers should be able to choose replacement parts or return unused material to its proper place by themselves. You can prevent a lot of general chaos with this simple measure. If you are accustomed to working by yourself where mass and riotous confusion often contributes to creativity and inspiration, you mustn't assume the same is true when communal activity is taking place. Keep work surfaces clean to the point of obsession. When working with others, efficiency is enhanced by clear surfaces and tools being returned to their proper places.

Start work at traditional hours. Many crafters keep odd hours and do their best work late at night when others are fast asleep. It is often tempting to try to duplicate this individualized schedule you may have developed on your own. However, with a multiplicity of shipping deadlines and upcoming shows hovering over your head, in the end it is best to get your crew there bright and early and be ready to start yourself when they arrive. Deadlines and emergencies tend to develop during the day, and if you are soaking in the tub at noon, the problems will pile up quickly.

Legal Considerations

In today's America, there are a number of stumbling blocks standing in the way of those who dream of establishing their own cottage industries. You will need to investigate before steaming full speed ahead even if you have saved a substantial amount of money to get started with or have access to financing. The law now requires that all employers carry liability, health, and unemployment insurance for their employees. There is also workers' compensation and disability insurance. The building in which you manufacture must be insured for fire and theft and have the required facilities, including the requisite number of bathrooms. Every vehicle used by your company needs to be fully insured under your corporate name.

In addition, there are questions of commercial zoning, acquiring the proper building permits, and getting the required environmental impact studies done and approved. These regulations and bureaucratic boondoggles are a factor in the crafts business, as in any other small business. As a result of these short-sighted policies, you will notice when you attend a craft show that you will see a much larger percentage of crafts today originating in Mexico, China, Korea, Taiwan, and other foreign countries, where labor costs and government regulation do not impede business investment and expansion, but, rather, encourage it. And sometimes, American crafters who want to expand their businesses are better off establishing ties with overseas workers, as the cautionary tale below, from the first edition, reveals.

Rosie's Business Adventures and Misadventures

Some years back, at the end of a financially miserable weekend, an entrepreneur who was interested in design artists and wondered if she would create bears for him approached Rosie Lamar. Rosie didn't take this proposal very seriously until he called again and informed her that he could provide her with some potentially big customers. He asked her to design two or three samples to present to buyers representing some nationally known chain-store outlets. Rosie agreed and provided them. The buyers liked the bears on presentation and agreed to purchase a certain number, setting the retail price at $19.95. (This was a much smaller bear than the one ordered by the Home Shopping Network.)

The question then became, could she produce the required number of bears that would sell at that price and still make a profit? Fortunately, the chain stores did not expect the markup that the Home Shopping Network required. If manufactured in the United States with that large a profit built into the price, Rosie's small bears would have had to retail for at least $60. Even with a smaller profit margin, domestically made bears could not have sold for $19.95.

To make a profit at the retail price of $19.95, the entrepreneur—now Rosie's partner—went to China and, with a Chinese partner, established a small factory. Rosie went to China to supervise the initial manufacturing process. She noted that Chinese laborers, who were inexperienced in making this type of product, needed meticulous schooling, but once they learned how to do it, they produced an especially fine product—of course, at a much lower cost than American labor. She also noted that the general quality of Chinese merchandise was constantly improving. So when Rosie was satisfied with the quality of product being produced, she returned home. The total cost of producing and shipping the bears was $4. Rosie received a profit of 3½ percent. So when all was said and done, Rosie netted $7,000. It was worth her effort, since she hadn't spent any of her own money upfront. It was a one-time-only deal, but Rosie's adventure was not over.

Successful in this endeavor, Rosie (who had grown tired of doing craft shows) and her new partner established a small factory in Twain Hart, California. She incorporated, hired five people, and purchased the necessary machinery. As Rosie will readily admit, she then made her biggest mistake by not immediately hiring at least a bookkeeper. The next obstacle she faced was finding people to hire at minimum wage who had the talent to produce beautiful bears. Her partner, having invested his money, went about his own business, not realizing that Rosie had no experience running a cottage industry or mass-marketing a product. The result was that the order for bears came in and Rosie simply could not fill them. Thousands of dollars went by the wayside, Rosie went deeply in debt, and her established reputation suffered. The sales reps out in the field lost their commissions because the orders weren't filled, and the merchants had no bears to fill their shelves.

A quick attempt to put a Band-Aid on the problem led to a return to China in hopes that the orders could be filled there, but the Chinese partner had gone belly-up in another business deal, so there was no salvaging the enterprise. Since Rosie never had a backup plan, both she and her partner lost a lot of money.

The lesson that Rosie learned from all this was that, as a creative, artistic person, she should have stuck to her area of expertise and hired the accounting, marketing, and advertising personnel necessary to run a successful business. As Rosie said, "I couldn't spread myself out any thinner. I got so scattered that I ended up doing everything 'half-assed.'" When the hats don't fit, don't try to wear them!

There is a happy ending to this tale, however. Rosie did learn from her mistakes and returned to her primary area of expertise—designing bears. Her financial backer secured contracts with three major distributors throughout the United States, each requiring a differently designed bear, something Rosie could easily create. A new factory has been established in China and Rosie now has orders for 900,000 bears.

Finding a Representative or Middle Man

For those who have chosen to wholesale their work and have come to terms with the issues of production, there often comes a time when you need to consider how many shows you are able to handle personally. One of the options to mull over is that of finding a professional representative or middleman. A representative will take samples of your merchandise to the large trade shows held in cities like New York, Chicago, and Los Angeles. Your product will be displayed to buyers from all over the United States, as well as buyers from department store chains and catalog houses. If a buyer likes your product and believes it will sell, he will submit orders and set a delivery date. However, these are not small orders. It could even be Macy's that wants to sell your work and may order 500 of this or 10,000 of that. So be aware of what you are getting yourself into.

There are many advantages to working with a rep, particularly for the craftsperson who is not comfortable with hard-core sales. A well-established rep will have the contacts and relationship with all the better boutiques in a region, as well as access to the head buyers in the department stores and catalog houses. With a simple phone call, a rep can get an appointment to show your work to the person who has actual control of the buying. After spending a week pounding the pavement and trying to show your product to stores, this itself can seem like a minor miracle.

It is a rep's job to follow up on any leads or signs of interest after a show and maintain the connection after a first order has been placed. Reps offer the continuous customer service you would like to afford all of your clients but just don't have the time to do. A good rep will expand your customer base at least 30 or 40 percent in the first year. Best of all, they will do this while you are home working on the part of the job you most enjoy. For these services, your rep will obviously take a percentage. The average commission is 15 to 20 percent. This has not changed in the last twenty years.

The first few years of expansion are very exciting, and many craftspeople are very grateful at the beginning. As they become more confident of their success, there tends to be a rising resentment of what is seen to be an unnecessary drain on the revenues of the business.

"A good rep will be out on the road four or five days out of seven in all weathers," says Genny Morley of Fireburst, a well-known New England rep company, "even on his birthday during a blizzard to get to a good account." Your rep is a partner in your business. Most businesses with a new and exciting product start with an upward curve during the introductory phase when enthusiasm is in full steam. The difficult part is to stay the course and even to continue the growth after the initial burst into the market. To do this, you need partnerships with others who have a long-term investment in seeing you grow. A good rep can do that for you, but he needs the incentive of being paid on time and kept properly up to date on your plans.

One of the best ways to find the kind of rep you will need is to ask your already existing wholesale customers who is their favorite rep. You can call or place a flyer in one of your orders. As always, it helps to offer a little incentive. Let them know that you will give them $150 off of their next order if you are still using the rep they recommend after six months. You can post your request for a rep from a specific region on designated bulletin boards during any trade show you are participating in. You can also put up a discreet sign in your booth, advertising the fact that you are seeking new reps.

As you are introducing yourself and interviewing reps, keep in mind that you are looking for someone who likes and understands your line. It is important that his customer base includes the type of venue you wish to sell your work in. Many artisans need a rep whose primary client list consists of galleries, museum shops, and high-end gift shops. Others will need someone who has general stores and country craft outlets. What you are looking for will depend on the type of craft you make. Even if a rep is excellent, it will not be a good match if you want to sell pottery and he sells exclusively to pharmacies, hair salons, and beauty product stores.

It is equally important to avoid starting out with a new rep. Many reps do not last. It is difficult for them to make enough money. They may be able to place your line as a novelty on a first time basis but then find it difficult to get repeat business. The mature rep will have the trust of the buyers who rely on their expertise and experience to recommend new lines. Their knowledge of an individual store's history, as well as regional patterns, are part of their appeal to a store owner.

What a Rep Looks For

From the very start of your relationship with a rep, you must always keep in mind that he is focused on his commission. He needs to know all his efforts to introduce your work will bear fruit in timely shipping, good presentation, and high-quality workmanship. Many reps have been burnt, having taken on a newbie and been disappointed. Therefore, they look at new prospects with a wary eye.

The first thing a rep will want to know is whether you have done wholesale before. Many new companies making the transition from large craft shows to wholesale fail to make adjustments in their shipping schedules and allow their production to come to a halt during a big craft show. Knowing that you are factoring in all your commitments when you quote your ship dates will give your rep the necessary assurance to go out on the road and plug your line without any niggling doubts. Remember as well that you must offer your product at the same uniform price in the general marketplace whether you are selling to the customer through your rep or directly at a show. If you sell at varying prices and undermine your rep by selling at a lower price than he is empowered to do, you will swiftly undermine your relationship and create questions about your creditability. There is a good chance that your rep will drop you like a hot potato.

The rep will also want to know that there is a way to re-order your product. A good color catalog is essential. The competition is putting out incredible catalogs. Yours will need to stand up in comparison. Go as far as you can with what you can afford. A catalog should go out with every first order you ship. Scale back the size of your catalog if it is too expensive. A catalog is of no use if only 25 percent of your customers receive it. This is your opportunity to encourage all of your customers to place a repeat order or consider ordering some untried items to fill in the gaps where merchandise has not sold. Catalogs can be inserted in the boxes when the orders are being packed or mailed off the same day.

Among the primary qualities a rep scrutinizes as he considers you as a candidate are your design capabilities and your ability to organize. "We've run into a lot of newbie's over the years who are either designers or business people. It is a rare company that is both." says Ginny Morley of Fireburst.

"You must understand what wholesale is. Don't rely on the rep to teach you as you go along. Gone are the days of the seventies and eighties and even the nineties when a rep would nurse you along. Times are tougher. Take a business course at a local community college. Learn the laws and local tax ordinances. Hire an accountant to help you set up your sales journal and payroll. Try to have a handle on the nuts and bolts before you start if you want to keep a rep," she concluded.

Once your line goes out on the road, you will quickly see that your work must be easily reproducible. While you may have been wholesaling on your own already, the little idiosyncrasies you have allowed yourself will immediately cause problems. Most reps will not carry one of a kind. They will not even be happy with minor variations that you may feel are part of the handmade charm. At the same time, your product needs to be cohesive with a look uniquely your own. Ginny explains, "The buyer looks at a piece of pottery, for example, recognizes the glaze and thinks 'Oh, that's Joe Blow's work.'"

Your work should be perceived as a definable entity that remains the same from one season to the next. The blue-green Grecian vase sample shown in January using a specific code number has to look the same when shipped in June. There can be no "product drift." Reps go crazy when they discover a product size, color, shape, or finish has shifted but in the crafter's view "is otherwise identical." If you need to change a design, design a new item with a new code number and have a new release. It is not acceptable to redesign a piece and just substitute the new piece in an order, even if you think it is superior or a better value for the money.

From the rep's point of view, his job is strictly to sell as much as he can to the widest market he can. A wholesale customer, whether she owns a small boutique or is buying for a catalog house, does not always care that your work is handcrafted at home at the kitchen table. She is searching for a look and a price. Until relatively recently, many buyers exclusively carried goods handcrafted in the U.S. and were able to make a good living. Now they are obliged to respond to the influx of globally made handcrafted crafts and imported craft-look products designed by Americans for the American market.

Crafts are no longer the oasis in the desert of commerce they once were. If you choose to work with a rep, you will have to open yourself to the demands of this new world market. Reps will ask you to present to them what they can sell and keep on selling. For those of us with an artistic temperament, this is one of the most difficult aspects of the entire process. Yet, even in this ever increasingly competitive atmosphere, there is room for creativity and individuality.

Retailers are forced to go further afield these days to find unique, fresh material. "You had better be very good at what you do and do your marketing before you start making your product," advises Gail Kessler of Gigi's At Home, a long-time crafts retailer in Florida. "Have a buyer in mind before you start trying to sell. A higher-end store featuring monkey items is likely to buy a beautiful monkey and pay a higher price. Now, I do chickens and I'll buy chickens but they need to be the right price. Most importantly, they need to absolutely not be out there in the mass market."

Epilogue

•　•　•　•　•

IN WRAPPING UP THIS package, and presenting it to you, the reader, a few words should be said about general courtesy, manners, deportment, and ethics. As in any respectable profession, how you conduct yourself is continually evaluated by your fellow craftspeople, promoters, and the public. Establishing your integrity and honesty is vital to your success.

Because of the physical and emotional strain of the business, your patience and endurance are constantly pushed to the breaking point. Exhibiting at a craft show is not unlike going on stage. The curtain goes up and you have a role to play. We saw many in the business who could not separate their role as an artist from their role as a seller. As a result, they lost many customers and a lot of money.

The public doesn't know or begin to appreciate the hard work you have put into creating your work, and you cannot allow them to know. They aren't interested in listening to verbal squabbling, nor are they at a show to be pressured, bullied, or insulted. You are not there to judge them.

The customer has paid to judge you and your product. So, when the show opens, it is time for you to become your most charming, effervescent self. Treat everyone—whether they make a purchase or not—like a guest you have invited into your home. This approach pays big dividends.

The same is true of your relationship with fellow artists. You will find that, very often, you will need their help and advice, and they will request yours. As the years pass, you will see many of them over and over again. Some will become great friends, others won't. You don't want any of them as an enemy.

Yes, you are in competition, but you are not at war. Help your neighbors out when they need assistance. There will come a day when your canopy collapses or the wind causes you a lot of breakage and you'll need their help. If they are selling successfully, be happy for them. Jealousy over their success does not improve yours.

Learn from your fellow artisans and from the mistakes you will naturally make. Share those mistakes, and the way you corrected them, with others. If you become financially successful, it will probably be, in large part, because of the helpful hints and tips you received voluntarily from many people you meet along the road.

We hope that the advice we have given will not discourage you from entering the crafts business. Our intent is to enlighten and inform, so that you may approach the business in a realistic and practical manner. Beyond that, the craft world is uncharted water. It is our desire that you jump in with your eyes wide open.

For all the work, frustration, and, sometimes, tedium, Judy and I also gained a great sense of achievement and considerable financial and emotional reward from our years in the crafts business. We never lost the feeling of satisfaction that comes when you create a product and then find that strangers are willing to spend their hard-earned money to purchase it, place it in their homes, or give it to a loved one or a special friend. We felt that excitement and wonderment the day we sold our first basket and we felt it when we sold our last.

During our seventeen years in the business, we met and sold to people from all over the world. As you wrap up a purchase and hand it to the customer, or pack it for shipping, it is a gratifying feeling to know that your creation will be placed in a home in Europe or Asia or Africa or Australia. Before we retired, The Three Basketeers had a home in about twenty-five countries. That satisfaction goes beyond making money. There is a feeling of closeness to the customers and, in talking to them about the work, a sense of commonality.

Judy and I found that no matter what the customer's place of origin, at heart, they were never really very different from us. They had the same concerns, loved and cried as we did, enjoyed the same beauty, got wet in the rain, and sweated in the heat, just as we did. In few occupations can you meet so many thousands of people, of such diverse backgrounds. That also holds true of the thousands of craftspeople that we met.

For all the wear and tear and planning that the travel entails, it also took us to cities and towns and countrysides that we would never have seen otherwise. We often worked in environments that were breathtakingly beautiful, met the people who lived there, and made friends of many as we returned to the same show each year.

Our business also made it possible for Judy and I to be together on a daily basis. We had the rare parental experience of being able to spend every day and evening with our youngest son Mark, something we could not do when we raised our two older children. We were there for him on a daily basis, in ways that are impossible in the normal workaday world. We could play tennis, golf, or go for a swim when we chose. As husband and wife, we forged a working relationship unique among married couples, and it contributed greatly to the stability of our twenty-six-year marriage.

We will never regret the years we gave to the business and we've never heard anyone who is successful regret theirs, either. Many of the friendships we made will last throughout our retirement years. That is why we have written this book. We want your craft adventure to be a similarly rewarding experience. Good luck! Have fun and have a great show.

About the Author

• • • • •

PHIL KADUBEC WAS BORN and raised in New York City. At age eighteen, he was a Roller Derby skater until he was drafted during the Korean War. Later, he worked in Chicago as a credit investigator, an insurance underwriter, and a dance instructor. In 1955, he graduated from the University of California at Berkeley with a major in psychology.

Following graduation, Phil took employment with the Alameda County Probation Department, in Oakland, California, where he worked for the next twenty-two years, retiring in 1982. Deciding to leave the Bay Area, Phil, his wife Judy, and their children built a home in Blue Lake Springs, California, where they first became interested in the craft business. Together, Phil and Judy developed The Three Basketeers, and for the next seventeen years, the couple and their son, Mark, traveled to hundreds of craft shows.

Retiring completely and selling their business in 1997, the family began a new phase of life, with Judy gardening their four acres in Smartville, California, and working for Nevada County as a court clerk, and Phil writing this book and pursuing a masters degree in the humanities at Cal State. Their son, Mark, is in the computer industry, their daughter Jenny is a homemaker in Sonora, California, and their son Jeff is a respiratory therapist in the U.S. Air Force.

Index

· · · · ·

location of, 113–114
in shops, 179–180
boredom, 61
building materials, for booth interior, 141
bulk ordering, 50
Burleigh, Rich, 12, 105
business
dividing tasks of, 149, 163–164
money goal of, 24
work routine and, 60
business card, 10, 11
business counter, 135–136, 137
business name, 8
business standards, 26
buyer, wholesale, 198–199

cabinets, 136, 137
California Victorian floral booth, 144–145
Campbell, Bill, 16
canopies, 122–125, 136
carnival/rodeo shows, 114–115
cash flow, 40–41, 61
cash register, 53–54, 135–136
catalog
sales through, 185
suppliers, 50
charge accounts, 57–59
chargebacks, 59
charity events, reasons to avoid, 116
checklist
booth set-up, 151
show planning, 155
children, 170, 216–217
closing time, 106
clothing booths, 143, 144
coding, wholesale product, 200
collections
payment, 204
wholesale manufacturing, 199
committee, jury, 107
competition, 73
craftsperson as, 14, 67
differentiating from, 20–21
evaluation of, 15
marketing techniques against, 6
overseas, 41, 100–101, 207
suppliers', 49–50
types of, 25
underselling, 37–38
competitors, 4
photographing by, 56–57
relations with neighboring, 215
confidence, 15
consignment, 180–181

contractors, employees v., 205–206
convention centers, 147
lighting problems in, 154, 156
cooperative craft gallery, 184–185
copycat, 22
copyrighting, 54–55
corporation, 4, 5, 17
costs of goods sold, 49
Cottage Crafts, 138
cottage industry, 204–207
Country Folk Art, 6, 12, 66, 95, 131, 132
craft business
adventure of, 216–217
beginners in, 25
billion dollar industry of, 3
as cottage industry, 204–207
financial reality of, 25
legalities of, 46, 54–55, 207
reevaluation of, 25–26
stress of, 2–3, 29–30, 149
supplementing income through, 1
trial and error process with, 2
craft marketplace, 22, 179
Internet, 188
realities of, 14–16
understanding, 179
craft show schedule, 29–30
advertising with, 12
building customer base with, 12, 174–178
closing time in, 106
law of diminishing returns with, 30
craft show selection. *See also* promoters
advertising and, 110
best method for, 71–72, 89
economy and, 65
environment factor in, 112
evaluation forms for, 77–82
goals in, 110
guide books for, 72–73, 76, 82–85
Internet guides for, 83–85
by invitation, 68–71
lifestyle and, 86–87
new/first annual shows and, 70–72
other crafters' feedback in, 76–77, 82–83
percentage shows and, 109
by word of mouth, 63–65, 66, 67
craft shows, 18–19. *See also* booth set-up; shows
acceptance into, 98, 114, 118
acceptance/rejection from, 96, 97, 98, 105, 118
letter explaining, 105
reasons for, 97
annual, 70–72
convention center, 147, 154, 156
entrance display at, 161

indoor v. outdoor, 136, 146, 152, 156, 157
new, risk of, 70–72
planning checklist for, 155
poor, 112, 113
rules/regulations for, promoters', 105–106,
  107, 119–121, 140, 144
service organization, 116–117
themes, 95
trade shows v., x
Crafts Fair Guide (Spiegel), 73, 76
craftsperson, xii, 5, 14, 23
liar type of, 67
Crawford, Tad, 46
creativity, 16, 17, 23
credit card purchase, 57–59
credit history, 203
critique, jurying as, 99–100
culture, pricing influenced by, 32
customers
  attitude toward, 14
  attracting/entertaining, 20, 152, 160,
    164–165, 169
  capturing imagination of, 16
  complementing, 160
  craft show invitations to, 12, 174–178
  desires of, 14, 27
  eccentricities of, 26–27
  gender and, 171–172
  giving schedule to, 12
  identity of, 7
  impulse buying and, 26, 90
  listening to, 19
  mailing lists of, 174–176
  personal connection with, 18, 160,
    167–168, 169–172, 215, 216
  pricing determined by, 35–36
  repeat, 142, 176, 194
  rudeness of, 23–24
  special orders by, 39–40
  today's, 101
  understanding, 6

deadlines, shipping, 202
deductions
  business use of home, 51–52
  business use of vehicle, 52–53
design
  booth interior, 142–144
  production line, 197–200
  stealing of, 17, 56
  Web site, 190–192
design patents, 54–55
designer, artisan v., 196
discounts, 169

display, 138–139
  business card, 10
  at craft-show entrance, 161
  eye-level, 157
  merchandise, 119, 151–157, 158–159
  sculpture, 128–129
Display Excellence, 138–139
division of tasks, 149, 163–164.
  See also work routine
Domanski, Kim, 95, 98–99
drapery, 138
  enclosures with, 139, 144
  fireproof, 140, 144

economy
  craft show selection and, 65
  pricing and, 32
ego
  artistic temperament and, 14
  flexibility of, 21
  knowing limitations of, 23–25
  pricing without, 35
electricity, 120, 156
e-mail, 176–178. *See also* Internet; Web sites
embellishment, product, 100–101
Emerson, Ralph Waldo, xiii
employees
  contractors v., 205–206
  legal issues and, 207
employers, legal requirements of, 207
enclosures, drapery, 139, 144
entrepreneur, home-based, 4
entry fees, 87–88, 89
  reasons for, 96, 111
environment, 216
  in craft show selection, 112
  flea market, 101
  travel and, 216
evaluation(s)
  competing booth displays, 15
  craft business re-, 25–26
  craft show selection using forms for,
    77–82
  of craft shows, 82–83
  self, 28–30
excuses, for poor shows, 112, 113
expenses. *See also* costs of goods sold; fees
  advertising, 95, 96, 111
  booth fee, 87–88, 89, 110–111
  deducting, 45–46, 51–52
  electricity, 156
  planning for, 88
  promoters', 88, 110–111
  travel, 89

self-reliance, 5–7
self-satisfaction, 16
senses, appealing to customers', 169
service organization craft shows, 116–117
set-up. *See* booth set-up
shelving, 125, 126, 127, 136
shipping, 39–40, 202–204
shop, renting space in, 179–180
shows
   antique car, 115
   carnival/rodeo, 114–115
   flea market, 101
   food and gift, 115
   gift, 196
   percentage, 109
   at Prime rib and chili cook-offs, 116
   rod and gun, 115
   trade, x, 197, 199
   wholesale, 195–197
signage, booth, 59, 160–161
Skelly, Heather, 42
skills
   marketing, 5–6
   public relations, 30
special order, 39–40
Spiegel, Lee/Dianne, 73, 76
stealing, 17, 22, 56
storage, 157–150
store(s)
   booth as, 163
   small, selling to, 195
   starting own, 182–184
street fair, 90–92, 97
stress, 2–3, 29–30, 149
success, 21, 66
   promoters', 88
   of Three Basketeers, 216
suppliers, 49–50

target market, 6
tax
   expense deductions and, 45–46, 51–52
   sales, 46–49
teamwork, 149, 163–164, 215, 216
tear down, 161–162
television market, 185–186
themes
   for booth display, 142, 143
   craft show, 95
   production line, 198–200
Three Basketeers, 1–3, 216, 218
tools, for indoor/outdoor set-up, 146
trade shows, 197, 199
   craft shows v., x
   promoters of, 68–71, 88

travel, 29, 86–87, 89, 216
trends, 18–20, 26, 27–28
   trade show, 199
Tritel, Jeff, 128–129

underselling, 37–38, 194
uniqueness, 16–20, 156
upright poles, 122

vacation, 29
variety
   environmental, 216
   marketing, 21–22
   pricing, 38
   promoter seeking, 114
   rejection and, 96, 97
   in wholesale manufacturing, 198
vehicle
   deductions for use of, 52–53
   loading/packing, 145–147, 150

weather, 112, 124
Weathervane Capital, 134–135
Weber, Beth, 24–25, 88, 106
Web sites. *See also* e-mail; Internet
   application, 95
   design of, 190–192
   for guides to craft shows, 83–85
   marketing and, 191–192
   promotion of, 188–190
   wholesale show, 196
Western Exhibitors, 95–96
wholesale
   pricing, retail v., 42–43, 193–194
   representatives, 209–213
   shipping, 202–204
   to small stores, 195
wholesale manufacturing, 209–213
   collections for, 199
   custom orders for, 200–201
   payment terms in, 202–204
   pitfalls of, 193–194
   production line in, 197–200, 204–207
   purchase orders in, 200
wholesale shows, 195–197
Williams, Nancy/Julien, 130
word of mouth, in craft-show selection,
   63–65, 66, 67
work routine, 60
working the crowd, 160

Zapplication, 94–95, 98–99
   Internet applications via, 98–99
   jurying through, 98–99
zero sum concept, 67

Books from Allworth Press

Allworth Press is an imprint of Allworth Communications, Inc. Selected titles are listed below.

Creative Careers in Crafts
by Susan Joy Sager (paperback, 6 × 9, 272 pages, $19.95)

Scrapbooking For Profit
by Rebecca Pitman (paperback, 6 × 9, 208 pages, $19.95)

Make Money Quilting
by Sylvia Ann Landman (paperback, 6 × 9, 256 pages, $19.95)

How to Start a Faux Painting or Mural Business
by Rebecca Pitman (paperback, 6 × 9, 208 pages, $19.95)

Selling Art Without Galleries
by Daniel Grant (paperback, 6 × 9, 256 pages, $19.95)

Fine Art Publicity, Second Edition
by Susan Abbott (paperback, 6 × 9, 192 pages, $19.95)

Selling Your Crafts, Revised Edition
by Susan Joy Sager (paperback, 6 × 9, 288 pages, $19.95)

Creating a Successful Crafts Business
by Rogene A. Robbins and Robert Robbins (paperback, 6 × 9, 256 pages, $19.95)

Business and Legal Forms for Crafts, Second Edition
by Tad Crawford (paperback, 8½ × 11, 144 pages, $29.95)

The Law (in Plain English), for Crafts, Sixth Edition
by Leonard DuBoff (paperback, 6 × 9, 224 pages, $19.95)

Legal Guide for the Visual Artist, Fourth Edition
by Tad Crawford (paperback, 8½ × 11, 272 pages, $19.95)

The Business of Being an Artist, Third Edition
by Daniel Grant (paperback, 6 × 9, 352 pages, $19.95)

To request our free catalog, or order by credit card, call 1-800-491-2808.
To see our complete catalog on the World Wide Web, or to order online, you can find us at
www.allworth.com.